THE SEARCH FOR THE
"MANCHURIAN CANDIDATE"

THE SEARCH FOR THE
"MANCHURIAN CANDIDATE"
THE CIA AND MIND CONTROL

John Marks

McGRAW-HILL BOOK COMPANY

New York   St. Louis   San Francisco   Bogotá   Düsseldorf   Madrid
Mexico   Montreal   Panama   Paris   São Paulo   Tokyo   Toronto

For Barbara and Daniel

Reprinted by arrangement with
Times Books

First McGraw-Hill Paperback edition, 1980

1 2 3 4 5 6 7 8 9 0   FGRFGR   8 7 6 5 4 3 2 1 0

Library of Congress Cataloging in Publication
Data
Marks, John D
The search for the "Manchurian candidate."
Reprint of the 1979 ed. published by Times
Books, New York.
Includes index.
1. United States. Central Intelligence Agency.
2. Behavior modification. I. Title.
[JK468.I6M4   1980]   327.1'2'06073
79-25637
ISBN 0-07-040397-X

AUTHOR'S NOTE

This book has grown out of the 16,000 pages of documents that the CIA released to me under the Freedom of Information Act. Without these documents, the best investigative reporting in the world could not have produced a book, and the secrets of CIA mind-control work would have remained buried forever, as the men who knew them had always intended. From the documentary base, I was able to expand my knowledge through interviews and readings in the behavioral sciences. Nevertheless, the final result is not the whole story of the CIA's attack on the mind. Only a few insiders could have written that, and they choose to remain silent. I have done the best I can to make the book as accurate as possible, but I have been hampered by the refusal of most of the principal characters to be interviewed and by the CIA's destruction in 1973 of many of the key documents.

I want to extend special thanks to the congressional sponsors of the Freedom of Information Act. I would like to think that they had my kind of research in mind when they passed into law the idea that information about the government belongs to the people, not to the bureaucrats. I am also grateful to the CIA officials who made what must have been a rather unpleasant decision to release the documents and to those in the Agency who worked on the actual mechanics of release. From my point of view, the system has worked extremely well.

I must acknowledge that the system worked almost not at all during the first six months of my three-year Freedom of Information struggle. Then in late 1975, Joseph Petrillo and Timothy Sullivan, two skilled and energetic lawyers with the firm of Fried, Frank, Shriver, Harris and Kampelman, entered the case. I had the distinct impression that the government attorneys took me much more seriously when my requests for documents started arriving on stationery with all those prominent partners at the top. An author should not need lawyers to write a book, but I would have had great difficulty without mine. I greatly appreciate their assistance.

What an author *does* need is editors, a publisher, researchers, consultants, and friends, and I have been particularly blessed with good ones. My very dear friend Taylor Branch edited the book, and I continue to be impressed with his great skill in making my ideas and language coherent. Taylor has also served as my agent, and in this capacity, too, he has done me great service.

I had a wonderful research team, without which I never could have sifted through the masses of material and run down leads in so many places. I thank them all, and I want to acknowledge their contributions. Diane St. Clair was the mainstay of the group. She put together a system for filing and cross-indexing that worked beyond all expectations. (Special thanks to *Newsday*'s Bob Greene, whose suggestions for organizing a large investigation came to us through the auspices of Investigative Reporters and Editors, Inc.) Not until a week before the book was finally finished did I fail to find a document which I needed; naturally, it was something I had misfiled myself. Diane also contributed greatly to the Cold War chapter. Richard Sokolow made similar contributions to the Mushroom and Safehouse chapters. His work was solid, and his energy boundless. Jay Peterzell delved deeply into Dr. Cameron's "depatterning" work in Montreal and stayed with it when others might have quit. Jay also did first-rate studies of brainwashing and sensory deprivation. Jim Mintz and Ken Cummins provided excellent assistance in the early research stage.

The Center for National Security Studies, under my good friend Robert Borosage, provided physical support and research aid, and I would like to express my appreciation. My thanks also to Morton Halperin who continued the support when he became director of the Center. I also appreciated the help of Penny Bevis, Hannah Delaney, Florence Oliver, Aldora Whittaker, Nick Fiore, and Monica Andres.

My sister, Dr. Patricia Greenfield, did excellent work on the CIA's interface with academia and on the Personality Assessment System. I want to acknowledge her contribution to the book and express my thanks and love.

There has been a whole galaxy of people who have provided specialized help, and I would like to thank them all: Jeff Kohan, Eddie Becker, Sam Zuckerman, Matthew Meselson, Julian Robinson, Milton Kline, Marty Lee, M. J. Conklin, Alan Scheflin, Bonnie Goldstein, Paul Avery, Bill Mills, John Lilly, Humphrey Osmond, Julie Haggerty, Patrick Oster, Norman Kempster, Bill Richards, Paul Magnusson, Andy Sommer, Mark Cheshire, Sidney Cohen, Paul Altmeyer, Fred and Elsa Kleiner, Dr. John Cavanagh, and Senator James Abourezk and his staff.

I sent drafts of the first ten chapters to many of the people I interviewed (and several who refused to be interviewed). My aim was to have them correct any inaccuracies or point out material taken out of context. The comments of those who responded aided me considerably in preparing the final book. My thanks for their assistance to Albert Hofmann, Telford Taylor, Leo Alexander, Walter Langer, John Stockwell, William Hood, Samuel Thompson, Sidney Cohen, Milton Greenblatt, Gordon Wasson, James Moore, Laurence Hinkle, Charles Osgood, John Gittinger (for Chapter 10 only), and all the others who asked not to be identified.

Finally, I would like to express my appreciation to my publisher, Times Books, and especially to my editor John J. Simon. John, Tom Lipscomb, Roger Jellinek, Gyorgyi Voros, and John Gallagher all believed in this book from the beginning and provided outstanding support. Thanks also go to Judith H. McQuown, who copyedited the manuscript, and Rosalyn T. Badalamenti, Times Books' Production Editor, who oversaw the whole production process.

John Marks
Washington, D.C.
October 26, 1978

CONTENTS

PART I ORIGINS OF MIND-CONTROL RESEARCH

1. WORLD WAR II   3
2. COLD WAR ON THE MIND   21
3. THE PROFESSOR AND THE "A" TREATMENT   34

PART II INTELLIGENCE OR "WITCHES POTIONS"

4. LSD   53
5. CONCERNING THE CASE OF DR. FRANK OLSON   73
6. THEM UNWITTING: THE SAFEHOUSES   87
7. MUSHROOMS TO COUNTERCULTURE   105

PART III SPELLS—ELECTRODES AND HYPNOSIS

8. BRAINWASHING   125
9. HUMAN ECOLOGY   147
10. THE GITTINGER ASSESSMENT SYSTEM   164
11. HYPNOSIS   182

PART IV   CONCLUSIONS

12. THE SEARCH FOR THE TRUTH   195

    NOTES   215

    INDEX   231

PART

I

ORIGINS OF MIND-CONTROL RESEARCH

If the doors of perception were cleansed, every thing would appear to man as it is, infinite.   —WILLIAM BLAKE.

It is far pleasanter to sit comfortably in the shade rubbing red pepper in a poor devil's eyes than to go about in the sun hunting up evidence.   —SIR JAMES STEPHENS, 1883.

If both the past and the external world exist only in the mind, and if the mind itself is controllable—what then?
                    —GEORGE ORWELL IN *1984*.

CHAPTER
1
WORLD WAR II

On the outskirts of Basel, Switzerland, overlooking the Rhine, lies the worldwide headquarters of the Sandoz drug and chemical empire. There, on the afternoon of April 16, 1943, Dr. Albert Hofmann made an extraordinary discovery—by accident.

At 37, with close-cropped hair and rimless glasses, Hofmann headed the company's research program to develop marketable drugs out of natural products. He was hard at work in his laboratory that warm April day when a wave of dizziness suddenly overcame him. The strange sensation was not unpleasant, and Hofmann felt almost as though he were drunk.

But he became quite restless. His nerves seemed to run off in different directions. The inebriation was unlike anything he had ever known before. Leaving work early, Hofmann managed a wobbly bicycle-ride home. He lay down and closed his eyes, still unable to shake the dizziness. Now the light of day was disagreeably bright. With the external world shut out, his mind raced along. He experienced what he would later describe as "an uninterrupted stream of fantastic images of extraordinary plasticity and vividness. . . . accompanied by an intense, kaleidoscope-like play of colors."

These visions subsided after a few hours, and Hofmann, ever the inquiring scientist, set out to find what caused them. He presumed he had somehow ingested one of the drugs with which he had been working that day, and his prime suspect was d-lysergic acid diethylamide, or LSD, a substance that he himself had first produced in the same lab five years earlier. As part of his search for a circulation stimulant, Hofmann had been examining derivatives of ergot, a fungus that attacks rye.

Ergot had a mysterious, contradictory reputation. In China and some Arab countries, it was thought to have medicinal powers, but in Europe it was associated with the horrible malady from the Middle Ages called St. Anthony's Fire, which struck periodically like the plague. The disease turned fingers and toes into blackened stumps and led to madness and death.

Hofmann guessed that he had absorbed some ergot derivative through his skin, perhaps while changing the filter paper in a suction bottle. To test his theory, he spent three days making up a fresh batch of LSD. Cautiously he swallowed 250 micrograms (less than 1/100,000 of an ounce). Hofmann planned to take more gradually through the day to obtain a result, since no known drug had any effect on the human body in such infinitesimal amounts. He had no way of knowing that because of LSD's potency, he had already taken several times what would later be termed an ordinary dose. Unexpectedly, this first speck of LSD took hold after about 40 minutes, and Hofmann was off on the first self-induced "trip" of modern times.*

Hofmann recalls he felt "horrific . . . I was afraid. I feared I was becoming crazy. I had the idea I was out of my body. I thought I had died. I did not know how it would finish. If you know you will come back from this very strange world, only then can you enjoy it." Of course, Hofmann had no way of knowing that he would return. While he had quickly recovered from his accidental trip three days earlier, he did not know how much LSD had caused it or whether the present dose was more than his body could detoxify. His mind kept veering off into an unknown dimension, but he was unable to appreciate much beyond his own terror.

Less than 200 miles from Hofmann's laboratory, doctors connected to the S.S. and Gestapo were doing experiments that led to the testing of mescaline (a drug which has many of the mind-changing qualities of LSD) on prisoners at Dachau. Germany's secret policemen had the notion, completely alien to Hofmann, that they could use drugs like mescaline to bring unwilling people under their control. According to research

---

*While Hofmann specifically used the word "trip" in a 1977 interview to describe his consciousness-altering experience, the word obviously had no such meaning in 1943 and is used here anachronistically.

team member Walter Neff, the goal of the Dachau experiments was "to eliminate the will of the person examined."

At Dachau, Nazis took the search for scientific knowledge of military value to its most awful extreme. There, in a closely guarded, fenced-off part of the camp, S.S. doctors studied such questions as the amount of time a downed airman could survive in the North Atlantic in February. Information of this sort was considered important to German security, since skilled pilots were in relatively short supply. So, at Heinrich Himmler's personal order, the doctors at Dachau simply sat by huge tubs of ice water with stopwatches and timed how long it took immersed prisoners to die. In other experiments, under the cover of "aviation medicine," inmates were crushed to death in high-altitude pressure chambers (to learn how high pilots could safely fly), and prisoners were shot, so that special blood coagulants could be tested on their wounds.

The mescaline tests at Dachau run by Dr. Kurt Plötner were not nearly so lethal as the others in the "aviation" series, but the drug could still cause grave damage, particularly to anyone who already had some degree of mental instability. The danger was increased by the fact that the mescaline was administered covertly by S.S. men who spiked the prisoners' drinks. Unlike Dr. Hofmann, the subjects had no idea that a drug was causing their extreme disorientation. Many must have feared they had gone stark mad all on their own. Always, the subjects of these experiments were Jews, gypsies, Russians, and other groups on whose lives the Nazis placed little or no value. In no way were any of them true volunteers, although some may have come forward under the delusion that they would receive better treatment.

After the war, Neff told American investigators that the subjects showed a wide variety of reactions. Some became furious; others were melancholy or gay, as if they were drunk. Not surprisingly, "sentiments of hatred and revenge were exposed in every case." Neff noted that the drug caused certain people to reveal their "most intimate secrets." Still, the Germans were not ready to accept mescaline as a substitute for their more physical methods of interrogation. They went on to try hypnosis in combination with the drug, but they apparently never felt confident that they had found a way to assume command of their victim's mind.

Even as the S.S. doctors were carrying on their experiments

at Dachau, the Office of Strategic Services (OSS), America's wartime intelligence agency, set up a "truth drug" committee under Dr. Winfred Overholser, head of St. Elizabeth's Hospital in Washington. The committee quickly tried and rejected mescaline, several barbiturates, and scopolamine. Then, during the spring of 1943, the committee decided that *cannabis indica* —or marijuana—showed the most promise, and it started a testing program in cooperation with the Manhattan Project, the TOP SECRET effort to build an atomic bomb. It is not clear why OSS turned to the bomb makers for help, except that, as one former Project official puts it, "Our secret was so great, I guess we were safer than anyone else." Apparently, top Project leaders, who went to incredible lengths to preserve security, saw no danger in trying out drugs on their personnel.

The Manhattan Project supplied the first dozen test subjects, who were asked to swallow a concentrated, liquid form of marijuana that an American pharmaceutical company furnished in small glass vials. A Project man who was present recalls: "It didn't work the way we wanted. Apparently the human system would not take it all at once orally. The subjects would lean over and vomit." What is more, they disclosed no secrets, and one subject wound up in the hospital.

Back to the drawing board went the OSS experts. They decided that the best way to administer the marijuana was inhalation of its fumes. Attempts were made to pour the solution on burning charcoal, and an OSS officer named George White (who had already succeeded in knocking himself out with an overdose of the relatively potent substance) tried out the vapor, without sufficient effect, at St. Elizabeth's. Finally, the OSS group discovered a delivery system which had been known for years to jazz musicians and other users: the cigarette. OSS documents reported that smoking a mix of tobacco and the marijuana essence brought on a "state of irresponsibility, causing the subject to be loquacious and free in his impartation of information."

The first field test of these marijuana-laced cigarettes took place on May 27, 1943. The subject was one August Del Gracio, who was described in OSS documents as a "notorious New York gangster."* George White, an Army captain who had come to

---

*Del Gracio's name was deleted by the CIA from the OSS document that described the incident, but his identity was learned from the papers of George

OSS from the Federal Bureau of Narcotics, administered the drug by inviting Del Gracio up to his apartment for a smoke and a chat. White had been talking to Del Gracio earlier about securing the Mafia's cooperation to keep Axis agents out of the New York waterfront and to prepare the way for the invasion of Sicily.*

Del Gracio had already made it clear to White that he personally had taken part in killing informers who had squealed to the Feds. The gangster was as tough as they came, and if he could be induced to talk under the influence of a truth drug, certainly German prisoners could—or so the reasoning went. White plied him with cigarettes until "subject became high and extremely garrulous." Over the next two hours, Del Gracio told the Federal agent about the ins and outs of the drug trade (revealing information so sensitive that the CIA deleted it from the OSS documents it released 34 years later). At one point in the conversation, after Del Gracio had begun to talk, the gangster told White, "Whatever you do, don't ever use any of the stuff I'm telling you." In a subsequent session, White packed the cigarettes with so much marijuana that Del Gracio became unconscious for about an hour. Yet, on the whole the experiment was considered a success in "loosening the subject's tongue."

While members of the truth-drug committee never believed that the concentrated marijuana could compel a person to confess his deepest secrets, they authorized White to push ahead with the testing. On the next stage, he and a Manhattan Project counterintelligence man borrowed 15 to 18 thick dossiers from the FBI and went off to try the marijuana on suspected Communist soldiers stationed in military camps outside Atlanta, Memphis, and New Orleans. According to White's Manhattan Project sidekick, a Harvard Law graduate and future judge, they worked out a standard interrogation technique:

White, whose widow donated them to Foothills College in Los Altos, California. CIA officials cut virtually all the names from the roughly 16,000 pages of its own papers and the few score pages from OSS that it released to me under the Freedom of Information Act. However, as in this case, many of the names could be found through collateral sources.

*Naval intelligence officers eventually made a deal in which mob leaders promised to cooperate, and as a direct result, New York Governor Thomas Dewey ordered Del Gracio's chief, boss of bosses, Charles "Lucky" Luciano freed from jail in 1946.

Before we went in, George and I would buy cigarettes, remove them from the bottom of the pack, use a hypodermic needle to put in the fluid, and leave the cigarettes in a shot glass to dry. Then, we resealed the pack. . . . We sat down with a particular soldier and tried to win his confidence. We would say something like "This is better than being overseas and getting shot at," and we would try to break them. We started asking questions from their [FBI] folder, and we would let them see that we had the folder on them . . . We had a pitcher of ice water on the table, and we knew the drug had taken effect when they reached for a glass. The stuff actually worked. . . . Everyone but one—and he didn't smoke—gave us more information than we had before.

The Manhattan Project lawyer remembers this swing through the South with George White as a "good time." The two men ate in the best restaurants and took in all the sights. "George was quite a guy," he says. "At the Roosevelt Hotel in New Orleans after we had interviewed our men, we were lying on the beds when George took out his pistol and shot his initials into the molding that ran along the ceiling. He used his .22 automatic, equipped with a silencer, and he emptied several clips." Asked if he tried out the truth drug himself, the lawyer says, "Yes. The cigarettes gave you a feeling of walking a couple of feet off the floor. I had a pleasant sensation of well-being. . . . The fellows from my office wouldn't take a cigarette from me for the rest of the war."

Since World War II, the United States government, led by the Central Intelligence Agency, has searched secretly for ways to control human behavior. This book is about that search, which had its origins in World War II. The CIA programs were not only an extension of the OSS quest for a truth drug, but they also echoed such events as the Nazi experiments at Dachau and Albert Hofmann's discovery of LSD.

By probing the inner reaches of consciousness, Hofmann's research took him to the very frontiers of knowledge. As never before in history, the warring powers sought ideas from scientists capable of reaching those frontiers—ideas that could make the difference between victory and defeat. While Hofmann himself remained aloof, in the Swiss tradition, other scientists, like Albert Einstein, helped turned the abstractions of the laboratory into incredibly destructive weapons. Jules Verne's notions of spaceships touching the moon stopped being absurd when Wernher von Braun's rockets started pounding London. With their creations, the scientists reached beyond the speculations of science fiction. Never before had their discoveries been so breathtaking and so frightening. Albert Hofmann's work touched upon the fantasies of the mind—accessible, in ancient legends, to witches and wizards who used spells and potions to bring people under their sway. In the early scientific age, the dream of controlling the brain took on a modern form in Mary Shelley's creation, Dr. Frankenstein's monster. The dream would be updated again during the Cold War era to become the Manchurian Candidate, the assassin whose mind was controlled by a hostile government.* Who could say for certain that such a fantasy would not be turned into a reality, like Verne's rocket stories or Einstein's calculations? And who should be surprised to learn that government agencies—specifically the CIA—would swoop down on Albert Hofmann's lab in an effort to harness the power over the mind that LSD seemed to hold?

From the Dachau experiments came the cruelty that man was capable of heaping upon his fellows in the name of advancing science and helping his country gain advantage in war. To say that the Dachau experiments are object lessons of how far people can stretch ends to justify means is to belittle by cliché what occurred in the concentration camps. Nothing the CIA ever did in its postwar search for mind-control technology came close to the callous killing of the Nazi "aviation research." Nevertheless, in their attempts to find ways to manipulate people, Agency officials and their agents crossed many of the same ethical barriers. They experimented with dangerous

*The term "Manchurian Candidate" came into the language in 1959 when author Richard Condon made it the title of his best-selling novel that later became a popular movie starring Laurence Harvey and Frank Sinatra. The story was about a joint Soviet-Chinese plot to take an American soldier captured in Korea, condition him at a special brainwashing center located in Manchuria, and create a remote-controlled assassin who was supposed to kill the President of the United States. Condon consulted with a wide variety of experts while researching the book, and some inside sources may well have filled him in on the gist of a discussion that took place at a 1953 meeting at the CIA on behavior control. Said one participant, ". . . individuals who had come out of North Korea across the Soviet Union to freedom recently apparently had a blank period of disorientation while passing through a special zone in Manchuria." The CIA and military men at this session promised to seek more information, but the matter never came up again in either the documents released by the Agency or in the interviews done for this book.

and unknown techniques on people who had no idea what was happening. They systematically violated the free will and mental dignity of their subjects, and, like the Germans, they chose to victimize special groups of people whose existence they considered, out of prejudice and convenience, less worthy than their own. Wherever their extreme experiments went, the CIA sponsors picked for subjects their own equivalents of the Nazis' Jews and gypsies: mental patients, prostitutes, foreigners, drug addicts, and prisoners, often from minority ethnic groups.

In the postwar era, American officials straddled the ethical and the cutthroat approaches to scientific research. After an Allied tribunal had convicted the first echelon of surviving Nazi war criminals—the Görings and Speers—American prosecutors charged the Dachau doctors with "crimes against humanity" at a second Nuremberg trial. None of the German scientists expressed remorse. Most claimed that someone else had carried out the vilest experiments. All said that issues of moral and personal responsibility are moot in state-sponsored research. What is critical, testified Dr. Karl Brandt, Hitler's personal physician, is "whether the experiment is important or unimportant." Asked his attitude toward killing human beings in the course of medical research, Brandt replied, "Do you think that one can obtain any worthwhile fundamental results without a definite toll of lives?" The judges at Nuremberg rejected such defenses and put forth what came to be known as the Nuremberg Code on scientific research.* Its main points were simple: Researchers must obtain full voluntary consent from all subjects; experiments should yield fruitful results for the good of society that can be obtained in no other way; researchers should not conduct tests where death or serious injury might occur, "except, perhaps" when the supervising doctors also serve as subjects. The judges—all Americans—sentenced seven of the Germans, including Dr. Brandt, to death by hanging. Nine others received long prison sentences. Thus, the U.S. government put its full moral force behind the idea that there were limits on what scientists could do to human subjects, even when a country's security was thought to hang in the balance.

The Nuremberg Code has remained official American pol-

---

*The Code was suggested in essentially its final form by prosecution team consultant, Dr. Leo Alexander, a Boston psychiatrist.

icy ever since 1946, but, even before the verdicts were in, special U.S. investigating teams were sifting through the experimental records at Dachau for information of military value. The report of one such team found that while part of the data was "inaccurate," some of the conclusions, if confirmed, would be "an important complement to existing knowledge." Military authorities sent the records, including a description of the mescaline and hypnosis experiments, back to the United States. None of the German mind-control research was ever made public.

Immediately after the war, large political currents began to shift in the world, as they always do. Allies became enemies and enemies became allies. Other changes were fresh and yet old. In the United States, the new Cold War against communism carried with it a piercing sense of fear and a sweeping sense of mission—at least as far as American leaders were concerned. Out of these feelings and out of that overriding American faith in advancing technology came the CIA's attempts to tame hostile minds and make spy fantasies real. Experiments went forward and the CIA's scientists—bitten, sometimes obsessed—kept going back to their laboratories for one last adjustment. Some theories were crushed, while others emerged in unexpected ways that would have a greater impact outside the CIA than in the world of covert operations. Only one aspect remained constant during the quarter-century of active research: The CIA's interest in controlling the human mind had to remain absolutely secret.

World War II provided more than the grand themes of the CIA's behavioral programs. It also became the formative life experience of the principal CIA officials, and, indeed, of the CIA itself as an institution. The secret derring-do of the OSS was new to the United States, and the ways of the OSS would grow into the ways of the CIA. OSS leaders would have their counterparts later in the Agency. CIA officials tended to have known the OSS men, to think like them, to copy their methods, and even, in some cases, to be the same people. When Agency officials wanted to launch their massive effort for mind control, for instance, they got out the old OSS documents and went about their goal in many of the same ways the OSS had. OSS leaders enlisted outside scientists; Agency officials also went to the most prestigious ones in academia and industry, soliciting aid for the good of the country. They even approached the same

George White who had shot his initials in the hotel ceiling while on OSS assignment.

Years later, White's escapades with OSS and CIA would carry with them a humor clearly unintended at the time. To those directly involved, influencing human behavior was a deadly serious business, but qualities like bumbling and pure craziness shine through in hindsight. In the CIA's campaign, some of America's most distinguished behavioral scientists would stick all kinds of drugs and wires into their experimental subjects—often dismissing the obviously harmful effects with theories reminiscent of the learned nineteenth-century physicians who bled their patients with leeches and belittled the ignorance of anyone who questioned the technique. If the schemes of these scientists to control the mind had met with more success, they would be much less amusing. But so far, at least, the human spirit has apparently kept winning. That—if anything—is the saving grace of the mind-control campaign.

World War II signaled the end of American isolation and innocence, and the United States found it had a huge gap to close, with its enemies and allies alike, in applying underhanded tactics to war. Unlike Britain, which for hundreds of years had used covert operations to hold her empire together, the United States had no tradition of using subversion as a secret instrument of government policy. The Germans, the French, the Russians, and nearly everyone else had long been involved in this game, although no one seemed as good at it as the British.

Clandestine lobbying by British agents in the United States led directly to President Franklin Roosevelt's creation of the organization that became OSS in 1942. This was the first American agency set up to wage secret, unlimited war. Roosevelt placed it under the command of a Wall Street lawyer and World War I military hero, General William "Wild Bill" Donovan. A burly, vigorous Republican millionaire with great intellectual curiosity, Donovan started as White House intelligence adviser even before Pearl Harbor, and he had direct access to the President.

Learning at the feet of the British who made available their expertise, if not all their secrets, Donovan put together an organization where nothing had existed before. A Columbia College and Columbia Law graduate himself, he tended to turn to the gentlemanly preserves of the Eastern establishment for re-

cruits. (The initials OSS were said to stand for "Oh So Social.")
Friends—or friends of friends—could be trusted. "Old boys"
were the stalwarts of the British secret service, and, as with
most other aspects of OSS, the Americans followed suit.

One of Donovan's new recruits was Richard Helms, a young
newspaper executive then best known for having gained an
interview with Adolf Hitler in 1936 while working for United
Press. Having gone to Le Rosey, the same Swiss prep school as
the Shah of Iran, and then on to clubby Williams College,
Helms moved easily among the young OSS men. He was already more taciturn than the jovial Donovan, but he was
equally ambitious and skilled as a judge of character. For
Helms, OSS spywork began a lifelong career. He would become
the most important sponsor of mind-control research within
the CIA, nurturing and promoting it throughout his steady
climb to the top position in the Agency.

Like every major wartime official from President Roosevelt
down, General Donovan believed that World War II was in
large measure a battle of science and organization. The idea
was to mobilize science for defense, and the Roosevelt administration set up a costly, intertwining network of research programs to deal with everything from splitting the atom to pre-
venting mental breakdowns in combat. Donovan named Boston
industrialist Stanley Lovell to head OSS Research and Development and to be the secret agency's liaison with the government
scientific community.

A Cornell graduate and a self-described "saucepan chemist,"
Lovell was a confident energetic man with a particular knack
for coming up with offbeat ideas and selling them to others.
Like most of his generation, he was an outspoken patriot. He
wrote in his diary shortly after Pearl Harbor: "As James Hilton
said, 'Once at war, to reason is treason.' My job is clear—to do
all that is in me to help America."

General Donovan minced no words in laying out what he
expected of Lovell: "I need every subtle device and every underhanded trick to use against the Germans and Japanese—
by our own people—but especially by the underground resistance programs in all the occupied countries. You'll have
to invent them all, Lovell, because you're going to be my
man." Thus Lovell recalled his marching orders from Donovan, which he instantly received on being introduced to the
blustery, hyperactive OSS chief. Lovell had never met any-

one with Donovan's personal magnetism.

Lovell quickly turned to some of the leading lights in the academic and private sectors. A special group—called Division 19—within James Conant's National Defense Research Committee was set up to produce "miscellaneous weapons" for OSS and British intelligence. Lovell's strategy, he later wrote, was "to stimulate the Peck's Bad Boy beneath the surface of every American scientist and to say to him, 'Throw all your normal law-abiding concepts out the window. Here's a chance to raise merry hell.'"

Dr. George Kistiakowsky, the Harvard chemist who worked on explosives research during the war (and who became science adviser to Presidents Eisenhower and Kennedy) remembers Stanley Lovell well: "Stan came to us and asked us to develop ways for camouflaging explosives which could be smuggled into enemy countries." Kistiakowsky and an associate came up with a substance which was dubbed "Aunt Jemima" because it looked and tasted like pancake mix. Says Kistiakowsky: "You could bake bread or other things out of it. I personally took it to a high-level meeting at the War Department and ate cookies in front of all those characters to show them what a wonderful invention it was. All you had to do was attach a powerful detonator, and it exploded with the force of dynamite." Thus disguised, "Aunt Jemima" could be slipped into occupied lands. It was credited with blowing up at least one major bridge in China.

Lovell encouraged OSS behavioral scientists to find something that would offend Japanese cultural sensibilities. His staff anthropologists reported back that nothing was so shameful to the Japanese soldier as his bowel movements. Lovell then had the chemists work up a skatole compound which duplicated the odor of diarrhea. It was loaded into collapsible tubes, flown to China, and distributed to children in enemy-occupied cities. When a Japanese officer appeared on a crowded street, the kids were encouraged to slip up behind him and squirt the liquid on the seat of his pants. Lovell named the product "Who? Me?" and he credited it with costing the Japanese "face."

Unlike most weapons, "Who? Me?" was not designed to kill or maim. It was a "harassment substance" designed to lower the morale of individual Japanese. The inspiration came from academicians who tried to make a science of human behavior.

During World War II, the behavioral sciences were still very much in their infancy, but OSS—well before most of the outside world—recognized their potential in warfare. Psychology and psychiatry, sociology, and anthropology all seemed to offer insights that could be exploited to manipulate the enemy.

General Donovan himself believed that the techniques of psychoanalysis might be turned on Adolf Hitler to get a better idea of "the things that made him tick," as Donovan put it. Donovan gave the job of being the Führer's analyst to Walter Langer, a Cambridge, Massachusetts psychoanalyst whose older brother William had taken leave from a chair of history at Harvard to head OSS Research and Analysis.* Langer protested that a study of Hitler based on available data would be highly uncertain and that conventional psychiatric and psychoanalytic methods could not be used without direct access to the patient. Donovan was not the sort to be deterred by such details. He told Langer to go ahead anyway.

With the help of a small research staff, Langer looked through everything he could find on Hitler and interviewed a number of people who had known the German leader. Aware of the severe limitations on his information, but left no choice by General Donovan, Langer plowed ahead and wrote up a final study. It pegged Hitler as a "neurotic psychopath" and proceeded to pick apart the Führer's psyche. Langer, since retired to Florida, believes he came "pretty close" to describing the real Adolf Hitler. He is particularly proud of his predictions that the Nazi leader would become increasingly disturbed as Germany suffered more and more defeats and that he would commit suicide rather than face capture.

One reason for psychoanalyzing Hitler was to uncover vulnerabilities that could be covertly exploited. Stanley Lovell seized upon one of Langer's ideas—that Hitler might have feminine tendencies—and got permission from the OSS hierarchy to see if he could push the Führer over the gender line.† "The

*Four months before Pearl Harbor, Donovan had enlisted Walter Langer to put together a nationwide network of analysts to study the morale of the country's young men, who, it was widely feared, were not enthusiastic about fighting a foreign war. Pearl Harbor seemed to solve this morale problem, but Langer stayed with Donovan as a part-time psychoanalytic consultant.

†Langer wrote that Hitler was "masochistic in the extreme inasmuch as he derives sexual pleasure from punishment inflicted on his own body. There is every reason to suppose that during his early years, instead of identifying himself with his father as most boys do, he identified with his mother. This was

hope was that his moustache would fall off and his voice become soprano," Lovell wrote. Lovell used OSS's agent network to try to slip female sex hormones into Hitler's food, but nothing apparently came of it. Nor was there ever any payoff to other Lovell schemes to blind Hitler permanently with mustard gas or to use a drug to exacerbate his suspected epilepsy. The main problem in these operations—all of which were tried—was to get Hitler to take the medicine. Failure of the delivery schemes also kept Hitler alive—OSS was simultaneously trying to poison him.*

Without question, murdering a man was a decisive way to influence his behavior, and OSS scientists developed an arsenal of chemical and biological poisons that included the incredibly potent botulinus toxin, whose delivery system was a gelatin capsule smaller than the head of a pin. Lovell and his associates also realized there were less drastic ways to manipulate an enemy's behavior, and they came up with a line of products to cause sickness, itching, baldness, diarrhea, and/or the odor thereof. They had less success finding a drug to compel truth-telling, but it was not for lack of trying.

Chemical and biological substances had been used in war-time long before OSS came on the scene. Both sides had used poison gas in World War I; during the early part of World War II, the Japanese had dropped deadly germs on China and caused epidemics; and throughout the war, the Allies and Axis powers alike had built up chemical and biological warfare (CBW) stockpiles, whose main function turned out, in the end, to be deterring the other side. Military men tended to look on CBW as a way of destroying whole armies and even populations. Like the world's other secret services, OSS individualized

---

perhaps easier for him than for most boys since, as we have seen, there is a large feminine component in his physical makeup. . . . His extreme sentimentality, his emotionality, his occasional softness, and his weeping, even after he became Chancellor, may be regarded as manifestations of a fundamental pattern that undoubtedly had its origin in his relationship to his mother."

*Although historians have long known that OSS men had been in touch with the German officers who tried to assassinate Hitler in 1944, the fact that OSS independently was trying to murder him has eluded scholars of the period. Stanley Lovell gave away the secret in his 1963 book, *Of Spies and Stratagems,* but he used such casual and obscure words that the researchers apparently did not notice. Lovell wrote: "I supplied now and then a carbamate or other quietus medication, all to be injected into *der Führer's* carrots, beets, or whatever." A "quietus medicine" is a generic term for a lethal poison, of which carbamates are one type.

CBW and made it into a way of selectively but secretly embarrassing, disorienting, incapacitating, injuring, or killing an enemy.

As diversified as were Lovell's scientific duties for OSS, they were narrow in comparison with those of his main counterpart in the CIA's postwar mind-control program, Dr. Sidney Gottlieb. Gottlieb would preside over investigations that ranged from advanced research in amnesia by electroshock to dragnet searches through the jungles of Latin America for toxic leaves and barks. Fully in the tradition of making Hitler moustacheless, Gottlieb's office would devise a scheme to make Fidel Castro's beard fall out; like Lovell, Gottlieb would personally provide operators with deadly poisons to assassinate foreign leaders like the Congo's Patrice Lumumba, and he would be equally at ease discussing possible applications of new research in neurology. On a much greater scale than Lovell's, Gottlieb would track down every conceivable gimmick that might give one person leverage over another's mind. Gottlieb would preside over arcane fields from handwriting analysis to stress creation, and he would rise through the Agency along with his bureaucratic patron, Richard Helms.

Early in the war, General Donovan got another idea from the British, whose psychologists and psychiatrists had devised a testing program to predict the performance of military officers. Donovan thought such a program might help OSS sort through the masses of recruits who were being rushed through training. To create an assessment system for Americans, Donovan called in Harvard psychology professor Henry "Harry" Murray. In 1938 Murray had written *Explorations of Personality,* a notable book which laid out a whole battery of tests that could be used to size up the personalities of individuals. "Spying is attractive to loonies," states Murray. "Psychopaths, who are people who spend their lives making up stories, revel in the field." The program's prime objective, according to Murray, was keeping out the crazies, as well as the "sloths, irritants, bad actors, and free talkers."

Always in a hurry, Donovan gave Murray and a distinguished group of colleagues only 15 days until the first candidates arrived to be assessed. In the interim, they took over a spacious estate outside Washington as their headquarters. In a series of hurried meetings, they put together an assessment system that combined German and British methods with Murray's earlier research. It tested a recruit's ability to stand up under pressure, to be a leader, to hold liquor, to lie skillfully, and to read a person's character by the nature of his clothing.

More than 30 years after the war, Murray remains modest in his claims for the assessment system, saying that it was only an aid in weeding out the "horrors" among OSS candidates. Nevertheless, the secret agency's leaders believed in its results, and Murray's system became a fixture in OSS, testing Americans and foreign agents alike. Some of Murray's young behavioral scientists, like John Gardner,* would go on to become prominent in public affairs, and, more importantly, the OSS assessment program would be recognized as a milestone in American psychology. It was the first systematic effort to evaluate an individual's personality in order to predict his future behavior. After the war, personality assessment would become a new field in itself, and some of Murray's assistants would go on to establish OSS-like systems at large corporations, starting with AT&T. They also would set up study programs at universities, beginning with the University of California at Berkley.† As would happen repeatedly with the CIA's mind-control research, OSS was years ahead of public developments in behavioral theory and application.

In the postwar years, Murray would be superseded by a young Oklahoma psychologist John Gittinger, who would rise in the CIA on the strength of his ideas about how to make a hard science out of personality assessment and how to use it to manipulate people. Gittinger would build an office within CIA that refined both Murray's assessment function and Walter Langer's indirect analysis of foreign leaders. Gittinger's methods would become an integral part of everyday Agency operations, and he would become Sid Gottlieb's protégé.

Stanley Lovell reasoned that a good way to kill Hitler—and the OSS man was always looking for ideas—would be to hypnoti-

---

*Gardner, a psychologist teaching at Mount Holyoke College, helped Murray set up the original program and went on to open the West Coast OSS assessment site at a converted beach club in San Juan Capistrano. After the war, he would become Secretary of HEW in the Johnson administration and founder of Common Cause.

†Murray is not at all enthusiastic with the spinoffs. "Some of the things done with it turn your stomach," he declares.

cally control a German prisoner to hate the Gestapo and the Nazi regime and then to give the subject a hypnotic suggestion to assassinate the Führer. The OSS candidate would be let loose in Germany where he would take the desired action, "being under a compulsion that might not be denied," as Lovell wrote.

Lovell sought advice on whether this scheme would work from New York psychiatrist Lawrence Kubie and from the famed Menninger brothers, Karl and William. The Menningers reported that the weight of the evidence showed hypnotism to be incapable of making people do anything that they would not otherwise do. Equally negative, Dr. Kubie added that if a German prisoner had a logical reason to kill Hitler or anyone else, he would not need hypnotism to motivate him.

Lovell and his coworkers apparently accepted this skeptical view of hypnosis, as did the overwhelming majority of psychologists and psychiatrists in the country. At the time, hypnosis was considered a fringe activity, and there was little recognition of either its validity or its usefulness for any purpose— let alone covert operations. Yet there were a handful of serious experimenters in the field who believed in its military potential. The most vocal partisan of this view was the head of the Psychology Department at Colgate University, George "Esty" Estabrooks. Since the early 1930s, Estabrooks had periodically ventured out from his sleepy upstate campus to advise the military on applications of hypnotism.

Estabrooks acknowledged that hypnosis did not work on everyone and that only one person in five made a good enough subject to be placed in a deep trance, or state of somnambulism. He believed that only these subjects could be made to do such things against their apparent will as reveal secrets or commit crimes. He had watched respected members of the community make fools of themselves in the hands of stage hypnotists, and he had compelled his own students to reveal fraternity secrets and the details of private love affairs—all of which the subjects presumably did not want to do.

Still his experience was limited. Estabrooks realized that the only certain way to know whether a person would commit a crime like murder under hypnosis was to have the person kill someone. Unwilling to settle the issue on his own by trying the experiment, he felt that government sanction of the process would relieve the hypnotist of personal responsibility. "Any 'accidents' that might occur during the experiments will simply be charged to profit and loss," he wrote, "a very trifling portion of that enormous wastage in human life which is part and parcel of war."

After Pearl Harbor, Estabrooks offered his ideas to OSS, but they were not accepted by anyone in government willing to carry them to their logical conclusion. He was reduced to writing books about the potential use of hypnotism in warfare. Cassandra-like, he tried to warn America of the perils posed by hypnotic control. His 1945 novel, *Death in the Mind,* concerned a series of seemingly treasonable acts committed by Allied personnel: an American submarine captain torpedoes one of our own battleships, and the beautiful heroine starts acting in an irrational way which serves the enemy. After a perilous investigation, secret agent Johnny Evans learns that the Germans have been hypnotizing Allied personnel and conditioning them to obey Nazi commands. Evans and his cohorts, shaken by the many ways hypnotism can be used against them, set up elaborate countermeasures and then cannot resist going on the offensive. Objections are heard from the heroine, who by this time has been brutally and rather graphically tortured. She complains that "doing things to people's minds" is "a loathsome way to fight." Her qualms are brushed aside by Johnny Evans, her lover and boss. He sets off after the Germans—"to tamper with their minds; Make them traitors; Make them work for us."

In the aftermath of the war, as the U.S. national security apparatus was being constructed, the leaders of the Central Intelligence Agency would adopt Johnny Evans' mission—almost in those very words. Richard Helms, Sid Gottlieb, John Gittinger, George White, and many others would undertake a far-flung and complicated assault on the human mind. In hypnosis and many other fields, scientists even more eager than George Estabrooks would seek CIA approval for the kinds of experiments they would not dare perform on their own. Sometimes the Agency men concurred; on other occasions, they reserved such experiments for themselves. They would tamper with many minds and inevitably cause some to be damaged. In the end, they would minimize and hide their deeds, and they would live to see doubts raised about the health of their own minds.

CHAPTER

2

COLD WAR
ON THE MIND

CIA officials started preliminary work on drugs and hypnosis shortly after the Agency's creation in 1947, but the behavior-control program did not really get going until the Hungarian government put Josef Cardinal Mindszenty on trial in 1949. With a glazed look in his eyes, Mindszenty confessed to crimes of treason he apparently did not commit. His performance recalled the Moscow purge trials of 1937 and 1938 at which tough and dedicated party *apparatchiks* had meekly pleaded guilty to long series of improbable offenses. These and a string of postwar trials in other Eastern European countries seemed staged, eerie, and unreal. CIA men felt they had to know how the Communists had rendered the defendants zombielike. In the Mindszenty case, a CIA Security Memorandum declared that "some unknown force" had controlled the Cardinal, and the memo speculated that the communist authorities had used hypnosis on him.

In the summer of 1949, the Agency's head of Scientific Intelligence made a special trip to Western Europe to find out more about what the Soviets were doing and "to apply special methods of interrogation for the purpose of evaluation of Russian practices." In other words, fearful that the communists might have used drugs and hypnosis on prisoners, a senior CIA official used exactly the same techniques on refugees and returned prisoners from Eastern Europe. On returning to the United

States, this official recommended two courses of action: first, that the Agency consider setting up an escape operation to free Mindszenty; and second, that the CIA train and send to Europe a team skilled in "special" interrogation methods of the type he had tried out in Europe.

By the spring of 1950, several other CIA branches were contemplating the operational use of hypnosis. The Office of Security, whose main job was to protect Agency personnel and facilities from enemy penetration, moved to centralize all activity in this and other behavioral fields. The Security chief, Sheffield Edwards, a former Army colonel who a decade later would personally handle joint CIA–Mafia operations, took the initiative by calling a meeting of all interested Agency parties and proposing that interrogation teams be formed under Security's command. Security would use the teams to check out agents and defectors for the whole CIA. Each team would consist of a psychiatrist, a polygraph (lie detector) expert trained in hypnosis, and a technician. Edwards agreed not to use the teams operationally without the permission of a high-level committee. He called the project BLUEBIRD, a code name which, like all Agency names, had no significance—except perhaps to the person who chose it. Edwards classified the program TOP SECRET and stressed the extraordinary need for secrecy. On April 20, 1950, CIA Director Roscoe Hillenkoetter approved BLUEBIRD and authorized the use of unvouchered funds to pay for its most sensitive areas. The CIA's behavior-control program now had a bureaucratic structure.

The chief of Scientific Intelligence attended the original BLUEBIRD meeting in Sheffield Edwards' office and assured those present that his office would keep trying to gather all possible data on foreign—particularly Russian—efforts in the behavioral field. Not long afterward, his representative arranged to inspect the Nuremberg Tribunal records to see if they contained anything useful to BLUEBIRD. According to a CIA psychologist who looked over the German research, the Agency did not find much of specific help. "It was a real horror story, but we learned what human beings were capable of," he recalls. "There were some experiments on pain, but they were so mixed up with sadism as not to be useful. . . . How the victim coped was very interesting."

At the beginning, at least, there was cooperation between the scientists and the interrogators in the CIA. Researchers from

Security (who had no special expertise but who were experienced in police work) and researchers from Scientific Intelligence (who lacked operational background but who had academic training) pored jointly over all the open literature and secret reports. They quickly realized that the only way to build an effective defense against mind control was to understand its offensive possibilities. The line between offense and defense—if it ever existed—soon became so blurred as to be meaningless. Nearly every Agency document stressed goals like "controlling an individual to the point where he will do our bidding against his will and even against such fundamental laws of nature as self-preservation." On reading one such memo, an Agency officer wrote to his boss: "If this is supposed to be covered up as a defensive feasibility study, it's pretty damn transparent."

Three months after the Director approved BLUEBIRD, the first team traveled to Japan to try out behavioral techniques on human subjects—probably suspected double agents. The three men arrived in Tokyo in July 1950, about a month after the start of the Korean War. No one needed to impress upon them the importance of their mission. The Security Office ordered them to conceal their true purpose from even the U.S. military authorities with whom they worked in Japan, using the cover that they would be performing "intensive polygraph" work. In stifling, debilitating heat and humidity, they tried out combinations of the depressant sodium amytal with the stimulant benzedrine on each of four subjects, the last two of whom also received a second stimulant, picrotoxin. They also tried to induce amnesia. The team considered the tests successful, but the CIA documents available on the trip give only the sketchiest outline of what happened.* Then around October 1950, the BLUEBIRD team used "advanced" techniques on 25 subjects, apparently North Korean prisoners of war.

By the end of that year, a Security operator, Morse Allen, had become the head of the BLUEBIRD program. Forty years old at the time, Allen had spent most of his earlier career rooting out the domestic communist threat, starting in the late 1930s when he had joined the Civil Service Commision and set up its first security files on communists. ("He knows their methods," wrote

---

*For a better-documented case of narcotherapy and narcohypnosis, see Chapter 3.

a CIA colleague.) During World War II, Allen had served with Naval intelligence, first pursuing leftists in New York and then landing with the Marines on Okinawa. After the war, he went to the State Department, only to leave in the late 1940s because he felt the Department was whitewashing certain communist cases. He soon joined the CIA's Office of Security. A suspicious man by inclination and training, Allen took nothing at face value. Like all counterintelligence or security operators, his job was to show why things are not what they seem to be. He was always thinking ahead and behind, punching holes in surface realities. Allen had no academic training for behavioral research (although he did take a short course in hypnotism, a subject that fascinated him). He saw the BLUEBIRD job as one that called for studying every last method the communists might use against the United States and figuring out ways to counter them.

The CIA had schooled Morse Allen in one field which in the CIA's early days became an important part of covert operations: the use of the polygraph. Probably more than any intelligence service in the world, the Agency developed the habit of strapping its foreign agents—and eventually, its own employees—into the "box." The polygraph measures physiological changes that might show lying—heartbeat, blood pressure, perspiration, and the like. It has never been foolproof. In 1949 the Office of Security estimated that it worked successfully on seven out of eight cases, a very high fraction but not one high enough for those in search of certainty. A psychopathic liar, a hypnotized person, or a specially trained professional can "beat" the machine. Moreover, the skill of the person running the polygraph and asking the questions determines how well the device will work. "A good operator can make brilliant use of the polygraph without plugging it in," claims one veteran CIA case officer. Others maintain only somewhat less extravagantly that its chief value is to deter agents tempted to switch loyalties or reveal secrets. The power of the machine—real and imagined —to detect infidelity and dishonesty can be an intimidating factor.* Nevertheless, the polygraph cannot compel truth. Like

*While the regular polygraphing of CIA career employees apparently never has turned up a penetration agent in the ranks, it almost certainly has a deterrent effect on those considering coming out of the homosexual closet or on those considering dipping into the large sums of cash dispensed from proverbial black bags.

Pinocchio's nose, it only indicates lying. In addition, the machine requires enough physical control over the subject to strap him in. For years, the CIA tried to overcome this limitation by developing a "super" polygraph that could be aimed from afar or concealed in a chair. In this field, as in many others, no behavior control scheme was too farfetched to investigate, and Agency scientists did make some progress.

In December 1950, Morse Allen told his boss, Paul Gaynor, a retired brigadier general with a long background in counterintelligence and interrogation, that he had heard of experiments with an "electro-sleep" machine in a Richmond, Virginia hospital. Such an invention appealed to Allen because it supposedly put people to sleep without shock or convulsions. The BLUEBIRD team had been using drugs to bring on a state similar to a hypnotic trance, and Allen hoped this machine would allow an operator to put people into deep sleep without having to resort to chemicals. In theory, all an operator had to do was to attach the electrode-tipped wires to the subject's head and let the machine do the rest. It cost about $250 and was about twice the size of a table-model dictating machine. "Although it would not be feasible to use it on any of our own people because there is at least a theoretical danger of temporary brain damage," Morse Allen wrote, "it would possibly be of value in certain areas in connection with POW interrogation or on individuals of interest to this Agency." The machine never worked well enough to get into the testing stage for the CIA.

At the end of 1951, Allen talked to a famed psychiatrist (whose name, like most of the others, the CIA has deleted from the documents released) about a gruesome but more practical technique. This psychiatrist, a cleared Agency consultant, reported that electroshock treatments could produce amnesia for varying lengths of time and that he had been able to obtain information from patients as they came out of the stupor that followed shock treatments. He also reported that a lower setting of the Reiter electroshock machine produced an "excruciating pain" that, while nontherapeutic, could be effective as "a third degree method" to make someone talk. Morse Allen asked if the psychiatrist had ever taken advantage of the "groggy" period that followed normal electroshock to gain hypnotic control of his patients. No, replied the psychiatrist, but he would try it in the near future and report back to the Agency. The psychiatrist also mentioned that continued electroshock treatments could gradually reduce a subject to the "vegetable level," and that these treatments could not be detected unless the subject was given EEG tests within two weeks. At the end of a memo laying out this information, Allen noted that portable, battery-driven electroshock machines had come on the market.

Shortly after this Morse Allen report, the Office of Scientific Intelligence recommended that this same psychiatrist be given $100,000 in research funds "to develop electric shock and hypnotic techniques." While Allen thought this subject worth pursuing, he had some qualms about the ultimate application of the shock treatments: "The objections would, of course, apply to the use of electroshock if the end result was creation of a 'vegetable.' [I] believe that these techniques should not be considered except in gravest emergencies, and neutralization by confinement and/or removal from the area would be far more appropriate and certainly safer."

In 1952 the Office of Scientific Intelligence proposed giving another private doctor $100,000 to develop BLUEBIRD-related "neurosurgical techniques"—presumably lobotomy-connected.* Similarly, the Security office planned to use outside consultants to find out about such techniques as ultrasonics, vibrations, concussions, high and low pressure, the uses of various gases in airtight chambers, diet variations, caffeine, fatigue, radiation, heat and cold, and changing light. Agency officials looked into all these areas and many others. Some they studied intensively; others they merely discussed with consultants.

The BLUEBIRD mind-control program began when Stalin was still alive, when the memory of Hitler was fresh, and the terrifying prospect of global nuclear war was just sinking into popular consciousness. The Soviet Union had subjugated most of Eastern Europe, and a Communist party had taken control over the world's most populous nation, China. War had broken out in Korea, and Senator Joseph McCarthy's anticommunist crusade was on the rise in the United States. In both foreign and domestic politics, the prevailing mood was one of fear—even paranoia.

American officials have pointed to the Cold War atmosphere ever since as an excuse for crimes and excesses committed then

---

*Whether the Agency ultimately funded this or the electric-shock proposal cited above cannot be determined from the documents.

and afterward. One recurring litany in national security investigations has been the testimony of the exposed official citing Cold War hysteria to justify an act that he or she would not otherwise defend. The apprehensions of the Cold War do not provide a moral or legal shield for such acts, but they do help explain them. Even when the apprehensions were not well founded, they were no less real to the people involved.

It was also a time when the United States had achieved a new preeminence in the world. After World War II, American officials wielded the kind of power that diplomats frequently dream of. They established new alliances, new rulers, and even new nations to suit their purposes. They dispensed guns, favors, and aid to scores of nations. Consequently, American officials were noticed, respected, and pampered wherever they went— as never before. Their new sense of importance and their Cold War fears often made a dangerous combination—it is a fact of human nature that anyone who is both puffed up and afraid is someone to watch out for.

In 1947 the National Security Act created not only the CIA but also the National Security Council—in sum, the command structure for the Cold War. Wartime OSS leaders like William Donovan and Allen Dulles lobbied feverishly for the Act. Officials within the new command structure soon put their fear and their grandiose notions to work. Reacting to the perceived threat, they adopted a ruthless and warlike posture toward anyone they considered an enemy—most especially the Soviet Union. They took it upon themselves to fight communism and things that might lead to communism everywhere in the world. Few citizens disagreed with them; they appeared to express the sentiments of most Americans in that era, but national security officials still preferred to act in secrecy. A secret study commision under former President Hoover captured the spirit of their call to clandestine warfare:

> It is now clear we are facing an implacable enemy whose avowed objective is world domination by whatever means and at whatever cost. There are no rules in such a game. Hitherto acceptable longstanding American concepts of "fair play" must be reconsidered. We must develop effective espionage and counterespionage services and must learn to subvert, sabotage, and destroy our enemies by more clever, more sophisticated, and more effective methods than those used against us.

The men in the new CIA took this job quite seriously. "We felt we were the first line of defense in the anticommunist crusade," recalls Harry Rositzke, an early head of the Agency's Soviet Division. "There was a clear and heady sense of mission —a sense of what a huge job this was." Michael Burke, who was chief of CIA covert operations in Germany before going on to head the New York Yankees and Madison Square Garden, agrees: "It was riveting. . . . One was totally absorbed in something that has become misunderstood now, but the Cold War in those days was a very real thing with hundreds of thousands of Soviet troops, tanks, and planes poised on the East German border, capable of moving to the English Channel in forty-eight hours." Hugh Cunningham, an Agency official who stayed on for many years, remembers that survival itself was at stake, "What you were made to feel was that the country was in desperate peril and we had to do whatever it took to save it."

BLUEBIRD and the CIA's later mind-control programs sprang from such alarm. As a matter of course, the CIA was also required to learn the methods and intentions of all possible foes. "If the CIA had not tried to find out what the Russians were doing with mind-altering drugs in the early 1950s, I think the then-Director should have been fired," says Ray Cline, a former Deputy Director of the Agency.

High Agency officials felt they had to know what the Russians were up to. Nevertheless, a careful reading of the contemporaneous CIA documents almost three decades later indicates that if the Russians were scoring breakthroughs in the behavior-control field—whose author they almost certainly were not —the CIA lacked intelligence to prove that. For example, a 1952 Security document, which admittedly had an ax to grind with the Office of Scientific Intelligence, called the data gathered on the Soviet programs "extremely poor." The author noted that the Agency's information was based on "second- or third-hand rumors, unsupported statements and non-factual data."* Apparently, the fears and fantasies aroused by the Mindszenty trial and the subsequent Korean War "brainwashing" furor outstripped the facts on hand. The prevalent CIA notion of a "mind-control gap" was as much of a myth as the later bomber and missile "gaps." In any case, beyond the defensive

---

*The CIA refused to supply either a briefing or additional material when I asked for more background on Soviet behavior-control programs.

curiosity, mind control took on a momentum of its own.

As unique and frightening as the Cold War was, it did not cause people working for the government to react much differently to each other or power than at other times in American history. Bureaucratic squabbling went on right through the most chilling years of the behavior-control program. No matter how alarmed CIA officials became over the Russian peril, they still managed to quarrel with their internal rivals over control of Agency funds and manpower. Between 1950 and 1952, responsibility for mind control went from the Office of Security to the Scientific Intelligence unit back to Security again. In the process, BLUEBIRD was rechristened ARTICHOKE. The bureaucratic wars were drawn-out affairs, baffling to outsiders; yet many of the crucial turns in behavioral research came out of essentially bureaucratic considerations on the part of the contending officials. In general, the Office of Security was full of pragmatists who were anxious to weed out communists (and homosexuals) everywhere. They believed the intellectuals from Scientific Intelligence had failed to produce *"one* new, usable paper, suggestion, drug, instrument, name of an individual, etc., etc.," as one document puts it. The learned gentlemen from Scientific Intelligence felt that the former cops, military men, and investigators in Security lacked the technical background to handle so awesome a task as controlling the human mind.

"Jurisdictional conflict was constant in this area," a Senate committee would state in 1976. A 1952 report to the chief of the CIA's Medical Staff (itself a participant in the infighting) drew a harsher conclusion: "There exists a glaring lack of cooperation among the various intra-Agency groups fostered by petty jealousies and personality differences that result in the retardation of the enhancing and advancing of the Agency as a body." When Security took ARTICHOKE back from Scientific Intelligence in 1952, the victory lasted only two and one-half years before most of the behavioral work went to yet another CIA outfit, full of Ph.D.s with operational experience—the Technical Services Staff (TSS).*

There was bureaucratic warfare outside the CIA as well, al-

---

*This Agency component, responsible for providing the supporting gadgets, disguises, forgeries, secret writing, and weapons, has been called during its history the Technical Services Division and the Office of Technical Services, as well as TSS, the name which will be used throughout this book.

though there were early gestures toward interagency cooperation. In April 1951 the CIA Director approved liaison with
Army, Navy, and Air Force intelligence to avoid duplication of
effort. The Army and Navy were both looking for truth drugs,
while the prime concern of the Air Force was interrogation
techniques used on downed pilots. Representatives of each service attended regular meetings to discuss ARTICHOKE matters. The Agency also invited the FBI, but J. Edgar Hoover's
men stayed away.

During their brief period of cooperation, the military and the
CIA also exchanged information with the British and Canadian
governments. At the first session in June 1951, the British representative announced at the outset that there had been nothing
new in the interrogation business since the days of the Inquisition and that there was little hope of achieving valuable results
through research. He wanted to concentrate on propaganda
and political warfare as they applied to such threats as communist penetration of trade unions. The CIA's minutes of the session record that this skeptical Englishman finally agreed to the
importance of behavioral research, but one doubts the sincerity
of this conversion. The minutes also record a consensus of "no
conclusive evidence" that either Western countries or the Soviets had made any "revolutionary progress" in the field, and
describe Soviet methods as "remarkably similar . . . to the age-
old methods." Nonetheless, the representatives of the three
countries agreed to continue investigating behavior-control
methods because of their importance to "cold war operations."
To what extent the British and Canadians continued cannot be
told. The CIA did not stop until the 1970s.

Bureaucratic conflict was not the only aspect of ordinary government life that persisted through the Cold War. Officials also
maintained their normal awareness of the ethical and legal
consequences of their decisions. Often they went through con-
torted rationalizations and took steps to protect themselves, but
at least they recognized and paused over the various ethical
lines before crossing them. It would be unfair to say that all
moral awareness evaporated. Officials agonized over the consequences of their acts, and much of the bureaucratic record of
behavior control is the history of officials dealing with moral
conflicts as they arose.

The Security office barely managed to recruit the team psychiatrist in time for the first mission to Japan, and for years, Agency officials had trouble attracting qualified medical men to the project. Speculating why, one Agency memo listed such reasons as the CIA's comparatively low salaries for doctors and ARTICHOKE's narrow professional scope, adding that a candidate's "ethics might be such that he might not care to cooperate in certain more revolutionary phases of our project." This consideration became explicit in Agency recruiting. During the talent search, another CIA memo stated why another doctor seemed suitable: "His ethics are such that he would be completely cooperative in any phase of our program, regardless of how revolutionary it may be."

The matter was even more troublesome in the task of obtaining guinea pigs for mind-control experiments. "Our biggest current problem," noted one CIA memo, "is to find suitable subjects." The men from ARTICHOKE found their most convenient source among the flotsam and jetsam of the international spy trade: "individuals of dubious loyalty, suspected agents or plants, subjects having known reason for deception, etc.," as one Agency document described them. ARTICHOKE officials looked on these people as "unique research material," from whom meaningful secrets might be extracted while the experiments went on.

It is fair to say that the CIA operators tended to put less value on the lives of these subjects than they did on those of American college students, upon whom preliminary, more benign testing was done. They tailored the subjects to suit the ethical sensitivity of the experiment. A psychiatrist who worked on an ARTICHOKE team stresses that no one from the Agency wanted subjects to be hurt. Yet he and his colleagues were willing to treat dubious defectors and agents in a way which not only would be professionally unethical in the United States but also an indictable crime. In short, these subjects were, if not expendable, at least not particularly prized as human beings. As a CIA psychologist who worked for a decade in the behavior-control program, puts it, "One did not put a high premium on the civil rights of a person who was treasonable to his own country or who was operating effectively to destroy us." Another ex-Agency psychologist observes that CIA operators did not have "a universal concept of mankind" and thus were willing to do things to foreigners that they would have been reluctant to try on

Americans. "It was strictly a patriotic vision," he says.

ARTICHOKE officials never seemed to be able to find enough subjects. The professional operators—particularly the traditionalists—were reluctant to turn over agents to the Security men with their unproved methods. The field men did not particularly want outsiders, such as the ARTICHOKE crew, getting mixed up in their operations. In the spy business, agents are very valuable property indeed, and operators tend to be very protective of them. Thus the ARTICHOKE teams were given mostly the dregs of the clandestine underworld to work on.

Inexorably, the ARTICHOKE men crossed the clear ethical lines. Morse Allen believed it proved little or nothing to experiment on volunteers who gave their informed consent. For all their efforts to act naturally, volunteers still knew they were playing in a make-believe game. Consciously or intuitively, they understood that no one would allow them to be harmed. Allen felt that only by testing subjects "for whom much is at stake (perhaps life and death)," as he wrote, could he get reliable results relevant to operations. In documents and conversation, Allen and his coworkers called such realistic tests "terminal experiments"—terminal in the sense that the experiment would be carried through to completion. It would not end when the subject felt like going home or when he or his best interest was about to be harmed. Indeed, the subject usually had no idea that he had ever been part of an experiment.

In every field of behavior control, academic researchers took the work only so far. From Morse Allen's perspective, somebody then had to do the terminal experiment to find out how well the technique worked in the real world: how drugs affected unwitting subjects, how massive electroshock influenced memory, how prolonged sensory deprivation disturbed the mind. By definition, terminal experiments went beyond conventional ethical and legal limits. The ultimate terminal experiments caused death, but ARTICHOKE sources state that those were forbidden.

For career CIA officials, exceeding these limits in the name of national security became part of the job, although individual operators usually had personal lines they would not cross. Most academics wanted no part of the game at this stage—nor did Agency men always like having these outsiders around. If academic and medical consultants were brought along for the terminal phase, they usually did the work overseas, in secret. As

Cornell Medical School's famed neurologist Harold Wolff explained in a research proposal he made to the CIA, when any of the tests involved doing harm to the subjects, "We expect the Agency to make available suitable subjects and a proper place for the performance of the necessary experiments." Any professional caught trying the kinds of things the Agency came to sponsor—holding subjects prisoner, shooting them full of unwanted drugs— probably would have been arrested for kidnapping or aggravated assault. Certainly such a researcher would have been disgraced among his peers. Yet, by performing the same experiment under the CIA's banner, he had no worry from the law. His colleagues could not censure him because they had no idea what he was doing. And he could take pride in helping his country.

Without having been there in person, no one can know exactly what it felt like to take part in a terminal experiment. In any case, the subjects probably do not have fond memories of the experience. While the researchers sometimes resembled Alphonse and Gaston, they took themselves and their work very seriously. Now they are either dead, or, for their own reasons, they do not want to talk about the tests. Only in the following case have I been able to piece together anything approaching a firsthand account of a terminal experiment, and this one is quite mild compared to the others the ARTICHOKE men planned.

CHAPTER

3

THE PROFESSOR AND THE "A" TREATMENT

The three men were all part of the same Navy team, traveling together to Germany. Their trip was so sensitive that they had been ordered to ignore each other, even as they waited in the terminal at Andrews Air Force Base outside Washington on a sweltering August morning in 1952. Just the month before, Gary Cooper had opened in *High Noon,* and the notion of showdown—whether with outlaws or communists—was in the air. With war still raging in Korea, security consciousness was high. Even so, the secrecy surrounding this Navy mission went well beyond ordinary TOP SECRET restrictions, for the team was slated to link up in Frankfurt with a contingent from the most hush-hush agency of all, the CIA. Then the combined group was going to perform dangerous experiments on human subjects. Both Navy and CIA officials believed that any disclosure about these tests would cause grave harm to the American national interest.

The Navy team sweated out a two-hour delay at Andrews before the four-engine military transport finally took off. Not until the plane touched down at the American field in the Azores did one of the group, a representative of Naval intelligence, flash a prearranged signal indicating that they were not being watched and they could talk. "It was all this cloak-and-dagger crap," recalls another participant, Dr. Samuel Thompson, a psychiatrist, physiologist, and pharmacologist who was also a Navy commander.

The third man in the party was G. Richard Wendt, chairman of the Psychology Department at the University of Rochester and a part-time Navy contractor. A small 46-year-old man with graying blond hair and a fair-sized paunch, Wendt had been the only one with companionship during the hours of decreed silence. He had brought along his attractive young assistant, ostensibly to help him with the experiments. She was not well received by the Navy men, nor would she be appreciated by the CIA operators in Frankfurt. The behavior-control field was very much a man's world, except when women subjects were used. The professor's relationship with this particular lady was destined to become a source of friction with his fellow experimenters, and, eventually, a topic of official CIA reporting.

In theory, Professor Wendt worked under Dr. Thompson's supervision in a highly classified Navy program called Project CHATTER, but the strong-minded psychologist did not take anyone's orders easily. Very much an independent spirit, Wendt ironically, had accepted CHATTER's goal of weakening, if not eliminating, free will in others. The Navy program, which had started in 1947, was aimed at developing a truth drug that would force people to reveal their innermost secrets.

Thompson, who inherited Wendt and CHATTER in 1951 when he became head of psychiatric research at the Naval Medical Research Institute, remembers Naval intelligence telling him of the need for a truth drug in case "someone planted an A-bomb in one of our cities and we had twelve hours to find out from a person where it was. What could we do to make him talk?" Thompson concedes he was always "negative" about the possibility that such a drug could ever exist, but he cites the fear that the Russians might develop their own miracle potion as reason enough to justify the program. Also, Thompson and the other U.S. officials could not resist looking for a pill or panacea that would somehow make their side all-knowing or all-powerful.

Professor Wendt had experimented with drugs for the Navy before he became involved in the search for a truth serum. His earlier work had been on the use of dramamine and other methods to prevent motion sickness, and now that he was doing more sensitive research, the Navy hid it under the cover of continuing his "motion sickness" study. At the end of 1950, the Navy gave Wendt a $300,000 contract to study such substances as barbiturates, amphetamines, alcohol, and heroin. To preserve secrecy, which often reached fetish proportions in mind-control research, the money flowed to him not through Navy channels but out of the Secretary of Defense's contingency fund. For those drugs that were not available from pharmaceutical companies, Navy officials went to the Federal Bureau of Narcotics. The Commissioner of Narcotics personally signed the papers, and special couriers carried pouches of illegal drugs through Washington streets and then up to the professor at Rochester. Receipts show that the Bureau sent the Navy 30 grams of pure heroin and 11 pounds of "Mexican grown" marijuana, among other drugs.

Like most serious drug researchers, Wendt sampled everything first before testing on assistants and students. The drug that took up the most space in his first progress report was heroin. He had became his own prime subject. At weekly intervals, he told the Navy, the psychologist gave himself heroin injections and then wrote down his reactions as he moved through the "full range" of his life: driving, shopping, recreation, manual work, family relations, and sexual activity. He noted in himself "slight euphoria . . . heightened aesthetic appreciation . . . absentminded behavior . . . lack of desire to operate at full speed . . . lack of desire for alcohol . . . possibly reduced sex interest . . . feeling of physical well-being." He concluded in his report that heroin could have "some, but slight value for interrogation" if used on someone "worked on for a long period of time."*

Wendt never had any trouble getting student volunteers. He simply posted a notice on a campus bulletin board, and he wound up with a long waiting list. He chose only men subjects over 21, and he paid everyone accepted after a long interview $1.00 an hour. With so much government money to spend, he hired over 20 staff assistants, and he built a whole new testing facility in the attic of the school library. Wendt was cautious with his students, and he apparently did not share the hard drugs with them. He usually tested subjects in small groups—

---

*What Wendt appears to have been getting at—namely, that repeated shots of heroin might have an effect on interrogation—was stated explicitly in a 1952 CIA document which declared the drug "can be useful in reverse because of the stresses produced when . . . withdrawn from those addicted." Wendt's interest in heroin seems to have lasted to his death in 1977, long after his experiments had stopped. The woman who cleaned out his safe at that time told the Rochester *Democrat and Chronicle* she found a quantity of the white powder, along with syringes and a good many other drugs.

four to eight at a time. He and his associates watched through a two-way mirror and wrote down the subjects' reactions. He always used both placebos (inert substances) and drugs; the students never knew what—if anything—they were taking. According to Dr. Thompson, to have alerted them in advance and thus given themselves a chance to steel themselves up "would have spoiled the experiment."

Nonetheless, Wendt's procedure was a far cry from true unwitting testing. Any drug that was powerful enough to break through an enemy's resistance could have a traumatic effect on the person taking it—particularly if the subject was totally unaware of what was happening. The Navy research plan was to do preliminary studies on subjects like Wendt's students, and then, as soon as the drug showed promise, to try it under field conditions. Under normal scientific research, the operational tests would not have been run before the basic work was finished. But the Navy could not wait. The drugs were to be tested on involuntary subjects. Thompson readily admits that this procedure was "unethical," but he says, "We felt we had to do it for the good of country."

During the summer of 1952, Professor Wendt announced that he had found a concoction "so special" that it would be *the* answer" to the truth-drug problem, as Thompson recalls it. "I thought it would be a good idea to call the Agency," says Thompson. "I thought they might have someone with something to spill." Wendt was adamant on one point: He would not tell anyone in the Navy or the CIA what his potion contained. He would only demonstrate. Neither the CHATTER nor ARTICHOKE teams could resist the bait. The Navy had no source of subjects for terminal experiments, but the CIA men agreed to furnish the human beings—in Germany—even though they had no idea what Wendt had in store for his guinea pigs. The CIA named the operation CASTIGATE.

After settling into a Frankfurt hotel, Wendt, Thompson, and the Naval Intelligence man set out to meet the ARTICHOKE crew at the local CIA headquarters. It was located in the huge, elongated building that had housed the I. G. Farben industrial complex until the end of the war. The frantic bustle of a U.S. military installation provided ideal cover for this CIA base, and the arrival of a few new Americans attracted no special attention. The Navy group passed quickly through the lobby and rode up the elevator. At the CIA outer office, the team members had to show identification, and Thompson says they were frisked. The Naval Intelligence man had to check his revolver.

A secretary ushered the Navy group in to meet the ARTI-CHOKE contingent, which had arrived earlier from Washington. The party included team leader Morse Allen, his boss in the Office of Security, Paul Gaynor, and a prominent Washington psychiatrist who regularly left his private practice to fly off on special missions for the Agency. Also present were case officers from the CIA's Frankfurt base who had taken care of the support arrangements—the most important of which was supplying the subjects.

Everyone at the meeting wanted to know what drugs Wendt was going to use on the five selected subjects, who included one known double agent, one suspected double, and the three defectors. The professor still was not talking. Dr. Thompson asked what would happen if something went wrong and the subject died. He recalls one of the Frankfurt CIA men replying, "Disposal of the body would be no problem."

After the session ended, Thompson took Wendt aside and pointed out that since the professor, unlike Thompson, was neither a psychiatrist nor a pharmacologist, he was acting irresponsibly in not having a qualified physician standing by with antidotes in case of trouble. Wendt finally relented and confided in Thompson that he was going to slip the subjects a combination of the depressant Seconal, the stimulant Dexedrine, and tetrahydrocannabinol, the active ingredient in marijuana. Thompson was dumbfounded. He remembers wanting to shoot Wendt on the spot. These were all well-known drugs that had been thoroughly tested. Indeed, even the idea of mixing Seconal and Dexedrine was not original: The combined drug already had its own brand name—Dexamyl (and it would eventually have a street name, "the goofball"). Thompson quickly passed on to the CIA men what Wendt had in mind.* They, too, were more than a little disappointed.

Nevertheless, there was never any thought of stopping the experiments. The ARTICHOKE team had its own methods to try, even if Wendt's proved a failure, and the whole affair had developed its own momentum. Since this was one of the early

*Being good undercover operators, the CIA men never let on to Wendt that they knew his secret, and Wendt was not about to give it away. Toward the end of the trip, he told the consultant he would feel "unpatriotic" if he were to share his secret because the ARTICHOKE team was "not competent" to use the drugs.

ARTICHOKE trips into the field, the team was still working to perfect the logistics of testing. It had reserved two CIA "safehouses" in the countryside not far from Frankfurt, and Americans had been assigned to guard the experimental sites. Agency managers had already completed the paperwork for the installation of hidden microphones and two-way mirrors, so all the team members could monitor the interrogations.

The first safehouse proved to be a solid old farmhouse set picturesquely in the middle of green fields, far from the nearest dwelling. The ARTICHOKE and CHATTER groups drove up just as the CIA's carpenters were cleaning up the mess they had made in ripping a hole through the building's thick walls. The house had existed for several hundred years without an observation glass peering in on the sitting room, and it had put up some structural resistance to the workmen.

Subject #1 arrived in the early afternoon, delivered in a CIA sedan by armed operators, who had handcuffed him, shackled his feet, and made him lie down on the floor of the back seat. Agency officials described him as a suspected Russian agent, about 40 years old, who had a "Don Juan complex." One can only imagine how the subject must have reacted to these rather inconsistent Americans who only a few hours earlier had literally grabbed him out of confinement, harshly bound him, and sat more or less on top of him as they wandered through idyllic German farm country, and who now were telling him to relax as they engaged him in friendly conversation and offered him a beer. He had no way of knowing that it would be the last unspiked drink he would have for quite some time.

On the following morning, the testing started in earnest. Wendt put 20 mg. of Seconal in the subject's breakfast and then followed up with 50 mg. of Dexedrine in each of his two morning cups of coffee. Wendt gave him a second dose of Seconal in his luncheon beer. The subject was obviously not his normal self—whatever that was. What was clear was that Wendt was in way over his head, and even the little professor seemed to realize it. "I don't know how to deal with these people," he told the CIA psychiatric consultant. Wendt flatly refused to examine the subject, leaving the interrogation to the consultant. For his part, the consultant had little success in extracting information not already known to the CIA.

The third day was more of the same: Seconal with breakfast,

Dexedrine and marijuana in a glass of water afterwards. The only break from the previous day's routine came at 10:10 A.M. when the subject was allowed to play a short poker game. Then he was given more of Wendt's drugs in two red capsules that were, he was told, "a prescription for his nerves." By 2:40 P.M., Wendt declared that this subject was not the right personality type for his treatment. He explained to his disgusted colleagues that if someone is determined to lie, these drugs will only make him a better liar. He said that the marijuana extract produced a feeling of not wanting to hold anything back and that it worked best on people who wanted to tell the truth but were afraid to. OSS had discovered the same thing almost a decade earlier.

Wendt retired temporarily from the scene, and the others concluded it would be a shame to waste a good subject. They decided to give him the "A" (for ARTICHOKE) treatment. This, too, was not very original. It had been used during the war to interrogate prisoners and treat shell-shocked soldiers. As practiced on the suspected Russian agent, it consisted of injecting enough sodium pentothal into the vein of his arm to knock him out and then, twenty minutes later, stimulating him back to semiconsciousness with a shot of Benzedrine. In this case, the benzedrine did not revive the subject enough to suit the psychiatric consultant and he told Dr. Thompson to give the subject another 10 mg. ten minutes later. This put the subject into a state somewhere between waking and sleeping—almost comatose and yet bug-eyed. In hypnotic tones that had to be translated into Russian by an interpreter, the consultant used the technique of "regression" to convince the subject he was talking to his wife Eva at some earlier time in his life. This was no easy trick, since a male interpreter was playing Eva. Nevertheless, the consultant states he could "create any fantasy" with 60 to 70 percent of his patients, using narcotherapy (as in this case) or hypnosis. For roughly an hour, the subject seemed to have no idea he was not speaking with his wife but with CIA operatives trying to find out about his relationship with Soviet intelligence. When the subject started to doze, the consultant had Thompson give him a doubled jolt of Benzedrine. A half hour later, the subject began to weep violently. The consultant decided to end the session, and in his most soothing voice, he urged the subject to fall asleep. As the subject calmed down, the consultant suggested, with friendly and soothing words, that the subject would remember nothing of the experience when he woke up.

Inducing amnesia was an important Agency goal. "From the ARTICHOKE point of view," states a 1952 document, "the greater the amnesia produced, the more effective the results." Obviously if a victim remembered the "A" treatment, it would stop being a closely guarded ARTICHOKE secret. Presumably, some subject who really did work for the Russians would tell them how the Americans had worked him over. This reality made "disposal" of ARTICHOKE subjects a particular problem. Killing them seems to have been ruled out, but Agency officials made sure that some stayed in foreign prisons for long periods of time. While in numerous specific cases, ARTICHOKE team members claimed success in making their subjects forget, their outside consultants had told them "that short of cutting a subject's throat, a true amnesia cannot be guaranteed." As early as 1950, the Agency had put out a contract to a private researcher to find a memory-destroying drug, but to no apparent avail.* In any case, it would be unreasonable to assume that over the years at least one ARTICHOKE subject did not shake off the amnesic commands and tell the Russians what happened to him. As was so often the case with CIA operations, the enemy probably had a much better idea of the Agency's activities than the folks back home.

Back at the safehouse, Wendt was far from through. Four more subjects would be brought to him. The next one was an alleged double agent whom the CIA had code-named EXPLOSIVE. Agency documents describe him as a Russian "professional agent type" and "a hard-boiled individual who apparently has the ability to lie consistently but not very effectively." He was no stranger to ARTICHOKE team members who, a few months before, had plied him with a mixture of drugs and hypnosis under the cover of a "psychiatric-medical" exam. At that time, a professional hypnotist had accompanied the team, and he had given his commands through an elaborate intercom system to an interpreter who, in turn, was apparently able to put EXPLOSIVE under.† Afterward, the team reported to the

---

*Homer reported the ancient Greeks had such a substance—nepenthe—"a drug to lull all pain and anger, and bring forgetfulness of every sorrow."
†Neither Morse Allen nor anyone else on the ARTICHOKE teams spoke any foreign languages. Allen believed that the difficulty in communicating with the guinea pigs hampered ARTICHOKE research.

CIA's Director that EXPLOSIVE had revealed "extremely valuable" information and that he had been made to forget his interrogation through a hypnotically induced amnesia. Since that time EXPLOSIVE had been kept in custody. Now he was being brought out to give Professor Wendt a crack at him with the Seconal-Dexedrine-marijuana combination.

This time, Wendt gave the subject all three drugs together in one beer, delivered at the cocktail hour. Next came Seconal in a dinner beer and then all three once more in a postprandial beer. There were little, if any, positive results. Wendt ended the session after midnight and commented, "At least we learned one thing from this experiment. The people you have to deal with here are different from American college students."

During the next week, the CIA men brought Wendt three more subjects, with little success. The general attitude toward Wendt became, in Thompson's words, "hostile as all hell." Both the Agency and the Navy groups questioned his competence. With one subject, the professor declared he had given too strong a dose; with the next, too weak. While he had advertised his drugs as tasteless, the subjects realized they had swallowed something. As one subject in the next room was being interrogated in Russian that no one was bothering to translate, Wendt took to playing the same pattern on the piano over and over for a half hour. While the final subject was being questioned, Wendt and his female assistant got a little tipsy on beer. Wendt became so distracted during this experiment that he finally admitted, "My thoughts are elsewhere." His assistant began to giggle. Her presence had become like an open sore—which was made more painful when Mrs. Wendt showed up in Frankfurt and the professor threatened to jump off a church tower, Thompson recalls.

Wendt is not alive to give his version of what happened, but both CIA and Navy sources are consistent in their description of him. ARTICHOKE team leader Morse Allen felt he had been the victim of "a fraud or at least a gross misinterpretation," and he described the trip as "a waste of time and money." A man who usually hid his feelings, Allen became livid when Wendt's assistant measured drugs out with a penknife. He recommended in his final report that those who develop drugs not be allowed to participate in future field testing. "This, of course, does not mean that experimental work is condemned by the ARTICHOKE team," he wrote, "but a common sense approach in this direction will preclude arguments, alibis, and complaints as in the recent situation." In keeping with this "common sense approach," he also recommended that as "an absolute rule," no women be allowed on ARTICHOKE missions —because of the possible danger and because "personal convenience, toilet facilities, etc., are complicated by the presence of women."

Morse Allen and his ARTICHOKE mates returned to the States still convinced that they could find ways to control human behavior, but the Navy men were shaken. Their primary contractor had turned out to be a tremendous embarrassment. Dr. Thompson stated he could never work with Wendt again. Navy officials soon summoned Wendt to Bethesda and told him they were canceling their support for his research. Adding insult to injury, they told him they expected refund of all unspent money. While the Navy managers made some effort to continue CHATTER at other institutions, the program never recovered from the Wendt fiasco. By the end of the next year, 1953, the Korean War had ended and the Navy abandoned CHATTER altogether.

Over the next two decades, the Navy would still sponsor large amounts of specialized behavioral research, and the Army would invest huge sums in schemes to incapacitate whole armies with powerful drugs. But the CIA clearly pulled far into the lead in mind control. In those areas in which military research continued, the Agency stayed way ahead. The CIA consistently was out on what was called the "cutting edge" of the research, sponsoring the lion's share of the most harrowing experiments. ARTICHOKE and its successor CIA programs became an enormous effort that harnessed the energies of hundreds of scientists.

The experience of the CIA psychiatric consultant provides a small personal glimpse of how it felt to be a soldier in the mind-control campaign. This psychiatrist, who insists on anonymity, estimates that he made between 125 and 150 trips overseas on Agency operations from 1952 through his retirement in 1966. "To be a psychiatrist chasing off to Europe instead of just seeing the same patients year after year, that was extraordinary," he reminisces. "I wish I was back in those days. I never got tired of it." He says his assignments called for "practicing psychiatry in an ideal way, which meant you didn't become involved with your patients. You weren't supposed to." Asked how he felt about using drugs on unwitting foreigners, he snaps, "Depends which side you were on. I never hurt anyone. . . . We were at war."

For the most part, the psychiatrist stopped giving the "A" treatment after the mid-1950s but he continued to use his professional skills to assess and manipulate agents and defectors. His job was to help find out if a subject was under another country's control and to recommend how the person could be switched to the CIA's. In this work, he was contributing to the mainstream of CIA activity that permeates its institutional existence from its operations to its internal politics to its social life: the notion of controlling people. Finding reliable ways to do that is a primary CIA goal, and the business is often a brutal one. As former CIA Director Richard Helms stated in Senate testimony, "The clandestine operator . . . is trained to believe you can't count on the honesty of your agent to do exactly what you want or to report accurately unless you own him body and soul."

   Like all the world's secret services, the CIA sought to find the best methods of owning people and making sure they stayed owned. How could an operator be sure of an agent's loyalties? Refugees and defectors were flooding Western Europe, and the CIA wanted to exploit them. Which ones were telling the truth? Who was a deception agent or a provocateur. The Anglo-American secret invasion of Albania had failed miserably. Had they been betrayed?* Whom could the CIA trust?

   One way to try to answer these questions is to use physical duress—or torture. Aside from its ethical drawbacks, however, physical brutality simply does not work very well. As a senior counterintelligence official explains, "If you have a blowtorch up someone's ass, he'll give you tactical information." Yet he will not be willing or able to play the modern espionage game on the level desired by the CIA. One Agency document excludes the use of torture "because such inhuman treatment is not only out of keeping with the traditions of this country, but of dubious

---

*The answer was yes, in the sense that Soviet agent Harold "Kim" Philby, working as British intelligence's liaison with the CIA apparently informed his spymasters of specific plans to set up anticommunist resistance movements in Albania and all over Eastern Europe. The Russians almost certainly learned about CIA plans to overthrow communist rule in Eastern Europe and in the Soviet Union itself. Knowing of such operations presumably increased Soviet hostility.

effectiveness as compared with various supplemental psychoanalytical techniques."

The second and most popular method to get answers is traditional spy tradecraft. Given enough time, a good interrogator can very often find out a person's secrets. He applies persuasion and mental seduction, mixed with psychological pressures of every description—emotional carrots and sticks. A successful covert operator uses the same sorts of techniques in recruiting agents and making sure they stay in line. While the rest of the population may dabble in this sort of manipulation, the professional operator does it for a living, and he operates mostly outside the system of restraints that normally govern personal relationships. "I never gave a thought to legality or morality," states a retired and quite cynical Agency case officer with over 20 years' experience. "Frankly, I did what worked."

The operator pursues people he can turn into "controlled sources"—agents willing to do his bidding either in supplying intelligence or taking covert action. He seeks people in a position to do something useful for the Agency—or who someday *might* be in such a position, perhaps with CIA aid. Once he picks his target, he usually looks for a weakness or vulnerability he can play on. Like a good fisherman, the clever operator knows that the way to hook his prey is to choose an appropriate bait, which the target will think he is seizing because he wants to. The hook has to be firmly implanted; the agent sometimes tries to escape once he understands the implications of betraying his country. While the case officer might try to convince him he is acting for the good of his homeland, the agent must still face up to being branded a traitor.

Does every man have his price? Not exactly, states the senior counterintelligence man, but he believes a shrewd operator can usually find a way to reach anyone, particularly through his family. In developing countries, the Agency has caused family members to be arrested and mistreated by the local police, given or withheld medical care for a sick child, and, more prosaically, provided scholarships for a relative to study abroad. This kind of tactic does not work as well on a Russian or Western European, who does not live in a society where the CIA can exert pressure so easily.

Like a doctor's bedside manner or a lawyer's courtroom style, spy tradecraft is highly personalized. Different case officers swear by different approaches, and successful methods are carefully observed and copied. Most CIA operators seem to prefer using an ideological lure if they can. John Stockwell, who left the Agency in 1977 to write a book about CIA operations in Angola, believes his best agents were "people convinced they were doing the right thing...who disliked communists and felt the CIA was the right organization." Stockwell recalls his Agency instructors "hammering away at the positive aspect of recruitment. This was where they established the myth of CIA case officers being good guys. They said we didn't use negative control, and we always made the relationship so that both parties were better off for having worked together." More cynical operators, like the one quoted above, take a different view: "You can't create real motivation in a person by waving the flag or by saying this is for the future good of democracy. You've got to have a firmer hold than that. . . . His opinions can change." This ex-operator favors approaches based either on revenge or helping the agent advance his career:

> Those are good motives because they can be created within the individual. . . . Maybe you start with a Communist party cell member and you help him become a district committee member by eliminating his competition, or you help him get a position where he can get even with someone. At the same time, he's giving you more and more information as he moves forward, and if you ever surface his reports, he's out of business. You've really got him wrapped up. You don't even have to tell him. He realizes it himself.

No matter what the approach to the prospective agent, the case officer tries to make money a factor in the relationship. Sometimes the whole recruiting pitch revolves around enrichment. In other instances, the case officer allows the target the illusion that he has sold out for higher motives. Always, however, the operator tries to use money to make the agent dependent. The situation can become sticky with money-minded agents when the case officer insists that part or all of the payments be placed in escrow, to prevent attracting undue attention. But even cash does not create control in the spy business. As the cynical case officer puts it, "Money is tenuous because somebody can always offer more."

Surprisingly, each of the CIA operators sampled agrees that overt blackmail is a highly overrated form of control. The senior counterintelligence man notes that while the Russians frequently use some variety of entrapment—sexual or otherwise—the CIA rarely did. "Very few [Agency] case officers were tough enough" to pull it off and sustain it, he says. "Anytime an agent has been forced to cooperate, you can take it for granted that he has two things on his mind: he is looking for a way out and for revenge. Given the slightest opportunity, he will hit you right between the eyes." Blackmail could backfire in unexpected ways. John Stockwell remembers an agent in Southeast Asia who wanted to quit: "The case officer leaned on the guy and said, 'Look, friend, we still need your intelligence, and we have receipts you signed which we can turn over to the local police.' The agent blew his brains out, leaving a suicide note regretting his cooperation with the CIA and telling how the Agency had tried to blackmail him. It caused some problems with the local government."

The case officer always tries to weave an ever-tightening web of control around his agent. His methods of doing so are so personal and so basic that they often reveal more about the case officer himself than the agent, reflecting his outlook and his personal philosophy. The cynical operator describes his usual technique, which turns out to be a form of false idealism: "You've got to treat a man as an equal and convince him you're partners in this thing. Even if he's a communist party member, you can't deal with him like a crumb. You sit down with him and ask how are the kids, and you remember that he told you last time that his son was having trouble in school. You build personal rapport. If you treat him like dirt or an object of use, eventually he'll turn on you or drop off the bandwagon."

John Stockwell's approach relies on the power of imagination in a humdrum world: "I always felt the real key was that you were offering something special—a real secret life—something that he and you only knew made him different from all the pedestrian paper shufflers in a government office or a boring party cell meeting. Everybody has a little of Walter Mitty in him—what a relief to know you really do work for the CIA in your spare time."

Sometimes a case officer wants to get the agent to do something he does not think he wants to do. One former CIA operator uses a highly charged metaphor to describe how he did it: "Sometimes one partner in a relationship wants to get into deviations from standard sex. If you have some control, you might be able to force your partner to try different things, but it's much better to lead her down the road a step at a time, to discuss it and fantasize until eventually she's saying, 'Let's try this thing.' If her inhibitions and moral reservations are eroded and she is turned on, it's much more fun and there's less chance of blowback [exposure, in spy talk]. . . . It's the same with an agent."

All case officers—and particularly counterintelligence men—harbor recurring fears that their agents will betray them. The suspicious professional looks for telltale signs like lateness, nervousness, or inconsistency. He relies on his intuition. "The more you've been around agents, the more likely you are to sense that something isn't what it should be," comments the senior counterintelligence man. "It's like with children."

No matter how skillfully practiced, traditional spycraft provides only incomplete answers to the nagging question of how much the Agency can really trust an agent. All the sixth sense, digging, and deductive reasoning in the world do not produce certainty in a field that is based on deception and lies. Whereas the British, who invented the game, have historically understood the need for patience and a stiff upper lip, Americans tend to look for quick answers, often by using the latest technology. "We were very gimmick-prone," says the senior counterintelligence official. Gimmicks—machines, drugs, technical tricks—comprise the third method of behavior control, after torture and tradecraft. Like safecrackers who swear by the skill in their fingertips, most of the Agency's mainstream operators disparage newfangled gadgets. Many now claim that drugs, hypnosis, and other exotic methods actually detract from good tradecraft because they make operators careless and lazy.

Nevertheless, the operators and their high-level sponsors, like Allen Dulles and Richard Helms, consistently pushed for the magic technique—the *deus ex machina*—that would solve their problems. Caught in the muck and frustration of ordinary spywork, operators hoped for a miracle tool. Faced with liars and deceivers, they longed for a truth drug. Surrounded by people who knew too much, they sought a way to create amnesia. They dreamed of finding means to make unwilling people carry out specific tasks, such as stealing documents, provoking a fight, killing someone, or otherwise committing an antisocial act. Secret agents recruited by more traditional appeals to idealism, greed, ambition, or fear had always done such deeds, but they usually gave their spymasters headaches in the process. Sometimes they balked. Moreover, first they had to agree to serve the CIA. The best tradecraft in the world seldom works against a well-motivated target. (The cynical operator recalls offering the head of Cuban intelligence $1,000,000—in 1966 at a Madrid hotel—only to receive a flat rejection.) Plagued by the unsureness, Agency officials hoped to take the randomness—indeed, the free will—out of agent handling. As one psychologist who worked on behavior control describes it, "The problem of every intelligence operation is how do you remove the human element? The operators would come to us and ask for the human element to be removed." Thus the impetus toward mind-control research came not only from the lure of science and the fantasies of science fiction, it also came from the heart of the spy business.

PART

II

INTELLIGENCE OR "WITCHES POTIONS"

And it seems to me perfectly in the cards that there will be within the next generation or so a pharmacological method of making people love their servitude, and producing . . . a kind of painless concentration camp for entire societies, so that people will in fact have their liberties taken away from them but will rather enjoy it, because they will be distracted from any desire to rebel by propaganda, brainwashing, or brainwashing enhanced by pharmacological methods.

—ALDOUS HUXLEY, 1959.

I had perfected LSD for medical use, not as a weapon. It can make you insane or even kill you if it is not properly used under medical supervision. In any case, the research should be done by medical people and not by soldiers or intelligence agencies.

—ALBERT HOFFMAN, 1977.

LSD—LBJ—FBI—CIA.

—LYRIC FROM *Hair,* 1968.

CHAPTER
4
LSD

Albert Hofmann's discovery of LSD in 1943 may have begun a new age in the exploration of the human mind, but it took six years for word to reach America. Even after Hofmann and his coworkers in Switzerland published their work in a 1947 article, no one in the United States seemed to notice. Then in 1949, a famous Viennese doctor named Otto Kauders traveled to the United States in search of research funds. He gave a conference at Boston Psychopathic Hospital,* a pioneering mental-health institution affiliated with Harvard Medical School, and he spoke about a new experimental drug called d-lysergic acid diethylamide. Milton Greenblatt, the hospital's research director, vividly recalls Kauders' description of how an infinitesimally small dose had rendered Dr. Hofmann temporarily "crazy." "We were very interested in anything that could make someone schizophrenic," says Greenblatt. If the drug really did induce psychosis for a short time, the Boston doctors reasoned, an antidote—which they hoped to find—might cure schizophrenia. It would take many years of research to show that LSD did not, in fact, produce a "model psychosis," but to the Boston doctors in 1949, the drug showed incredible promise. Max Rinkel, a neuropsychiatrist and refugee from Hitler's Germany, was so intrigued by Kauders' presentation that he quickly contacted Sandoz, the huge Swiss pharmaceutical firm where Al-

*During the 1950s, Boston Psychopathic changed its name to Massachusetts Mental Health Center, the name it bears today.

bert Hofmann worked. Sandoz officials arranged to ship some LSD across the Atlantic.

The first American trip followed. The subject was Robert Hyde, a Vermont-born psychiatrist who was Boston Psychopathic's number-two man. A bold, innovative sort, Hyde took it for granted that there would be no testing program until he tried the drug. With Rinkel and the hospital's senior physician, H. Jackson DeShon looking on, Hyde drank a glass of water with 100 micrograms of LSD in it—less than half Hofmann's dose, but still a hefty jolt. DeShon describes Hyde's reaction as "nothing very startling." The perpetually active Hyde insisted on making his normal hospital rounds while his colleagues tagged along. Rinkel later told a scientific conference that Hyde became "quite paranoiac, saying that we had not given him anything. He also berated us and said the company had cheated us, given us plain water. That was not Dr. Hyde's normal behavior; he is a very pleasant man." Hyde's first experience was hardly as dramatic as Albert Hofmann's, but then the Boston psychiatrist had not, like Hofmann, set off on a voyage into the complete unknown. For better or worse, LSD had come to America in 1949 and had embarked on a strange trip of its own. Academic researchers would study it in search of knowledge that would benefit all mankind. Intelligence agencies, particularly the CIA, would subsidize and shape the form of much of this work to learn how the drug could be used to break the will of enemy agents, unlock secrets in the minds of trained spies, and otherwise manipulate human behavior. These two strains—of helping people and of controlling them—would coexist rather comfortably through the 1950s. Then, in the 1960s, LSD would escape from the closed world of scholar and spy, and it would play a major role in causing a cultural upheaval that would have an impact both on global politics and on intimate personal beliefs. The trip would wind up—to borrow some hyperbole from the musical *Hair*— with "the youth of America on LSD."

The counterculture generation was not yet out of the nursery, however, when Bob Hyde went tripping: Hyde himself would not become a secret CIA consultant for several years. The CIA and the military intelligence agencies were just setting out on their quest for drugs and other exotic methods to take possession of people's minds. The ancient desire to control enemies through magical spells and potions had come alive again, and several offices within the CIA competed to become the head controllers. Men from the Office of Security's ARTICHOKE program were struggling—as had OSS before them—to find a truth drug or hypnotic method that would aid in interrogation. Concurrently, the Technical Services Staff (TSS) was investigating in much greater depth the whole area of applying chemical and biological warfare (CBW) to covert operations. TSS was the lineal descendent of Stanley Lovell's Research and Development unit in OSS, and its officials kept alive much of the excitement and urgency of the World War II days when Lovell had tried to bring out the Peck's Bad Boy in American scientists. Specialists from TSS furnished backup equipment for secret operations: false papers, bugs, taps, suicide pills, explosive seashells, transmitters hidden in false teeth, cameras in tobacco pouches, invisible inks, and the like. In later years, these gadget wizards from TSS would become known for supplying some of history's more ludicrous landmarks, such as Howard Hunt's ill-fitting red wig; but in the early days of the CIA, they gave promise of transforming the spy world.

Within TSS, there existed a Chemical Division with functions that few others—even in TSS—knew about. These had to do with using chemicals (and germs) against specific people. From 1951 to 1956, the years when the CIA's interest in LSD peaked, Sidney Gottlieb, a native of the Bronx with a Ph.D. in chemistry from Cal Tech, headed this division. (And for most of the years until 1973, he would oversee TSS's behavioral programs from one job or another.) Only 33 years old when he took over the Chemical Division, Gottlieb had managed to overcome a pronounced stammer and a clubfoot to rise through Agency ranks. Described by several acquaintances as a "compensator," Gottlieb prided himself on his ability, despite his obvious handicaps, to pursue his cherished hobby, folk dancing. On returning from secret missions overseas, he invariably brought back a new step that he would dance with surprising grace. He could call out instructions for the most complicated dances without a break in his voice, infecting others with enthusiasm. A man of unorthodox tastes, Gottlieb lived in a former slave cabin that he had remodeled himself—with his wife, the daughter of Presbyterian missionaries in India, and his four children. Each morning, he rose at 5:30 to milk the goats he kept on his 15 acres outside Washington. The Gottliebs drank only goat's milk, and they made their own cheese. They also raised Christmas trees which they sold to the outside world. Greatly respected by his former colleagues, Gottlieb, who refused to be interviewed for this book, is described as a humanist, a man of intellectual humility and strength, willing to carry out, as one ex-associate puts it, "the tough things that had to be done." This associate fondly recalls, "When you watched him, you gained more and more respect because he was willing to work so hard to get an idea across. He left himself totally exposed. It was more important for us to get the idea than for him not to stutter." One idea he got across was that the Agency should investigate the potential use of the obscure new drug, LSD, as a spy weapon.

At the top ranks of the Clandestine Services (officially called the Directorate of Operations but popularly known as the "dirty tricks department"), Sid Gottlieb had a champion who appreciated his qualities, Richard Helms. For two decades, Gottlieb would move into progressively higher positions in the wake of Helms' climb to the highest position in the Agency. Helms, the tall, smooth "preppie," apparently liked the way the Jewish chemist, who had started out at Manhattan's City College, could thread his way through complicated technical problems and make them understandable to nonscientists. Gottlieb was loyal and he followed orders. Although many people lay in the chain of command between the two men, Helms preferred to avoid bureaucratic niceties by dealing directly with Gottlieb.

On April 3, 1953, Helms proposed to Director Allen Dulles that the CIA set up a program under Gottlieb for "covert use of biological and chemical materials." Helms made clear that the Agency could use these methods in "present and future clandestine operations" and then added, "Aside from the offensive potential, the development of a comprehensive capability in this field . . . gives us a thorough knowledge of the enemy's theoretical potential, thus enabling us to defend ourselves against a foe who might not be as restrained in the use of these techniques as we are." Once again, as it would throughout the history of the behavioral programs, defense justified offense. Ray Cline, often a bureaucratic rival of Helms, notes the spirit in which the future Director pushed this program: "Helms fancied himself a pretty tough cookie. It was fashionable among that group to fancy they were rather impersonal about dangers, risks, and human life. Helms would think it sentimental and foolish to be against something like this."

On April 13, 1953—the same day that the Pentagon announced that any U.S. prisoner refusing repatriation in Korea would be listed as a deserter and shot if caught—Allen Dulles approved the program, essentially as put forth by Helms. Dulles took note of the "ultra-sensitive work" involved and agreed that the project would be called MKULTRA.* He approved an initial budget of $300,000, exempted the program from normal CIA financial controls, and allowed TSS to start up research projects "without the signing of the usual contracts or other written agreements." Dulles ordered the Agency's bookkeepers to pay the costs blindly on the signatures of Sid Gottlieb and Willis Gibbons, a former U.S. Rubber executive who headed TSS.

As is so often the case in government, the activity that Allen Dulles approved with MKULTRA was already under way, even before he gave it a bureaucratic structure. Under the code name MKDELTA, the Clandestine Services had set up procedures the year before to govern the use of CBW products. (MKDELTA now became the operational side of MKULTRA.) Also in 1952, TSS had made an agreement with the Special Operations Division (SOD) of the Army's biological research center at Fort Detrick, Maryland whereby SOD would produce germ weapons for the CIA's use (with the program called MKNAOMI). Sid Gottlieb later testified that the purpose of these programs was "to investigate whether and how it was possible to modify an individual's behavior by covert means. The context in which this investigation was started was that of the height of the Cold War with the Korean War just winding down; with the CIA organizing its resources to liberate Eastern Europe by paramilitary means; and with the threat of Soviet aggression very real and tangible, as exemplified by the recent Berlin airlift" (which occurred in 1948).

In the early days of MKULTRA, the roughly six TSS professionals who worked on the program spent a good deal of their time considering the possibilities of LSD.† "The most fascinat-

---

*Pronounced M-K-ULTRA. The MK digraph simply identified it as a TSS project. As for the ULTRA part, it may have had its etymological roots in the most closely guarded Anglo-American World War II intelligence secret, the ULTRA program, which handled the cracking of German military codes. While good espionage tradecraft called for cryptonyms to have no special meaning, wartime experiences were still very much on the minds of men like Allen Dulles.
†By no means did TSS neglect other drugs. It looked at hundreds of others from cocaine to nicotine, with special emphasis on special-purpose substances. One

ing thing about it," says one of them, "was that such minute quantities had such a terrific effect." Albert Hofman had gone off into another world after swallowing less than 1/100,000 of an ounce. Scientists had known about the mind-altering qualities of drugs like mescaline since the late nineteenth century, but LSD was several thousand times more potent. Hashish had been around for millennia, but LSD was roughly a million times stronger (by weight). A two-suiter suitcase could hold enough LSD to turn on every man, woman, and child in the United States. "We thought about the possibility of putting some in a city water supply and having the citizens wander around in a more or less happy state, not terribly interested in defending themselves," recalls the TSS man. But incapacitating such large numbers of people fell to the Army Chemical Corps, which also tested LSD and even stronger hallucinogens. The CIA was concentrating on individuals. TSS officials understood that LSD distorted a person's sense of reality, and they felt compelled to learn whether it could alter someone's basic loyalties. Could the CIA make spies out of tripping Russians—or vice versa? In the early 1950s, when the Agency developed an almost desperate need to know more about LSD, almost no outside information existed on the subject. Sandoz had done some clinical studies, as had a few other places, including Boston Psychopathic, but the work generally had not moved much beyond the horse-and-buggy stage. The MKULTRA team had literally hundreds of questions about LSD's physiological, psychological, chemical, and social effects. Did it have any antidotes? What happened if it were combined with other drugs? Did it affect everyone the same way? What was the effect of doubling the dose? And so on.

TSS first sought answers from academic researchers, who, on the whole, gladly cooperated and let the Agency pick their brains. But CIA officials realized that no one would undertake a quick and systematic study of the drug unless the Agency itself paid the bill. Almost no government or private money was then available for what had been dubbed "experimental psychiatry." Sandoz wanted the drug tested, for its own commercial reasons, but beyond supplying it free to researchers, it

---

1952 memo talked about the urgent operational need for a chemical "producing general listlessness and lethargy." Another mentioned finding—as TSS later did—a potion to accelerate the effects of liquor, called an "alcohol extender."

would not assume the costs. The National Institutes of Mental Health had an interest in LSD's relationship to mental illness, but CIA officials wanted to know how the drug affected normal people, not sick ones. Only the military services, essentially for the same reasons as the CIA, were willing to sink much money into LSD, and the Agency men were not about to defer to them. They chose instead to take the lead—in effect to create a whole new field of research.

Suddenly there was a huge new market for grants in academia, as Sid Gottlieb and his aides began to fund LSD projects at prestigious institutions. The Agency's LSD pathfinders can be identified: Bob Hyde's group at Boston Psychopathic, Harold Abramson at Mt. Sinai Hospital and Columbia University in New York, Carl Pfeiffer at the University of Illinois Medical School, Harris Isbell of the NIMH-sponsored Addiction Research Center in Lexington, Kentucky, Louis Jolyon West at the University of Oklahoma, and Harold Hodge's group at the University of Rochester. The Agency disguised its involvement by passing the money through two conduits: the Josiah Macy, Jr. Foundation, a rich establishment institution which served as a cutout (intermediary) only for a year or two, and the Geschickter Fund for Medical Research, a Washington, D.C. family foundation, whose head, Dr. Charles Geschickter, provided the Agency with a variety of services for more than a decade. Reflexively, TSS officials felt they had to keep the CIA connection secret. They could only "assume," according to a 1955 study, that Soviet scientists understood the drug's "strategic importance" and were capable of making it themselves. They did not want to spur the Russians into starting their own LSD program or into devising countermeasures.

The CIA's secrecy was also clearly aimed at the folks back home. As a 1963 Inspector General's report stated, "Research in the manipulation of human behavior is considered by many authorities in medicine and related fields to be professionally unethical"; therefore, openness would put "in jeopardy" the reputations of the outside researchers. Moreover, the CIA Inspector General declared that disclosure of certain MKULTRA activities could result in "serious adverse reaction" among the American public.

At Boston Psychopathic, there were various levels of concealment. Only Bob Hyde and his boss, the hospital superintendant, knew officially that the CIA was funding the hospital's LSD program from 1952 on, to the tune of about $40,000 a year. Yet, according to another member of the Hyde group, Dr. DeShon, all senior staff understood where the money really came from. "We agreed not to discuss it," says DeShon. "I don't see any objection to this. We never gave it to anyone without his consent and without explaining it in detail." Hospital officials told the volunteer subjects something about the nature of the experiments but nothing about their origins or purpose. None of the subjects had any idea that the CIA was paying for the probing of their minds and would use the results for its own purposes; most of the staff was similarly ignorant.

Like Hyde, almost all the researchers tried LSD on themselves. Indeed, many believed they gained real insight into what it felt like to be mentally ill, useful knowledge for health professionals who spent their lives treating people supposedly sick in the head. Hyde set up a multidisciplinary program—virtually unheard of at the time—that brought together psychiatrists, psychologists, and physiologists. As subjects, they used each other, hospital patients, and volunteers—mostly students—from the Boston area. They worked through a long sequence of experiments that served to isolate variable after variable. Palming themselves off as foundation officials, the men from MKULTRA frequently visited to observe and suggest areas of future research. One Agency man, who himself tripped several times under Hyde's general supervision, remembers that he and his colleagues would pass on a nugget that another contractor like Harold Abramson had gleaned and ask Hyde to perform a follow-up test that might answer a question of interest to the Agency. Despite these tangents, the main body of research proceeded in a planned and orderly fashion. The researchers learned that while some subjects seemed to become schizophrenic, many others did not. Surprisingly, true schizophrenics showed little reaction at all to LSD, unless given massive doses. The Hyde group found out that the quality of a person's reaction was determined mainly by the person's basic personality structure (set) and the environment (setting) in which he or she took the drug. The subject's expectation of what would happen also played a major part. More than anything else, LSD tended to intensify the subject's existing characteristics—often to extremes. A little suspicion could grow into major paranoia, particularly in the company of people perceived as threatening.

Unbeknownst to his fellow researchers, the energetic Dr. Hyde also advised the CIA on using LSD in covert operations. A CIA officer who worked with him recalls: "The idea would be to give him the details of what had happened [with a case], and he would speculate. As a sharp M.D. in the old-school sense, he would look at things in ways that a lot of recent bright lights couldn't get. . . . He had a good sense of make-do." The Agency paid Hyde for his time as a consultant, and TSS officials eventually set aside a special MKULTRA subproject as Hyde's private funding mechanism. Hyde received funds from yet another MKULTRA subproject that TSS men created for him in 1954, so he could serve as a cutout for Agency purchases of rare chemicals. His first buy was to be $32,000 worth of corynanthine, a possible antidote to LSD, that would not be traced to the CIA.

Bob Hyde died in 1976 at the age of 66, widely hailed as a pacesetter in mental health. His medical and intelligence colleagues speak highly of him both personally and professionally. Like most of his generation, he apparently considered helping the CIA a patriotic duty. An Agency officer states that Hyde never raised doubts about his covert work. "He wouldn't moralize. He had a lot of trust in the people he was dealing with [from the CIA]. He had pretty well reached the conclusion that if they decided to do something [operationally], they had tried whatever else there was and were willing to risk it."

Most of the CIA's academic researchers published articles on their work in professional journals, but those long, scholarly reports often gave an incomplete picture of the research. In effect, the scientists would write openly about how LSD affects a patient's pulse rate, but they would tell only the CIA how the drug could be used to ruin that patient's marriage or memory. Those researchers who were aware of the Agency's sponsorship seldom published anything remotely connected to the instrumental and rather unpleasant questions the MKULTRA men posed for investigation. That was true of Hyde and of Harold Abramson, the New York allergist who became one of the first Johnny Appleseeds of LSD by giving it to a number of his distinguished colleagues. Abramson documented all sorts of experiments on topics like the effects of LSD on Siamese fighting fish and snails,* but he never wrote a word about one

*As happened to Albert Hofmann the first time, Abramson once unknowingly

of his early LSD assignments from the Agency. In a 1953 document, Sid Gottlieb listed subjects he expected Abramson to investigate with the $85,000 the Agency was furnishing him. Gottlieb wanted "operationally pertinent materials along the following lines: a. Disturbance of Memory; b. Discrediting by Aberrant Behavior; c. Alteration of Sex Patterns; d. Eliciting of Information; e. Suggestibility; f. Creation of Dependence."

Dr. Harris Isbell, whose work the CIA funded through Navy cover with the approval of the Director of the National Institutes of Health, published his principal findings, but he did not mention how he obtained his subjects. As Director of the Addiction Research Center at the huge Federal drug hospital in Lexington, Kentucky, he had access to a literally captive population. Inmates heard on the grapevine that if they volunteered for Isbell's program, they would be rewarded either in the drug of their choice or in time off from their sentences. Most of the addicts chose drugs—usually heroin or morphine of a purity seldom seen on the street. The subjects signed an approval form, but they were not told the names of the experimental drugs or the probable effects. This mattered little, since the "volunteers" probably would have granted their informed consent to virtually anything to get hard drugs.

Given Isbell's almost unlimited supply of subjects, TSS officials used the Lexington facility as a place to make quick tests of promising but untried drugs and to perform specialized experiments they could not easily duplicate elsewhere. For instance, Isbell did one study for which it would have been impossible to attract student volunteers. He kept seven men on LSD for 77 straight days.* Such an experiment is as chilling as

ingested some LSD, probably by swallowing water from his spiked snail tank. He started to feel bad, but with his wife's help, he finally pinpointed the cause. According to brain and dolphin expert John Lilly, who heard the story from Mrs. Abramson, Harold was greatly relieved that his discomfort was not grave. "Oh, it's nothing serious," he said. "It's just an LSD psychosis. I'll just go to bed and sleep it off."

*Army researchers, as usual running about five years behind the CIA, became interested in the sustained use of LSD as an interrogation device during 1961 field tests (called Operation THIRD CHANCE). The Army men tested the drug in Europe on nine foreigners and one American, a black soldier named James Thornwell, accused of stealing classified documents. While Thornwell was reacting to the drug under extremely stressful conditions, his captors threatened "to extend the state indefinitely, even to a permanent condition of insanity," according to an Army document. Thornwell is now suing the U.S. government for $30 million.

In one of those twists that Washington insiders take for granted and outsiders it is astonishing—both to lovers and haters of LSD. Nearly 20 years after Dr. Isbell's early work, counterculture journalist Hunter S. Thompson delighted and frightened his readers with accounts of drug binges lasting a few days, during which Thompson felt his brain boiling away in the sun, his nerves wrapping around enormous barbed wire forts, and his remaining faculties reduced to their reptilian antecedents. Even Thompson would shudder at the thought of 77 days straight on LSD, and it is doubtful he would joke about the idea. To Dr. Isbell, it was just another experiment. "I have had seven patients who have now been taking the drug for more than 42 days," he wrote in the middle of the test, which he called "the most amazing demonstration of drug tolerance I have ever seen." Isbell tried to "break through this tolerance" by giving triple and quadruple doses of LSD to the inmates.

Filled with intense curiosity, Isbell tried out a wide variety of unproven drugs on his subjects. Just as soon as a new batch of scopolamine, rivea seeds, or bufontenine arrived from the CIA or NIMH, he would start testing. His relish for the task occasionally shone through the dull scientific reports. "I will write you a letter as soon as I can get the stuff into a man or two," he informed his Agency contact.

No corresponding feeling shone through for the inmates, however. In his few recorded personal comments, he complained that his subjects tended to be afraid of the doctors and were not as open in describing their experiences as the experimenters would have wished. Although Isbell made an effort to "break through the barriers" with the subjects, who were nearly all black drug addicts, Isbell finally decided "in all probability, this type of behavior is to be expected with patients of this type." The subjects have long since scattered, and no one apparently has measured the aftereffects of the more extreme experiments on them.

One subject who could be found spent only a brief time with Dr. Isbell. Eddie Flowers was 19 years old and had been in Lexington for about a year when he signed up for Isbell's program. He lied about his age to get in, claiming he was 21. All he cared about was getting some drugs. He moved into the

---

do not quite believe, Terry Lenzner, a partner of the same law firm seeking this huge sum for Thornwell, is the lawyer for Sid Gottlieb, the man who oversaw the 77-day trips at Lexington and even more dangerous LSD testing.

experimental wing of the hospital where the food was better and he could listen to music. He loved his heroin but knew nothing about drugs like LSD. One day he took something in a graham cracker. No one ever told him the name, but his description sounds like it made him trip—badly, to be sure. "It was the worst shit I ever had," he says. He hallucinated and suffered for 16 or 17 hours. "I was frightened. I wouldn't take it again." Still, Flowers earned enough "points" in the experiment to qualify for his "payoff" in heroin. All he had to do was knock on a little window down the hall. This was the drug bank. The man in charge kept a list of the amount of the hard drug each inmate had in his account. Flowers just had to say how much he wanted to withdraw and note the method of payment. "If you wanted it in the vein, you got it there," recalls Flowers who now works in a Washington, D.C. drug rehabilitation center.

Dr. Isbell refuses all request for interviews. He did tell a Senate subcommittee in 1975 that he inheritied the drug payoff system when he came to Lexington and that "it was the custom in those days. . . . The ethical codes were not so highly developed, and there was a great need to know in order to protect the public in assessing the potential use of narcotics. . . . I personally think we did a very excellent job."

For every Isbell, Hyde, or Abramson who did TSS contract work, there were dozens of others who simply served as casual CIA informants, some witting and some not. Each TSS project officer had a skull session with dozens of recognized experts several times a year. "That was the only way a tiny staff like Sid Gottlieb's could possibly keep on top of the burgeoning behavioral sciences," says an ex-CIA official. "There would be no way you could do it by library research or the Ph.D. dissertation approach." The TSS men always asked their contacts for the names of others they could talk to, and the contacts would pass them on to other interesting scientists.

In LSD research, TSS officers benefited from the energetic intelligence gathering of their contractors, particularly Harold Abramson. Abramson talked regularly to virtually everyone interested in the drug, including the few early researchers not funded by the Agency or the military, and he reported his findings to TSS. In addition, he served as reporting secretary of two conference series sponsored by the Agency's sometime conduit, the Macy Foundation. These series each lasted over five year periods in the 1950s; one dealt with "Problems of Consciousness" and the other with "Neuropharmacology." Held once a year in the genteel surroundings of the Princeton Inn, the Macy Foundation conferences brought together TSS's (and the military's) leading contractors, as part of a group of roughly 25 with the multidisciplinary background that TSS officials so loved. The participants came from all over the social sciences and included such luminaries as Margaret Mead and Jean Piaget. The topics discussed usually mirrored TSS's interests at the time, and the conferences served as a spawning ground for ideas that allowed researchers to engage in some healthy cross-fertilization.

Beyond the academic world, TSS looked to the pharmaceutical companies as another source on drugs—and for a continuing supply of new products to test. TSS's Ray Treichler handled the liaison function, and this secretive little man built up close relationships with many of the industry's key executives. He had a particular knack for convincing them he would not reveal their trade secrets. Sometimes claiming to be from the Army Chemical Corps and sometimes admitting his CIA connection, Treichler would ask for samples of drugs that were either highly poisonous, or, in the words of the onetime director of research of a large company, "caused hypertension, increased blood pressure, or led to other odd physiological activity."

Dealing with American drug companies posed no particular problems for TSS. Most cooperated in any way they could. But relations with Sandoz were more complicated. The giant Swiss firm had a monopoly on the Western world's production of LSD until 1953. Agency officials feared that Sandoz would somehow allow large quantities to reach the Russians. Since information on LSD's chemical structure and effects was publicly available from 1947 on, the Russians could have produced it any time they felt it worthwhile. Thus, the Agency's phobia about Sandoz seems rather irrational, but it unquestionably did exist.

On two occasions early in the Cold War, the entire CIA hierarchy went into a dither over reports that Sandoz might allow large amounts of LSD to reach Communist countries. In 1951 reports came in through military channels that the Russians had obtained some 50 million doses from Sandoz. Horrendous visions of what the Russians might do with such a stockpile circulated in the CIA, where officials did not find out the intelligence was false for several years. There was an even greater uproar in 1953 when more reports came in, again through military intelligence, that Sandoz wanted to sell the astounding quantity of 10 kilos (22 pounds) of LSD—enough for about 100 million doses—on the open market.

A top-level coordinating committee which included CIA and Pentagon representatives unanimously recommended that the Agency put up $240,000 to buy it all. Allen Dulles gave his approval, and off went two CIA representatives to Switzerland, presumably with a black bag full of cash. They met with the president of Sandoz and other top executives. The Sandoz men stated that the company had never made anything approaching 10 kilos of LSD and that, in fact, since the discovery of the drug 10 years before, its total production had been only 40 grams (about 1½ ounces).* The manufacturing process moved quite slowly at that time because Sandoz used real ergot, which could not be grown in large quantities. Nevertheless, Sandoz executives, being good Swiss businessmen, offered to supply the U.S. Government with 100 grams weekly for an indefinite period, if the Americans would pay a fair price. Twice the Sandoz president thanked the CIA men for being willing to take the nonexistent 10 kilos off the market. While he said the company now regretted it had ever discovered LSD in the first place, he promised that Sandoz would not let the drug fall into communist hands. The Sandoz president mentioned that various Americans had in the past made "covert and sideways" approaches to Sandoz to find out about LSD, and he agreed to keep the U.S. Government informed of all future production and shipping of the drug. He also agreed to pass on any intelligence about Eastern European interest in LSD. The Sandoz executives asked only that their arrangement with the CIA be kept "in the very strictest confidence."

All around the world, the CIA tried to stay on top of the LSD supply. Back home in Indianapolis, Eli Lilly & Company was even then working on a process to synthesize LSD. Agency offi-

---

*A 1975 CIA document clears up the mystery of how the Agency's military sources could have made such a huge error in estimating Sandoz's LSD supply (and probably also explains the earlier inaccurate report that the Russians had bought 50,000,000 doses). What happened, according to the document, was that the U.S. military attaché in Switzerland did not know the difference between a milligram (1/1,000 of a gram) and a kilogram (1,000 grams). This mix-up threw all his calculations off by a factor of 1,000,000.

cials felt uncomfortable having to rely on a foreign company for their supply, and in 1953 they asked Lilly executives to make them up a batch, which the company subsequently donated to the government. Then, in 1954, Lilly scored a major breakthrough when its researchers worked out a complicated 12- to 15-step process to manufacture first lysergic acid (the basic building block) and then LSD itself from chemicals available on the open market. Given a relatively sophisticated lab, a competent chemist could now make LSD without a supply of the hard-to-grow ergot fungus. Lilly officers confidentially informed the government of their triumph. They also held an unprecedented press conference to trumpet their synthesis of lysergic acid, but they did not publish for another five years their success with the closely related LSD.

TSS officials soon sent a memo to Allen Dulles, explaining that the Lilly discovery was important because the government henceforth could buy LSD in "tonnage quantities," which made it a potential chemical-warfare agent. The memo writer pointed out, however, that from the MKULTRA point of view, the discovery made no difference since TSS was working on ways to use the drug only in small-scale covert operations, and the Agency had no trouble getting the limited amounts it needed. But now the Army Chemical Corps and the Air Force could get their collective hands on enough LSD to turn on the world.

Sharing the drug with the Army here, setting up research programs there, keeping track of it everywhere, the CIA generally presided over the LSD scene during the 1950s. To be sure, the military services played a part and funded their own research programs.* So did the National Institutes of Health, to a lesser extent. Yet both the military services and the NIH allowed themselves to be co-opted by the CIA—as funding con-

---

*Military security agencies supported the LSD work of such well-known researchers as Amedeo Marrazzi of the University of Minnesota and Missouri Institute of Psychiatry, Henry Beecher of Harvard and Massachusetts General Hospital, Charles Savage while he was at the Naval Medical Research Institute, James Dille of the University of Washington, Gerald Klee of the University of Maryland Medical School, Neil Burch of Baylor University (who performed later experiments for the CIA), and Paul Hoch and James Cattell of the New York State Psychiatric Institute, whose forced injections of a mescaline derivative led to the 1953 death of New York tennis professional Harold Blauer. (Dr. Cattell later told Army investigators, "We didn't know whether it was dog piss or what it was we were giving him.")

duits and intelligence sources. The Food and Drug Administration also supplied the Agency with confidential information on drug testing. Of the Western world's two LSD manufacturers, one—Eli Lilly—gave its entire (small) supply to the CIA and the military. The other—Sandoz—informed Agency representatives every time it shipped the drug. If somehow the CIA missed anything with all these sources, the Agency still had its own network of scholar-spies, the most active of whom was Harold Abramson who kept it informed of all new developments in the LSD field. While the CIA may not have totally cornered the LSD market in the 1950s, it certainly had a good measure of control —the very power it sought over human behavior.

Sid Gottlieb and his colleagues at MKULTRA soaked up pools of information about LSD and other drugs from all outside sources, but they saved for themselves the research they really cared about: operational testing. Trained in both science and espionage, they believed they could bridge the huge gap between experimenting in the laboratory and using drugs to outsmart the enemy. Therefore the leaders of MKULTRA initiated their own series of drug experiments that paralleled and drew information from the external research. As practical men of action, unlimited by restrictive academic standards, they did not feel the need to keep their tests in strict scientific sequence. They wanted results now—not next year. If a drug showed promise, they felt no qualms about trying it out operationally before all the test results came in. As early as 1953, for instance, Sid Gottlieb went overseas with a supply of a hallucinogenic drug—almost certainly LSD. With unknown results, he arranged for it to be slipped to a speaker at a political rally, presumably to see if it would make a fool of him.

These were freewheeling days within the CIA—then a young agency whose bureaucratic arteries had not started to harden. The leaders of MKULTRA had high hopes for LSD. It appeared to be an awesome substance, whose advent, like the ancient discovery of fire, would bring out primitive responses of fear and worship in people. Only a speck of LSD could take a strong-willed man and turn his most basic perceptions into willowy shadows. Time, space, right, wrong, order, and the notion of what was possible all took on new faces. LSD was a frightening weapon, and it took a swashbuckling boldness for the leaders of MKULTRA to prepare for operational testing the way they first did: by taking it themselves. They tripped at the office. They tripped at safehouses, and sometimes they traveled to Boston to trip under Bob Hyde's penetrating gaze. Always they observed, questioned, and analyzed each other. LSD seemed to remove inhibitions, and they thought they could use it to find out what went on in the mind underneath all the outside acts and pretensions. If they could get at the inner self, they reasoned, they could better manipulate a person—or keep him from being manipulated.

The men from MKULTRA were trying LSD in the early 1950s —when Stalin lived and Joe McCarthy raged. It was a foreboding time, even for those not professionally responsible for doomsday poisons. Not surprisingly, Sid Gottlieb and colleagues who tried LSD did not think of the drug as something that might enhance creativity or cause transcendental experiences. Those notions would not come along for years. By and large, there was thought to be only one prevailing and hardheaded version of reality, which was "normal," and everything else was "crazy." An LSD trip made people temporarily crazy, which meant potentially vulnerable to the CIA men (and mentally ill, to the doctors). The CIA experimenters did not trip for the experience itself, or to get high, or to sample new realities. They were testing a weapon; for their purposes, they might as well have been in a ballistics lab.

Despite this prevailing attitude in the Agency, at least one MKULTRA pioneer recalls that his first trip expanded his conception of reality: "I was shaky at first, but then I just experienced it and had a high. I felt that everything was working right. I was like a locomotive going at top efficiency. Sure there was stress, but not in a debilitating way. It was like the stress of an engine pulling the longest train it's ever pulled." This CIA veteran describes seeing all the colors of the rainbow growing out of cracks in the sidewalk. He had always disliked cracks as signs of imperfection, but suddenly the cracks became natural stress lines that measured the vibrations of the universe. He saw people with blemished faces, which he had previously found slightly repulsive. "I had a change of values about faces," he says. "Hooked noses or crooked teeth would become beautiful for that person. Something had turned loose in me, and all I had done was shift my attitude. Reality hadn't changed, but I had. That was all the difference in the world between seeing something ugly and seeing truth and beauty."

At the end of this day of his first trip, the CIA man and his colleagues had an alcohol party to help come down. "I had a lump in my throat," he recalls wistfully. Although he had never done such a thing before, he wept in front of his coworkers. "I didn't want to leave it. I felt I would be going back to a place where I wouldn't be able to hold on to this kind of beauty. I felt very unhappy. The people who wrote the report on me said I had experienced depression, but they didn't understand why I felt so bad. They thought I had had a bad trip."

This CIA man says that others with his general personality tended to enjoy themselves on LSD, but that the stereotypical CIA operator (particularly the extreme counterintelligence type who mistrusts everyone and everything) usually had negative reactions. The drug simply exaggerated his paranoia. For these operators, the official notes, "dark evil things would begin to lurk around," and they would decide the experimenters were plotting against them.

The TSS team understood it would be next to impossible to allay the fears of this ever-vigilant, suspicious sort, although they might use LSD to disorient or generally confuse such a person. However, they toyed with the idea that LSD could be applied to better advantage on more trusting types. Could a clever foe "re-educate" such a person with a skillful application of LSD? Speculating on this question, the CIA official states that while under the influence of the drug, "you tend to have a more global view of things. I found it awfully hard when stoned to maintain the notion: I am a U.S. citizen—my country right or wrong. . . . You tend to have these good higher feelings. You are more open to the brotherhood-of-man idea and more susceptible to the seamy sides of your own society. . . . I think this is exactly what happened during the 1960s, but it didn't make people more communist. It just made them less inclined to identify with the U.S. They took a plague-on-both-your-houses position."

As to whether his former colleagues in TSS had the same perception of the LSD experience, the man replies, "I think everybody understood that if you had a good trip, you had a kind of above-it-all look into reality. What we subsequently found was that when you came down, you remembered the experience, but you didn't switch identities. You really didn't have that kind of feeling. You weren't as suspicious of people. You listened to them, but you also saw through them more easily and clearly. We decided that this wasn't the kind of thing that was going to make a guy into a turncoat to his own country. The more we worked with it, the less we became convinced this was what the communists were using for brainwashing."

The early LSD tests—both outside and inside the Agency—had gone well enough that the MKULTRA scientists moved forward to the next stage on the road to "field" use: They tried the drug out on people by surprise. This, after all, would be the way an operator would give—or get—the drug. First they decided to spring it on each other without warning. They agreed among themselves that a coworker might slip it to them at any time. (In what may be an apocryphal story, a TSS staff man says that one of his former colleagues always brought his own bottle of wine to office parties and carried it with him at all times.) Unwitting doses became an occupational hazard.

MKULTRA men usually took these unplanned trips in stride, but occasionally they turned nasty. Two TSS veterans tell the story of a coworker who drank some LSD-laced coffee during his morning break. Within an hour, states one veteran, "he sort of knew he had it, but he couldn't pull himself together. Sometimes you take it, and you start the process of maintaining your composure. But this grabbed him before he was aware, and it got away from him." Filled with fear, the CIA man fled the building that then housed TSS, located on the edge of the Mall near Washington's great monuments. Having lost sight of him, his colleagues searched frantically, but he managed to escape. The hallucinating Agency man worked his way across one of the Potomac bridges and apparently cut his last links with rationality. "He reported afterwards that every automobile that came by was a terrible monster with fantastic eyes, out to get him personally," says the veteran. "Each time a car passed, he would huddle down against the parapet, terribly frightened. It was a real horror trip for him. I mean, it was hours of agony. It was like a dream that never stops—with someone chasing you."

After about an hour and a half, the victim's coworkers found him on the Virginia side of the Potomac, crouched under a fountain, trembling. "It was awfully hard to persuade him that his friends were his friends at that point," recalls the colleague. "He was alone in the world, and everyone was hostile. He'd become a full-blown paranoid. If it had lasted for two weeks, we'd have plunked him in a mental hospital." Fortunately for him, the CIA man came down by the end of the day. This was not the first, last, or most tragic bad trip in the Agency's testing program.*

By late 1953, only six months after Allen Dulles had formally created MKULTRA, TSS officials were already well into the last stage of their research: systematic use of LSD on "outsiders" who had no idea they had received the drug. These victims simply felt their moorings slip away in the midst of an ordinary day, for no apparent reason, and no one really knew how they would react.

Sid Gottlieb was ready for the operational experiments. He considered LSD to be such a secret substance that he gave it a private code name ("serunim") by which he and his colleagues often referred to the drug, even behind the CIA's heavily guarded doors. In retrospect, it seems more than bizarre that CIA officials—men responsible for the nation's intelligence and alertness when the hot and cold wars against the communists were at their peak—would be sneaking LSD into each other's coffee cups and thereby subjecting themselves to the unknown frontiers of experimental drugs. But these side trips did not seem to change the sense of reality of Gottlieb or of high CIA officials, who took LSD on several occasions. The drug did not transform Gottlieb out of the mind set of a master scientist-spy, a protégé of Richard Helms in the CIA's inner circle. He never stopped milking his goats at 5:30 every morning.

The CIA leaders' early achievements with LSD were impressive. They had not invented the drug, but they had gotten in on the American ground floor and done nearly everything else. They were years ahead of the scientific literature—let alone the public—and spies win by being ahead. They had monopolized the supply of LSD and dominated the research by creating much of it themselves. They had used money and other blandishments to build a network of scientists and doctors whose work they could direct and turn to their own use. All that remained between them and major espionage successes was the performance of the drug in the field.

That, however, turned out to be a considerable stumbling block. LSD had an incredibly powerful effect on people, but not in ways the CIA could predict or control.

*TSS officials had long known that LSD could be quite dangerous. In 1952, Harvard Medical School's Henry Beecher, who regularly gave the Agency information on his talks with European colleagues, reported that a Swiss doctor had suffered severe depression after taking the drug and had killed herself three weeks later.

CHAPTER
5
CONCERNING THE CASE
OF DR. FRANK OLSON

In November 1953, Sid Gottlieb decided to test LSD on a group of scientists from the Army Chemical Corps' Special Operations Division (SOD) at Fort Detrick in Frederick, Maryland. Although the Clandestine Services hierarchy had twice put TSS under strict notice not to use LSD without permission from above, Gottlieb must have felt that trying the drug on SOD men was not so different from giving it to his colleagues at the office. After all, officials at TSS and SOD worked intimately together, and they shared one of the darkest secrets of the Cold War: that the U.S. government maintained the capability—which it would use at times—to kill or incapacitate selected people with biological weapons. Only a handful of the highest CIA officials knew that TSS was paying SOD about $200,000 a year in return for operational systems to infect foes with disease.

Gottlieb planned to drop the LSD on the SOD men in the splendid isolation of a three-day working retreat. Twice a year, the SOD and TSS men who collaborated on MKNAOMI, their joint program, held a planning session at a remote site where they could brainstorm without interruption. On November 18, 1953, they gathered at Deep Creek Lodge, a log building in the woods of Western Maryland. It had been built as a Boy Scout camp 25 years earlier. Surrounded by the water of a mountain lake on three sides, with the peaks of the Appalachian chain looking down over the thick forest, the lodge was isolated enough for even the most security conscious spy. Only an occasional hunter was likely to wander through after the summer months.

Dr. John Schwab, who had founded SOD in 1950, Lt. Colonel Vincent Ruwet, its current chief, and Dr. Frank Olson, its temporary head earlier that year, led the Detrick group. These germ warriors came under the cover of being wildlife writers and lecturers off on a busman's holiday. They carefully removed the Fort Detrick parking stickers from their cars before setting out. Sid Gottlieb brought three co-workers from the Agency, including his deputy Robert Lashbrook.

They met in the living room of the lodge, in front of a roaring blaze in the huge walk-in fireplace. Then they split off into smaller groups for specialized meetings. The survivors among those who attended these sessions remain as tight-lipped as ever, willing to share a few details of the general atmosphere but none of the substance. However, from other sources at Fort Detrick and from government documents, the MKNAOMI research can be pieced together. It was this program that was discussed during the fateful retreat.

Under MKNAOMI, the SOD men developed a whole arsenal of toxic substances for CIA use. If Agency operators needed to kill someone in a few seconds with, say, a suicide pill, SOD provided super-deadly shellfish toxin.* On his ill-fated U-2 flight over the Soviet Union in 1960, Francis Gary Powers carried—and chose not to use—a drill bit coated with this poison concealed in a silver dollar. While perfect for someone anxious to die—or kill—instantly, shellfish toxin offered no time to escape and could be traced easily. More useful for assassination, CIA and SOD men decided, was botulinum. With an incubation period of 8 to 12 hours, it allowed the killer time to separate himself from the deed. Agency operators would later supply pills laced with this lethal food poison to its Mafia allies for inclusion in Fidel Castro's milkshake. If CIA officials wanted an assassination to look like a death from natural causes, they could choose

---

*Toxins are chemical substances, not living organisms, derived from biological agents. While they can make people sick or dead, they cannot reproduce themselves like bacteria. Because of their biological origin, toxins came under the responsibility of Fort Detrick rather than Edgewood Arsenal, the facility which handled the chemical side of America's chemical and biological warfare (CBW) programs.

from a long list of deadly diseases that normally occurred in particular countries. Thus in 1960, Clandestine Services chief Richard Bissell asked Sid Gottlieb to pick out an appropriate malady to kill the Congo's Patrice Lumumba. Gottlieb told the Senate investigators that he selected one that "was supposed to produce a disease that was . . . indigenous to that area [of West Africa] and that could be fatal." Gottlieb personally carried the bacteria to the Congo, but this murderous operation was scrubbed before Lumumba could be infected. (The Congolese leader was killed shortly thereafter under circumstances that still are not clear.)

When CIA operators merely wanted to be rid of somebody temporarily, SOD stockpiled for them about a dozen diseases and toxins of varying strengths. At the relatively benign end of the SOD list stood *Staph. enterotoxin,* a mild form of food poisoning—mild compared to botulinum. This *Staph.* infection almost never killed and simply incapacitated its victim for 3 to 6 hours. Under the skilled guidance of Sid Gottlieb's wartime predecessor, Stanley Lovell, OSS had used this very substance to prevent Nazi official Hjalmar Schacht from attending an economic conference during the war. More virulent in the SOD arsenal was *Venezuelan equine encephalomyelitis* virus. It usually immobilized a person for 2 to 5 days and kept him in a weakened state for several more weeks. If the Agency wanted to incapacitate someone for a period of months, SOD had two different kinds of brucellosis.*

A former senior official at Fort Detrick was kind enough to run me through all the germs and toxins SOD kept for the CIA, listing their advantages and disadvantages. Before doing so, he emphasized that SOD was also trying to work out ways to protect U.S. citizens and installations from attack with similar substances. "You can't have a serious defense," he says, "unless someone has thought about offense." He stated that Japan made repeated biological attacks against China during World War II—which was one reason for starting the American pro-

---

*Brucellosis may well have been the disease that Gottlieb selected in the spring of 1960 when the Clandestine Services' Health Alteration Committee approved an operation to disable an Iraqi colonel, said to be "promoting Soviet-bloc political interests" for at least three months. Gottlieb told the Church committee that he had a monogrammed handkerchief treated with the incapacitating agency, and then mailed it to the colonel. CIA officials told the committee that the colonel was shot by a firing squad—which the Agency had nothing to do with—before the handkerchief arrived.

gram.* He knows of no use since by the Soviet Union or any other power.

According to the Detrick official, anyone contemplating use of a biological product had to consider many other factors besides toxicity and incubation period.

Can the germ be detected easily and countered with a vaccine? He notes that anthrax, a fatal disease (when inhaled) that SOD stored for CIA, has the advantage of symptoms that resemble pneumonia; similarly, Venezuelan equine encephalomyelitis can be mistaken for the grippe. While vaccines do exist for many of the stockpiled diseases, SOD was forever developing more virulent strains. "I don't know of any organism susceptible to a drug that can't be made more resistant," states the Detrick man.

Did the disease have a high degree of secondary spread? SOD preferred it not to, because these germ warfare men did not want to start epidemics—that was the job of others at Fort Detrick.

Was the organism stable? How did humidity affect it? SOD considered these and many other factors.

To the CIA, perhaps the most important question was whether it could covertly deliver the germ to infect the right person. One branch of SOD specialized in building delivery systems, the most famous of which now is the dart gun fashioned out of a .45 pistol that ex-CIA Director William Colby displayed to the world at a 1975 Senate hearing. The Agency had long been after SOD to develop a "non-discernible microbioinoculator" which could give people deadly shots that, according to a CIA document, could not be "easily detected upon a detailed autopsy." SOD also rigged up aerosol sprays that could be fired by remote control, including a fluorescent starter that was activated by turning on the light, a cigarette lighter that sprayed when lit, and an engine head bolt that shot off as the engine heated. "If you're going to infect people, the most likely way is respiratory," notes the high Detrick official. "Everybody breathes, but you might not get them to eat."

---

*For some reason, the U.S. government has made it a point not to release information about Japanese use of biological warfare. The senior Detrick source says, "We knew they sprayed Manchuria. We had the results of how they produced and disseminated [the biological agents, including anthrax]. . . . I read the autopsy reports myself. We had people who went over to Japan after the war."

Frank Olson specialized in the airborne delivery of disease. He had been working in the field ever since 1943, when he came to Fort Detrick as one of the original military officers in the U.S. biological warfare program. Before the end of the war, he developed a painful ulcer condition that led him to seek a medical discharge from the uniformed military, but he had stayed on as a civilian. He joined SOD when it started in 1950. Obviously good at what he did, Olson served for several months as acting chief of SOD in 1952–53 but asked to be relieved when the added stress caused his ulcer to flare up. He happily returned to his lesser post as a branch chief, where he had fewer administrative duties and could spend more time in the laboratory. A lover of practical jokes, Olson was very popular among his many friends. He was an outgoing man, but, like most of his generation, he kept his inner feelings to himself. His great passion was his family, and he spent most of his spare time playing with his three kids and helping around the house. He had met his wife while they both studied at the University of Wisconsin.

Olson attended all the sessions and apparently did everything expected of him during the first two days at the lodge. After dinner on Thursday, November 19, 1953—the same day that a Washington *Post* editorial decried the use of dogs in chemical experiments—Olson shared a drink of Cointreau with all but two of the men present. (One had a heart condition; the other, a reformed alcoholic, did not drink.) Unbeknownst to the SOD men, Sid Gottlieb had decided to spike the liqueur with LSD.*

"To me, everyone was pretty normal," says SOD's Benjamin Wilson. "No one was aware anything had happened until Gottlieb mentioned it. [20 minutes after the drink] Gottlieb asked if we had noticed anything wrong. Everyone was aware, once it was brought to their attention." They tried to continue their discussion, but once the drug took hold, the meeting deteriorated into laughter and boisterous conversation. Two of the SOD men apparently got into an all-night philosophical conversation that had nothing to do with biological warfare.

---

*Gottlieb stated just after Olson's death, at a time when he was trying to minimize his own culpability, that he had talked to the SOD men about LSD and that they had agreed in general terms to the desirability of unwitting testing. Two of the SOD group in interviews and a third in congressional testimony flatly deny the Gottlieb version. Gottlieb and the SOD men all agree Gottlieb gave no advance warning that he was giving them a drug in their liqueur.

Ruwet remembers it as "the most frightening experience I ever had or hope to have." Ben Wilson recalls that "Olson was psychotic. He couldn't understand what happened. He thought someone was playing tricks on him. . . . One of his favorite expressions was 'You guys are a bunch of thespians.' "

Olson and most of the others became increasingly uncomfortable and could not sleep.* When the group gathered in the morning, Olson was still agitated, obviously disturbed, as were several of his colleagues. The meeting had turned sour, and no one really wanted to do more business. They all straggled home during the day.

Alice Olson remembers her husband coming in before dinner that evening: "He said nothing. He just sat there. Ordinarily when he came back from a trip, he'd tell me about the things he could—what they had to eat, that sort of thing. During dinner, I said, 'It's a damned shame the adults in this family don't communicate anymore.' He said, 'Wait until the kids get to bed and I'll talk to you.' " Later that night, Frank Olson told his wife he had made "a terrible mistake," that his colleagues had laughed at him and humiliated him. Mrs. Olson assured him that the others were his friends, that they would not make fun of him. Still, Olson would not tell her any more. He kept his fears bottled up inside, and he shared nothing of his growing feeling that someone was out to get him. Alice Olson was accustomed to his keeping secrets. Although she realized he worked on biological warfare, they never talked about it. She had had only little glimpses of his profession. He complained about the painful shots he was always taking.† He almost never took a bath at home because he showered upon entering and leaving his office every day. When a Detrick employee died of anthrax (one of three fatalities in the base's 27-year history), Frank

---

*For the very reason that most trips last about eight hours no matter what time a subject takes the drug, virtually all experimenters, including TSS's own contractors, give LSD in the morning to avoid the discomfort of sleepless nights.
†To enter the SOD building, in addition to needing an incredibly hard-to-get security clearance, one had to have an up-to-date shot card with anywhere from 10 to 20 immunizations listed. The process was so painful and time consuming that at one point in the 1960s the general who headed the whole Army Chemical Corps decided against inspecting SOD and getting an on-the-spot briefing. When asked about this incident, an SOD veteran who had earlier resigned said, "That's the way we kept them out. Those [military] types didn't need to know. Most of the security violations came from the top level. . . . He could have gone in without shots if he had insisted. The safety director would have protested, but he could have."

Olson told his wife the man had died of pneumonia.

Alice Olson had never even seen the building where her husband worked. Fort Detrick was built on the principle of concentric circles, with secrets concealed inside secrets. To enter the inner regions where SOD operated, one needed not only the highest security clearance but a "need to know" authorization. Her husband was not about to break out of a career of government-imposed secrecy to tell her about the TOP SECRET experiment that Sid Gottlieb had performed on him.

The Olsons spent an uncommunicative weekend together. On Sunday they sat on the davenport in their living room, holding hands—something they had not done for a long time. "It was a rotten November day," recalls Mrs. Olson. "The fog outside was so thick you could hardly see out the front door. Frank's depression was dreadful." Finally, she recalls, they packed up the three young children, and went off to the local theater. The film turned out to be *Luther.* "It was a very serious movie," remembers Mrs. Olson, "not a good one to see when you're depressed."

The following day, Olson appeared at 7:30 A.M. in the office of his boss, Lieutenant Colonel Ruwet. To Ruwet, Olson seemed "agitated." He told Ruwet he wanted either to quit or be fired. Taken aback, Ruwet reassured Olson that his conduct at the lodge had been "beyond reproach." Seemingly satisfied and relieved, Olson agreed to stay on and spent the rest of the day on routine SOD business. That evening, the Olsons spent their most lighthearted evening since before the retreat to Deep Creek Lodge, and they planned a farewell party for a colleague the following Saturday night.

Tuesday morning, Ruwet again arrived at his office to find a disturbed Frank Olson waiting for him. Olson said he felt "all mixed up" and questioned his own competence. He said that he should not have left the Army during the war because of his ulcer and that he lacked the ability to do his present work. After an hour, Ruwet decided Olson needed "psychiatric attention." Ruwet apparently felt that the CIA had caused Olson's problem in the first place, and instead of sending him to the base hospital, he called Gottlieb's deputy Robert Lashbrook to arrange for Olson to see a psychiatrist.

After a hurried conference, Lashbrook and Gottlieb decided to send Olson to Dr. Harold Abramson in New York. Abramson had no formal training in psychiatry and did not hold himself out to be a psychiatrist. He was an allergist and immunologist interested in treating the problems of the mind. Gottlieb chose him because he had a TOP SECRET CIA security clearance and because he had been working with LSD—under Agency contract—for several years. Gottlieb was obviously protecting his own bureaucratic position by not letting anyone outside TSS know what he had done. Having failed to observe the order to seek higher approval for LSD use, Gottlieb proceeded to violate another CIA regulation. It states, in effect, that whenever a potential flap arises that might embarrass the CIA or lead to a break in secrecy, those involved should immediately call the Office of Security. For health problems like Olson's, Security and the CIA medical office keep a long list of doctors (and psychiatrists) with TOP SECRET clearance who can provide treatment.

Gottlieb had other plans for Frank Olson, and off to New York went the disturbed SOD biochemist in the company of Ruwet and Lashbrook. Olson alternately improved and sank deeper and deeper into his feelings of depression, inadequacy, guilt, and paranoia. He began to think that the CIA was putting a stimulant like Benzedrine in his coffee to keep him awake and that it was the Agency that was out to get him. That first day in New York, Abramson saw Olson at his office. Then at 10:30 in the evening, the allergist visited Olson in his hotel room, armed with a bottle of bourbon and a bottle of the sedative Nembutal—an unusual combination for a doctor to give to someone with symptoms like Olson's.

Before Olson's appointment with Dr. Abramson the following day, he and Ruwet accompanied Lashbrook on a visit to a famous New York magician named John Mulholland, whom TSS had put under contract to prepare a manual that would apply "the magician's art to covert activities." An expert at pulling rabbits out of hats could easily find new and better ways to slip drugs into drinks, and Gottlieb signed up Mulholland to work on, among other things, "the delivery of various materials to unwitting subjects." Lashbrook thought that the magician might amuse Olson, but Olson became "highly suspicious." The group tactfully cut their visit short, and Lashbrook dropped Olson off at Abramson's office. After an hour's consultation with Abramson that afternoon the allergist gave Olson permission to return to Frederick the following day, Thanksgiving, to be with his family.

Olson, Ruwet, and Lashbrook had plane reservations for Thursday morning, so that night, in a preholiday attempt to lift spirits, they all went to see the Rodgers and Hammerstein hit musical, *Me and Juliet.* Olson became upset during the first act and told Ruwet that he knew people were waiting outside the theater to arrest him. Olson and Ruwet left the show at intermission, and the two old friends walked back to the Statler Hotel, near Penn Station. Later, while Ruwet slept in the next bed, Olson crept out of the hotel and wandered the streets. Gripped by the delusion that he was following Ruwet's orders, he tore up all his paper money and threw his wallet down a chute. At 5:30 A.M., Ruwet and Lashbrook found him sitting in the Statler lobby with his hat and coat on.

They checked out of the hotel and caught the plane back to Washington. An SOD driver picked Olson and Ruwet up at National Airport and started to drive them back to Frederick. As they drove up Wisconsin Avenue, Olson had the driver pull into a Howard Johnson's parking lot. He told Ruwet that he was "ashamed" to see his family in his present state and that he feared he might become violent with his children. Ruwet suggested he go back to see Abramson in New York, and Olson agreed. Ruwet and Olson drove back to Lashbrook's apartment on New Hampshire Avenue off Dupont Circle, and Lashbrook summoned Sid Gottlieb from Thanksgiving dinner in Virginia. All agreed that Lashbrook would take Olson back to New York while Ruwet would go back to Frederick to explain the situation to Mrs. Olson and to see his own family. (Ruwet was Olson's friend, whereas Lashbrook was no more than a professional acquaintance. Olson's son Eric believes that his father's mental state suffered when Ruwet left him in the hands of the CIA's Lashbrook, especially since Olson felt the CIA was "out to get him.") Olson and Lashbrook flew to LaGuardia airport and went to see Abramson at his Long Island office. Then the two men ate a joyless Thanksgiving dinner at a local restaurant. Friday morning Abramson drove them into Manhattan. Abramson, an allergist, finally realized that he had more on his hands with Olson than he could handle, and he recommended hospitalization. He wrote afterward that Olson "was in a psychotic state . . . with delusions of persecution."

Olson agreed to enter Chestnut Lodge, a Rockville, Maryland sanitarium that had CIA-cleared psychiatrists on the staff. They could not get plane reservations until the next morning, so Olson and Lashbrook decided to spend one last night at the Statler. They took a room on the tenth floor. With his spirits revived, Olson dared to call his wife for the first time since he had left originally for New York. They had a pleasant talk, which left her feeling better.

In the early hours of the morning, Lashbrook woke up just in time to see Frank Olson crash through the drawn blinds and closed window on a dead run.

Within seconds, as a crowd gathered around Olson's shattered body on the street below, the cover-up started. Lashbrook called Gottlieb to tell him what had happened before he notified the police. Next, Lashbrook called Abramson, who, according to Lashbrook, "wanted to be kept out of the thing completely." Abramson soon called back and offered to assist. When the police arrived, Lashbrook told them he worked for the Defense Department. He said he had no idea why Olson killed himself, but he did know that the dead man had "suffered from ulcers." The detectives assigned to the case later reported that getting information out of Lashbrook was "like pulling teeth." They speculated to each other that the case could be a homicide with homosexual overtones, but they soon dropped their inquiries when Ruwet and Abramson verified Lashbrook's sketchy account and invoked high government connections.

Back in Washington, Sid Gottlieb finally felt compelled to tell the Office of Security about the Olson case. Director Allen Dulles personally ordered Inspector General Lyman Kirkpatrick to make a full investigation, but first, Agency officials tried to make sure that no outsider would tie Olson's death either to the CIA or LSD. Teams of Security officers were soon scurrying around New York and Washington, making sure the Agency had covered its tracks. One interviewed Lashbrook and then accompanied him to a meeting with Abramson. When Lashbrook and Abramson asked the security officer to leave them alone, he complied and then, in the best traditions of his office, listened in on the conversation covertly. From his report on their talk, it can safely be said that Lashbrook and Abramson conspired to make sure they told identical stories. Lashbrook dictated to Abramson, who made a recording of the symptoms that Olson was supposed to be suffering from and the problems that were bothering him. Lashbrook even stated that Mrs. Olson had suggested her husband see a psychiatrist months before the LSD incident.* Lashbrook's comments appeared in three reports Abramson submitted to the CIA, but these reports were internally inconsistent. In one memo, Abramson wrote that Olson's "psychotic state . . . seemed to have been crystallized by [the LSD] experiment." In a later report, Abramson called the LSD dose "therapeutic" and said he believed "this dosage could hardly have had any significant role in the course of events that followed.†

The CIA officially—but secretly—took the position that the LSD had "triggered" Olson's suicide. Agency officials worked industriously behind the scenes to make sure that Mrs. Olson received an adequate government pension—two-thirds of her husband's base pay. Ruwet, who had threatened to expose the whole affair if Mrs. Olson did not get the pension, submitted a form saying Olson had died of a "classified illness." Gottlieb and Lashbrook kept trying to have it both ways in regard to giving Olson LSD, according to the CIA's General Counsel. They acknowledged LSD's triggering function in his death, but they also claimed it was "practically impossible" for the drug to have harmful aftereffects. The General Counsel called these two positions "completely inconsistent," and he wrote he was "not happy with what seems to me a very casual attitude on the part of TSS representatives to the way this experiment was conducted and to their remarks that this is just one of the risks running with scientific investigation."

As part of his investigation, Inspector General Kirkpatrick sequestered Gottlieb's LSD files, which Kirkpatrick remembers did not make Gottlieb at all happy. "I brought out his stutter," says Kirkpatrick with a wry smile. "He was quite concerned about his future." Kirkpatrick eventually recommended that some form of reprimand be given to Gottlieb, TSS chief Willis Gibbons, and TSS deputy chief James "Trapper" Drum, who had waited 20 days after Olson's death to admit that Gottlieb

---

*Mrs. Olson says that this is an outright lie.
†Nonpsychiatrist Abramson who allowed chemist Lashbrook to tell him about his patient's complexes clearly had a strange idea what was "therapeutic"—or psychotherapeutic, for that matter. In Abramson's 1953 proposal to the CIA for $85,000 to study LSD, he wrote that over the next year he "hoped" to give hospital patients "who are essentially normal from a psychiatric point of view . . . unwitting doses of the drug for psychotherapeutic purposes." His treatment brings to mind the William Burroughs character in *Naked Lunch* who states; "Now, boys, you won't see this operation performed very often, and there's a reason for that . . . you see, it has absolutely no medical value."

had cleared the experiment with him. Others opposed Kirkpatrick's recommendation. Admiral Luis deFlorez, the Agency's Research Chairman, sent a personal memo to Allen Dulles saying reprimands would be an "injustice" and would hinder "the spirit of initiative and enthusiasm so necessary in our work." The Director's office went along, and Kirkpatrick began the tortuous process of preparing letters for Dulles' signature that would say Gottlieb, Gibbons, and Drum had done something wrong, but nothing *too* wrong. Kirkpatrick went through six drafts of the Gottlieb letter alone before he came up with acceptable wording. He started out by saying TSS officials had exercised "exceedingly bad judgment." That was too harsh for high Agency officials, so Kirkpatrick tried "very poor judgment." Still too hard. He settled for "poor judgment." The TSS officials were told that they should not consider the letters to be reprimands and that no record of the letters would be put in their personnel files where they could conceivably harm future careers.

The Olson family up in Frederick did not get off so easily. Ruwet told them Olson had jumped or fallen out of the window in New York, but he mentioned not a word about the LSD, whose effects Ruwet himself believed had led to Olson's death. Ever the good soldier, Ruwet could not bring himself to talk about the classified experiment—even to ease Alice Olson's sorrow. Mrs. Olson did not want to accept the idea that her husband had willfully committed suicide. "It was very important to me—almost the core of my life—that my children not feel their father had walked out on them," recalls Mrs. Olson.

For the next 22 years, Alice Olson had no harder evidence than her own belief that her husband did not desert her and the family. Then in June 1975, the Rockefeller Commission studying illegal CIA domestic operations reported that a man fitting Frank Olson's description had leaped from a New York hotel window after the CIA had given him LSD without his knowledge. The Olson family read about the incident in the Washington *Post.* Daughter Lisa Olson Hayward and her husband went to see Ruwet, who had retired from the Army and settled in Frederick. In an emotional meeting, Ruwet confirmed that Olson was the man and said he could not tell the family earlier because he did not have permission. Ruwet tried to discourage them from going public or seeking compensation from the government, but the Olson family did both.* On national television, Alice Olson and each of her grown children took turns reading from a prepared family statement:

> We feel our family has been violated by the CIA in two ways," it said. "First, Frank Olson was experimented upon illegally and negligently. Second, the true nature of his death was concealed for twenty-two years. . . . In telling our story, we are concerned that neither the personal pain this family has experienced nor the moral and political outrage we feel be slighted. Only in this way can Frank Olson's death become part of American memory and serve the purpose of political and ethical reform so urgently needed in our society.

The statement went on to compare the Olsons with families in the Third World "whose hopes for a better life were destroyed by CIA intervention." Although Eric Olson read those words in behalf of the whole family, they reflected more the politics of the children than the feelings of their mother, Alice Olson. An incredibly strong woman who seems to have made her peace with the world, Mrs. Olson went back to college after her husband's death, got a degree, and held the family together while she taught school. She has no malice in her heart toward Vin Ruwet, her friend who withheld that vital piece of information from her all those years. He comforted her and gave support during the most difficult of times, and she deeply appreciates that. Mrs. Olson defends Ruwet by saying he was in "a bad position," but then she stops in mid-sentence and says, "If I had only been given some indication that it was the pressure of work. . . . If only I had had something I could have told the kids. I don't know how [Ruwet] could have done it either. It was a terrible thing for a man who loved him."

"I'm not vindicative toward Vin [Ruwet]," reflects Mrs. Olson. "Gottlieb is a different question. He was despicable." She tells how Gottlieb and Lashbrook both attended Olson's funeral in Frederick and contributed to a memorial fund. A week or two later, the two men asked to visit her. She knew they did not work at Detrick, but she did not really understood where they came from or their role. "I didn't want to see them," she notes. "Vin told me it would make them feel better. I didn't want an

---

*President Gerald Ford later personally apologized to the Olson family, and Congress passed a bill in 1976 to pay $750,000 in compensation to Mrs. Olson and her three children. The family voluntarily abandoned the suit.

ounce of flesh from them. I didn't think it was necessary, but, okay, I agreed. In retrospect, it was so bizarre, it makes me sick . . . I was a sucker for them."

Gottlieb and Lashbrook apparently never returned to the biological warfare offices at SOD. Little else changed, however. Ray Treichler and Henry Bortner took over CIA's liaison with SOD. SOD continued to manufacture and stockpile bacteriological agents for the CIA until 1969, when President Richard Nixon renounced the use of biological warfare tactics.

And presumably, someone replaced Frank Olson.

CHAPTER
6
THEM UNWITTING: THE SAFEHOUSES

Frank Olson's death could have been a major setback for the Agency's LSD testing, but the program, like Sid Gottlieb's career, emerged essentially unscathed. High CIA officials did call a temporary halt to all experiments while they investigated the Olson case and re-examined the general policy. They cabled the two field stations that had supplies of the drug (Manila and Atsugi, Japan) not to use it for the time being, and they even took away Sid Gottlieb's own private supply and had it locked up in his boss' safe, to which no one else had the combination. In the end, however, Allen Dulles accepted the view Richard Helms put forth that the only "operationally realistic" way to test drugs was to try them on unwitting people. Helms noted that experiments which gave advance warning would be *"pro forma* at best and result in a false sense of accomplishment and readiness." For Allen Dulles and his top aides, the possible importance of LSD clearly outweighed the risks and ethical problem of slipping the drug to involuntary subjects. They gave Gottlieb back his LSD.

Once the CIA's top echelon had made its decision to continue unwitting testing, there remained, in Richard Helms' words, "only then the question of how best to do it." The Agency's role in the Olson affair had come too perilously close to leaking out for the comfort of the security-minded, so TSS officials simply had to work out a testing system with better cover. That meant finding subjects who could not be so easily traced back to the Agency.

Well before Olson's death, Gottlieb and the MKULTRA crew had started pondering how best to do unwitting testing. They considered using an American police force to test drugs on prisoners, informants, and suspects, but they knew that some local politicians would inevitably find out. In the Agency view, such people could not be trusted to keep sensitive secrets. TSS officials thought about trying Federal prisons or hospitals, but, when sounded out, the Bureau of Prisons refused to go along with true unwitting testing (as opposed to the voluntary, if coercive, form practiced on drug addicts in Kentucky). They contemplated moving the program overseas, where they and the ARTICHOKE teams were already performing operational experiments, but they decided if they tested on the scale they thought was necessary, so many foreigners would have to know that it would pose an unacceptable security risk.

Sid Gottlieb is remembered as the brainstorming genius of the MKULTRA group—and the one with a real talent for showing others, without hurting their feelings, why their schemes would not work. States an ex-colleague who admires him greatly, "In the final analysis, Sid was like a good soldier—if the job had to be done, he did it. Once the decision was made, he found the most effective way."

In this case, Gottlieb came up with the solution after reading through old OSS files on Stanley Lovell's search for a truth drug. Gottlieb noted that Lovell had used George White, a pre-war employee of the Federal Bureau of Narcotics, to test concentrated marijuana. Besides trying the drug out on Manhattan Project volunteers and unknowing suspected Communists, White had slipped some to August Del Gracio, the Lucky Luciano lieutenant. White had called the experiment a great success. If it had not been—if Del Gracio had somehow caught on to the drugging—Gottlieb realized that the gangster would never have gone to the police or the press. His survival as a criminal required he remain quiet about even the worst indignities heaped upon him by government agents.

To Gottlieb, underworld types looked like ideal test subjects. Nevertheless, according to one TSS source, "We were not about to fool around with the Mafia." Instead, this source says they chose "the borderline underworld"—prostitutes, drug addicts, and other small-timers who would be powerless to seek any sort of revenge if they ever found out what the CIA had done to them. In addition to their being unlikely whistle-blowers, such people lived in a world where an unwitting dose of some drug —usually knockout drops—was an occupational hazard anyway. They would therefore be better equipped to deal with— and recover from—a surprise LSD trip than the population as a whole. Or so TSS officials rationalized. "They could at least say to themselves, 'Here I go again. I've been slipped a mickey,'" says a TSS veteran. Furthermore, this veteran remembers, his former colleagues reasoned that if they had to violate the civil rights of anyone, they might as well choose a group of marginal people.

George White himself had left OSS after the war and returned to the Narcotics Bureau. In 1952 he was working in the New York office. As a high-ranking narcotics agent, White had a perfect excuse to be around drugs and people who used them. He had proved during the war that he had a talent for clandestine work, and he certainly had no qualms when it came to unwitting testing. With his job, he had access to all the possible subjects the Agency would need, and if he could use LSD or any other drug to find out more about drug trafficking, so much the better. From a security viewpoint, CIA officials could easily deny any connection to anything White did, and he clearly was not the crybaby type. For Sid Gottlieb, George White was clearly the one. The MKULTRA chief decided to contact White directly to see if he might be interested in picking up with the CIA where he had left off with OSS.

Always careful to observe bureaucratic protocol, Gottlieb first approached Harry Anslinger, the longtime head of the Federal Bureau of Narcotics, and got permission to use White on a part-time basis. Then Gottlieb traveled to New York and made his pitch to the narcotics agent, who stood 5'7", weighed over 200 pounds, shaved his head, and looked something like an extremely menacing bowling ball. After an early-morning meeting, White scrawled in his sweat-stained, leather-bound diary for that day, June 9, 1952: "Gottlieb proposed I be a CIA consultant—I agree." By writing down such a thing and using Gottlieb's true name,* White had broken CIA security regula-

---

*CIA operators and agents all had cover names by which they were supposed to be called—even in classified documents. Gottlieb was "Sherman R. Grifford." George White became "Morgan Hall."

tions even before he started work. But then, White was never known as a man who followed rules.

Despite the high priority that TSS put on drug testing, White's security approval did not come through until almost a year later. "It was only last month that I got cleared," the outspoken narcotics agent wrote to a friend in 1953. "I then learned that a couple of crew-cut, pipe-smoking punks had either known me—or heard of me—during OSS days and had decided I was 'too rough' for their league and promptly blackballed me. It was only when my sponsors discovered the root of the trouble they were able to bypass the blockade. After all, fellas, I didn't go to Princeton."

People either loved or hated George White, and he had made some powerful enemies, including New York Governor Thomas Dewey and J. Edgar Hoover. Dewey would later help block White from becoming the head of the Narcotics Bureau in New York City, a job White sorely wanted. For some forgotten reason, Hoover had managed to stop White from being hired by the CIA in the Agency's early days, at a time when he would have preferred to leave narcotics work altogether. These were two of the biggest disappointments of his life. White's previous exclusion from the CIA may explain why he jumped so eagerly at Gottlieb's offer and why at the same time he privately heaped contempt on those who worked for the Agency. A remarkably heavy drinker, who would sometimes finish off a bottle of gin in one sitting, White often mocked the CIA crowd over cocktails. "He thought they were a joke," recalls one long-time crony. "They were too complicated, and they had other people do their heavy stuff."

Unlike his CIA counterparts, White loved the glare of publicity. A man who gloried in talking about himself and cultivating a hard-nosed image, White knew how to milk a drug bust for all it was worth—a skill that grew out of early years spent as a newspaper reporter in San Francisco and Los Angeles. In search of a more financially secure profession, he had joined the Narcotics Bureau in 1934, but he continued to pal around with journalists, particularly those who wrote favorably about him. Not only did he come across in the press as a cop hero, but he helped to shape the picture of future Kojaks by serving as a consultant to one of the early-television detective series. To start a raid, he would dramatically tip his hat to signal his agents—and to let the photographers know that the time had come to snap his picture. "He was sort of vainglorious," says another good friend, "the kind of guy who if he did something, didn't mind having the world know about it."*

The scientists from TSS, with their Ph.D.s and lack of street experience, could not help admiring White for his swashbuckling image. Unlike the men from MKULTRA, who, for all their pretensions, had never worked as real-live spies, White had put his life on the line for OSS overseas and had supposedly killed a Japanese agent with his bare hands. The face of one ex-TSS man lit up, like a little boy's on Christmas morning, as he told of racing around New York in George White's car and parking illegally with no fear of the law. "We were Ivy League, white, middle-class," notes another former TSSer. "We were naïve, totally naïve about this, and he felt pretty expert. He knew the whores, the pimps, the people who brought in the drugs. He'd purportedly been in a number of shootouts where he'd captured millions of dollars worth of heroin. . . . He was a pretty wild man. I know I was afraid of him. You couldn't control this guy . . . I had a little trouble telling who was controlling who in those days."

White lived with extreme personal contradictions. As could be expected of a narcotics agent, he violently opposed drugs. Yet he died largely because his beloved alcohol had destroyed his liver. He had tried everything else, from marijuana to LSD, and wrote an acquaintance, "I did feel at times I was having a 'mind-expanding' experience but this vanished like a dream immediately after the session." He was a law-enforcement official who regularly violated the law. Indeed, the CIA turned to him because of his willingness to use the power of his office to ride roughshod over the rights of others—in the name of "na-

---

*One case which put White in every newspaper in the country was his 1949 arrest of blues singer Billie Holliday on an opium charge. To prove she had been set up and was not then using drugs, the singer checked into a California sanitarium that had been recommended by a friend of a friend, Dr. James Hamilton. The jury then acquitted her. Hamilton's involvement is bizarre because he had worked with George White testing truth drugs for OSS, and the two men were good friends. White may have put his own role in perspective when he told a 1970 interviewer he "enjoyed" chasing criminals. "It was a game for me," he said. "I felt quite a bit of compassion for a number of the people that I found it necessary to put in jail, particularly when you'd see the things that would happen to their families. I'd give them a chance to stay out of jail and take care of their families by giving me information, perhaps, and they would stubbornly refuse to do so. They wouldn't be a rat, as they would put it."

tional security," when he tested LSD for the Agency, in the name of stamping out drug abuse, for the Narcotics Bureau. As yet another close associate summed up White's attitude toward his job, "He really believed the ends justified the means."

George White's "pragmatic" approach meshed perfectly with Sid Gottlieb's needs for drug testing. In May 1953 the two men, who wound up going folk dancing together several times, formally joined forces. In CIA jargon, White became MKULTRA subproject #3. Under this arrangement, White rented two adjacent Greenwich Village apartments, posing as the sometime artist and seaman "Morgan Hall." White agreed to lure guinea pigs to the "safehouse"—as the Agency men called the apartments—slip them drugs, and report the results to Gottlieb and the others in TSS. For its part, the CIA let the Narcotics Bureau use the place for undercover activities (and often for personal pleasure) whenever no Agency work was scheduled, and the CIA paid all the bills, including the cost of keeping a well-stocked liquor cabinet—a substantial bonus for White. Gottlieb personally handed over the first $4,000 in cash, to cover the initial costs of furnishing the safehouse in the lavish style that White felt befitted him.

Gottlieb did not limit his interest to drugs. He and other TSS officials wanted to try out surveillance equipment. CIA technicians quickly installed see-through mirrors and microphones through which eavesdroppers could film, photograph, and record the action. "Things go wrong with listening devices and two-way mirrors, so you build these things to find out what works and what doesn't," says a TSS source. "If you are going to entrap, you've got to give the guy pictures [*flagrante delicto*] and voice recordings. Once you learn how to do it so that the whole thing looks comfortable, cozy, and safe, then you can transport the technology overseas and use it." This TSS man notes that the Agency put to work in the bedrooms of Europe some of the techniques developed in the George White safehouse operation.

In the safehouse's first months, White tested LSD, several kinds of knockout drops, and that old OSS standby, essence of marijuana. He served up the drugs in food, drink, and cigarettes and then tried to worm information—usually on narcotics matters—from his "guests." Sometimes MKULTRA men came up from Washington to watch the action. A September

1953 entry in White's diary noted: "Lashbrook at 81 Bedford Street—Owen Winkle and LSD surprise—can wash." Sid Gottlieb's deputy, Robert Lashbrook, served as "project monitor" for the New York safehouse.*

White had only been running the safehouse six months when Olson died (in Lashbrook's company), and Agency officials suspended the operation for re-evaluation. They soon allowed him to restart it, and then Gottlieb had to order White to slow down again. A New York State commissioner had summoned the narcotics agent to explain his role in the deal that wound up with Governor Dewey pardoning Lucky Luciano after the war. The commissioner was asking questions that touched on White's use of marijuana on Del Gracio, and Gottlieb feared that word of the CIA's current testing might somehow leak out. This storm also soon passed, but then, in early 1955, the Narcotics Bureau transferred White to San Francisco to become chief agent there. Happy with White's performance, Gottlieb decided to let him take the entire safehouse operation with him to the Coast. White closed up the Greenwich Village apartments, leaving behind unreceipted "tips" for the landlord "to clear up any difficulties about the alterations and damages," as a CIA document put it.†

White soon rented a suitable "pad" (as he always called it) on Telegraph Hill, with a stunning view of San Francisco Bay, the Golden Gate Bridge, and Alcatraz. To supplement the furniture he brought from the New York safehouse, he went out and bought items that gave the place the air of the brothel it was to become: Toulouse-Lautrec posters, a picture of a French can-can dancer, and photos of manacled women in black stockings. "It was supposed to look rich," recalls a narcotics agent who regularly visited, "but it was furnished like crap."

White hired a friend's company to install bugging equip-

*Despite this indication from White's diary that Lashbrook came to the New York safehouse for an "LSD surprise" and despite his signature on papers authorizing the subproject, Lashbrook flatly denied all firsthand knowledge of George White's testing in 1977 Senate testimony. Subcommittee chairman Edward Kennedy did not press Lashbrook, nor did he refer the matter to the Justice Department for possible perjury charges.
†This was just one of many expenditures that would drive CIA auditors wild while going over George White's accounts. Others included $44.04 for a telescope, liquor bills over $1,000 "with no record as to the necessity of its use," and $31.75 to make an on-the-spot payment to a neighborhood lady whose car he hit. The reason stated for using government funds for the last expense: "It was important to maintain security and forestall an insurance investigation."

ment, and William Hawkins, a 25-year-old electronics whiz then studying at Berkley put in four DD-4 microphones disguised as electrical wall outlets and hooked them up to two F-301 tape recorders, which agents monitored in an adjacent "listening post." Hawkins remembers that White "kept a pitcher of martinis in the refrigerator, and he'd watch me for a while as I installed a microphone and then slip off." For his own personal "observation post," White had a portable toilet set up behind a two-way mirror, where he could watch the proceedings, usually with drink in hand.

The San Francisco safehouse specialized in prostitutes. "But this was before *The Hite Report* and before any hooker had written a book," recalls a TSS man, "so first we had to go out and learn about their world. In the beginning, we didn't know what a john was or what a pimp did." Sid Gottlieb decided to send his top staff psychologist, John Gittinger, to San Francisco to probe the demimonde.

George White supplied the prostitutes for the study, although White, in turn, delegated much of the pimping function to one of his assistants, Ira "Ike" Feldman. A muscular but very short man, whom even the 5′7″ White towered over, Feldman tried even harder than his boss to act tough. Dressed in suede shoes, a suit with flared trousers, a hat with a turned-up brim, and a huge zircon ring that was supposed to look like a diamond, Feldman first came to San Francisco on an undercover assignment posing as an East Coast mobster looking to make a big heroin buy. Using a drug-addicted prostitute name Janet Jones, whose common-law husband states that Feldman paid her off with heroin, the undercover man lured a number of suspected drug dealers to the "pad" and helped White make arrests.

As the chief Federal narcotics agent in San Francisco, White was in a position to reward or punish a prostitute. He set up a system whereby he and Feldman provided Gittinger with all the hookers the psychologist wanted. White paid off the women with a fixed number of "chits." For each chit, White owed one favor. "So the next time the girl was arrested with a john," says an MKULTRA veteran, "she would give the cop George White's phone number. The police all knew White and cooperated with him without asking questions. They would release the girl if he said so. White would keep good records of how many chits each person had and how many she used. No money was exchanged, but five chits were worth $500 to $1,000." Prostitutes were not the only beneficiaries of White's largess. The narcotics agent worked out a similar system to forgive the transgressions of small time drug pushers when the MKULTRA men wanted to talk to them about "the rules of their game," according to the source.

TSS officials wanted to find out everything they could about how to apply sex to spying, and the prostitute project became a general learning and then training ground for CIA carnal operations. After all, states one TSS official, "We did quite a study of prostitutes and their behavior. . . . At first nobody really knew how to use them. How do you train them? How do you work them? How do you take a woman who is willing to use her body to get money out of a guy to get things which are much more important, like state secrets. I don't care how beautiful she is—educating the ordinary prostitute up to that level is not a simple task."

The TSS men continually tried to refine their knowledge. They realized that prostitutes often wheedled extra money out of a customer by suggesting some additional service as male orgasm neared. They wondered if this might not also be a good time to seek sensitive information. "But no," says the source, "we found the guy was focused solely on hormonal needs. He was not thinking of his career or anything else at that point." The TSS experts discovered that the postsexual, light-up-a-cigarette period was much better suited to their ulterior motives. Says the source:

> Most men who go to prostitutes are prepared for the fact that [after the act] she's beginning to work to get herself out of there, so she can get back on the street to make some more money. . . . To find a prostitute who is willing to stay is a hell of a shock to anyone used to prostitutes. It has a tremendous effect on the guy. It's a boost to his ego if she's telling him he was really neat, and she wants to stay for a few more hours. . . . Most of the time, he gets pretty vulnerable. What the hell's he going to talk about? Not the sex, so he starts talking about his business. It's at this time she can lead him gently. But you have to train prostitutes to do that. Their natural inclination is to do exactly the opposite.

The men from MKULTRA learned a great deal about varying sexual preferences. One of them says:

We didn't know in those days about hidden sadism and all that sort of stuff. We learned a lot about human nature in the bedroom. We began to understand that when people wanted sex, it wasn't just what we had thought of—you know, the missionary position. . . . We started to pick up knowledge that could be used in operations, but with a lot of it we never figured out any way to use it operationally. We just learned. . . . All these ideas did not come to us at once. But evolving over three or four years in which these studies were going on, things emerged which we tried. Our knowledge of prostitutes' behavior became pretty damn good. . . . This comes across now that somehow we were just playing around and we just found all these exotic ways to waste the taxpayers' money on satisfying our hidden urges. I'm not saying that watching prostitutes was not exciting or something like that. But what I am saying was there was a purpose to the whole business.*

In the best tradition of Mata Hari, the CIA did use sex as a clandestine weapon, although apparently not so frequently as the Russians. While many in the Agency believed that it simply did not work very well, others like CIA operators in Berlin during the mid-1960s felt prostitutes could be a prime source of intelligence. Agency men in that city used a network of hookers to good advantage—or so they told visitors from headquarters. Yet, with its high proportion of Catholics and Mormons—not to mention the Protestant ethic of many of its top leaders—the Agency definitely had limits beyond which prudery took over. For instance, a TSS veteran says that a good number of case officers wanted no part of homosexual entrapment operations. And to go a step further, he recalls one senior KGB man who told too many sexual jokes about young boys. "It didn't take too long to recognize that he was more than a little fascinated by youths," says the source. "I took the trouble to point out he was probably too good, too well-trained, to be either entrapped or to give away secrets. But he would have been tempted toward a compromising position by a preteen. I mentioned this, and they said, 'As a psychological observer, you're probably quite right. But what the hell are we going to do about it? Where are we going to get a twelve-year-old boy?' " The source believes that if the Russian had had a taste for older men, U.S. intelligence

---

*In *1984,* George Orwell wrote about government-encouraged prostitution: "Mere debauchery did not matter very much, so long as it was furtive and joyless, and only involved the women of a submerged and despised class."

might have mounted an operation, "but the idea of a twelve-year-old boy was just more than anybody could stomach."

As the TSS men learned more about the San Francisco hustlers, they ventured outside the safehouse to try out various clandestine-delivery gimmicks in public places like restaurants, bars, and beaches. They practiced ways to slip LSD to citizens of the demimonde while buying them a drink or lighting up a cigarette, and they then tried to observe the effects when the drug took hold. Because the MKULTRA scientists did not move smoothly among the very kinds of people they were testing, they occasionally lost an unwitting victim in a crowd—thereby sending a stranger off alone with a head full of LSD.

In a larger sense, *all* the test victims would become lost. As a matter of policy, Sid Gottlieb ordered that virtually no records be kept of the testing. In 1973, when Gottlieb retired from the Agency, he and Richard Helms agreed to destroy what they thought were the few existing documents on the program. Neither Gottlieb nor any other MKULTRA man has owned up to having given LSD to an unknowing subject, or even to observing such an experiment—except of course in the case of Frank Olson. Olson's death left behind a paper trail outside of Gottlieb's control and that hence could not be denied. Otherwise, Gottlieb and his colleagues have put all the blame for actual testing on George White, who is not alive to defend himself. One reason the MKULTRA veterans have gone to such lengths to conceal their role is obvious: fear of lawsuits from victims claiming damaged health.

At the time of the experiments, the subjects' health did not cause undue concern. At the safehouse, where most of the testing took place, doctors were seldom present. Dr. James Hamilton, a Stanford Medical School psychiatrist and White's OSS colleague, visited the place from time to time, apparently for studies connected to unwitting drug experiments and deviant sexual practices. Yet neither Hamilton nor any other doctor provided much medical supervision. From his perch atop the toilet seat, George White could do no more than make surface observations of his drugged victims. Even an experienced doctor would have had difficulty handling White's role. In addition to LSD, which they knew could cause serious, if not fatal problems, TSS officials gave White even more exotic experimental drugs to test, drugs that other Agency contractors may or may not have already used on human subjects. "If we were scared enough of a drug not to try it out on ourselves, we sent it to San Francisco," recalls a TSS source. According to a 1963 report by CIA Inspector General John Earman, "In a number of instances, however, the test subject has become ill for hours or days, including hospitalization in at least one case, and [White] could only follow up by guarded inquiry after the test subject's return to normal life. Possible sickness and attendant economic loss are inherent contingent effects of the testing."

The Inspector General noted that the whole program could be compromised if an outside doctor made a "correct diagnosis of an illness." Thus, the MKULTRA team not only made some people sick but had a vested interest in keeping doctors from finding out what was really wrong. If that bothered the Inspector General, he did not report his qualms, but he did say he feared "serious damage to the Agency" in the event of public exposure. The Inspector General was only somewhat reassured by the fact that George White "maintain[ed] close working relations with local police authorities which could be utilized to protect the activity in critical situations."

If TSS officials had been willing to stick with their original target group of marginal underworld types, they would have had little to fear from the police. After all, George White *was* the police. But increasingly they used the safehouse to test drugs, in the Inspector General's words, "on individuals of all social levels, high and low, native American and foreign." After all, they were looking for an operational payoff, and they knew people reacted differently to LSD according to everything from health and mood to personality structure. If TSS officials wanted to slip LSD to foreign leaders, as they contemplated doing to Fidel Castro, they would try to spring an unwitting dose on somebody as similar as possible. They used the safehouse for "dry runs" in the intermediate stage between the laboratory and actual operations.

For these dress rehearsals, George White and his staff procurer, Ike Feldman, enticed men to the apartment with prostitutes. An unsuspecting john would think he had bought a night of pleasure, go back to a strange apartment, and wind up zonked. A CIA document that survived Sid Gottlieb's shredding recorded this process. Its author, Gottlieb himself, could not break a lifelong habit of using nondescriptive language. For the MKULTRA chief, the whores were "certain individuals who covertly administer this material to other people in accordance with [White's] instructions." White normally paid the women $100 in Agency funds for their night's work, and Gottlieb's prose reached new bureaucratic heights as he explained why the prostitutes did not sign for the money: "Due to the highly unorthodox nature of these activities and the considerable risk incurred by these individuals, it is impossible to require that they provide a receipt for these payments or that they indicate the precise manner in which the funds were spent." The CIA's auditors had to settle for canceled checks which White cashed himself and marked either "Stormy" or, just as appropriately, "Undercover Agent." The program was also referred to as "Operation Midnight Climax."

TSS officials found the San Francisco safehouse so successful that they opened a branch office, also under George White's auspices, across the Golden Gate on the beach in Marin County.* Unlike the downtown apartment, where an MKULTRA man says "you could bring people in for quickies after lunch," the suburban Marin County outlet proved useful for experiments that required relative isolation. There, TSS scientists tested such MKULTRA specialties as stink bombs, itching and sneezing powders, and diarrhea inducers. TSS's Ray Treichler, the Stanford chemist, sent these "harassment substances" out to California for testing by White, along with such delivery systems as a mechanical launcher that could throw a foul-smelling object 100 yards, glass ampules that could be stepped on in a crowd to release any of Treichler's powders, a fine hypodermic needle to inject drugs through the cork in a wine bottle, and a drug-coated swizzle stick.

TSS men also planned to use the Marin County safehouse for an ill-fated experiment that began when staff psychologists David Rhodes and Walter Pasternak spent a week circulating in bars, inviting strangers to a party. They wanted to spray LSD from an acrosol can on their guests, but according to Rhodes' Senate testimony, "the weather defeated us." In the heat of the summer, they could not close the doors and windows long enough for the LSD to hang in the air and be inhaled. Sensing

*In 1961 MKULTRA officials started a third safehouse in New York, also under the Narcotics Bureau's supervision. This one was handled by Charles Siragusa, who, like White, was a senior agent and OSS veteran.

a botched operation, their MKULTRA colleague, John Gittinger (who brought the drug out from Washington) shut himself in the bathroom and let go with the spray. Still, Rhodes
testified, Gittinger did not get high, and the CIA men apparently scrubbed the party.*

The MKULTRA crew continued unwitting testing until the
summer of 1963 when the Agency's Inspector General stumbled across the safehouses during a regular inspection of TSS
activities. This happened not long after Director John McCone
had appointed John Earman to the Inspector General position.†
Much to the displeasure of Sid Gottlieb and Richard Helms,
Earman questioned the propriety of the safehouses, and he
insisted that Director McCone be given a full briefing. Although President Kennedy had put McCone in charge of the
Agency the year before, Helms—the professional's professional
—had not bothered to tell his outsider boss about some of the
CIA's most sensitive activities, including the safehouses and
the CIA–Mafia assassination plots.‡ Faced with Earman's demands, Helms—surely one of history's most clever bureaucrats
—volunteered to tell McCone himself about the safehouses
(rather than have Earman present a negative view of the program). Sure enough, Helms told Earman afterward, McCone
raised no objections to unwitting testing (as Helms described
it). A determined man and a rather brave one, Earman countered with a full written report to McCone recommending that
the safehouses be closed. The Inspector General cited the risks

*Rhodes' testimony about this incident, which had been set up in advance with
Senator Edward Kennedy's staff, brought on the inevitable "Gang That
Couldn't Spray Straight" headline in the Washington *Post*. This approach
turned the public perception of a deadly serious program into a kind of practical joke carried out badly by a bunch of bumblers.
†Lyman Kirkpatrick, the longtime Inspector General who had then recently
left the job to take a higher Agency post, had personally known of the safehouse
operation since right after Olson's death and had never raised any noticeable
objection. He now states he was "shocked" by the unwitting testing, but that he
"didn't have the authority to follow up . . . I was trying to determine what the
tolerable limits were of what I could do and still keep my job."
‡Trying to explain why he had specifically decided not to inform the CIA
Director about the Agency's relationship with the mob, Helms stated to the
Church committee, "Mr. McCone was relatively new to this organization, and
I guess I must have thought to myself, well this is going to look peculiar to him
. . . This was, you know not a very savory effort." Presumably, Helms had
similar reasons for not telling McCone about the unwitting drug-testing in the
safehouses.

of exposure and pointed out that many people both inside and outside the Agency found "the concepts involved in manipulating human behavior . . . to be distasteful and unethical." McCone reacted by putting off a final decision but suspending unwitting testing in the meantime. Over the next year, Helms, who then headed the Clandestine Services, wrote at least three memos urging resumption. He cited "indications . . . of an apparent Soviet aggressiveness in the field of covertly administered chemicals which are, to say the least, inexplicable and disturbing," and he claimed the CIA's "positive operational capacity to use drugs is diminishing owing to a lack of realistic testing."* To Richard Helms, the importance of the program exceeded the risks and the ethical questions, although he did admit, "We have no answer to the moral issue." McCone simply did nothing for two years. The director's indecision had the effect of killing the program, nevertheless. TSS officials closed the San Francisco safehouse in 1965 and the New York one in 1966.

Years later in a personal letter to Sid Gottlieb, George White wrote an epitaph for his role with the CIA: "I was a very minor missionary, actually a heretic, but I toiled wholeheartedly in the vineyards because it was fun, fun, fun. Where else could a red-blooded American boy lie, kill, cheat, steal, rape, and pillage with the sanction and blessing of the All-Highest?"

After 10 years of unwitting testing, the men from MKULTRA apparently scored no major breakthroughs with LSD or other drugs. They found no effective truth drug, recruitment pill, or aphrodisiac. LSD had not opened up the mind to CIA control. "We had thought at first that this was the secret that was going to unlock the universe," says a TSS veteran. "We found that human beings had resources far greater than imagined."

Yet despite the lack of precision and uncertainty, the CIA still made field use of LSD and other drugs that had worked their way through the MKULTRA testing progression. A 1957 report showed that TSS had already moved 6 drugs out of the experi-

---

*Helms was a master of telling different people different stories to suit his purposes. At the precise time he was raising the Soviet menace to push McCone into letting the unwitting testing continue, he wrote the Warren Commission that not only did Soviet behavioral research lag five years behind the West's, but that "there is no present evidence that the Soviets have any singular, new, potent, drugs . . . to force a course of action on an individual."

mental stage and into active use. Up to that time, CIA operators had utilized LSD and other psychochemicals against 33 targets in 6 different operations. Agency officials hoped in these cases either to discredit the subject by making him seem insane or to "create within the individual a mental and emotional situation which will release him from the restraint of self-control and induce him to reveal information willingly under adroit manipulation." The Agency has consistently refused to release details of these operations, and TSS sources who talk rather freely about other matters seem to develop amnesia when the subject of field use comes up. Nevertheless, it can be said that the CIA did establish a relationship with an unnamed foreign secret service to interrogate prisoners with LSD-like drugs. CIA operators participated directly in these interrogations, which continued at least until 1966. Often the Agency showed more concern for the safety of its operational targets abroad than it did for its unwitting victims in San Francisco, since some of the foreign subjects were given medical examinations before being slipped the drug.*

In these operations, CIA men sometimes brought in local doctors for reasons that had nothing to do with the welfare of the patient. Instead, the doctor's role was to certify the apparent insanity of a victim who had been unwittingly dosed with LSD or an even more durable psychochemical like BZ (which causes trips lasting a week or more and which tends to induce violent behavior). If a doctor were to prescribe hospitalization or other severe treatment, the effect on the subject could be devastating. He would suffer not only the experience itself, including possible confinement in a mental institution, but also social stigma. In most countries, even the suggestion of mental problems severely damages an individual's professional and personal standing (as Thomas Eagleton, the recipient of some shock therapy, can testify). "It's an old technique," says an MKULTRA veteran. "You neutralize someone by having their constituency doubt them." The Church committee confirms

---

*TSS officials led by Sid Gottlieb, who were responsible for the operational use of LSD abroad, took the position that there was "no danger medically" in unwitting doses and that neither giving a medical exam or having a doctor present was necessary. The Agency's Medical Office disagreed, saying the drug was "medically dangerous." In 1957 Inspector General Lyman Kirkpatrick noted it would be "unrealistic" to give the Medical Office what amounted to veto power over covert operations by letting Agency doctors rule on the health hazard to subjects in the field.

that the Agency used this technique at least several times to assassinate a target's character.*

Still, the Clandestine Services did not frequently call on TSS for LSD or other drugs. Many operators had practical and ethical objections. In part to overcome such objections and also to find better ways to use chemical and biological substances in covert operations, Sid Gottlieb moved up in 1959 to become Assistant for Scientific Matters to the Clandestine Services chief. Gottlieb found that TSS had kept the MKULTRA programs so secret that many field people did not even know what techniques were available. He wrote that tight controls over field use in MKDELTA operations "may have generated a general defeatism among case officers," who feared they would not receive permission or that the procedure was not worth the effort. Gottlieb tried to correct these shortcomings by providing more information on the drug arsenal to senior operators and by streamlining the approval process. He had less luck in overcoming views that drugs do not work or are not reliable, and that their operational use leads to laziness and poor tradecraft.

If the MKULTRA program had ever found that LSD or any other drug really did turn a man into a puppet, Sid Gottlieb would have had no trouble surmounting all those biases. Instead, Gottlieb and his fellow searchers came frustratingly close but always fell short of finding a reliable control mechanism. LSD certainly penetrated to the innermost regions of the mind. It could spring loose a whole gamut of feelings, from

---

*While I was doing the research for this book, many people approached me claiming to be victims of CIA drugging plots. Although I listened carefully to all and realized that some might be authentic victims, I had no way of distinguishing between someone acting strangely and someone *made* to act strangely. Perhaps the most insidious aspect of this whole technique is that anyone blaming his aberrant behavior on a drug or on the CIA gets labeled a hopeless paranoid and his case is thrown into the crank file. There is no better cover than operating on the edge of madness.

One leftist professor in a Latin American university who had opposed the CIA says that he was working alone in his office one day in 1974 when a strange woman entered and jabbed his wrist with a pin stuck in a small round object. Almost immediately, he become irrational, broke glasses, and threw water in colleagues' faces. He says his students spotted an ambulance waiting for him out front. They spirited him out the back door and took him home, where he tripped (or had psychotic episodes) for more than a week. He calls the experience a mix of "heaven and hell," and he shudders at the thought that he might have spent the time in a hospital "with nurses and straitjackets." Although he eventually returned to his post at the university, he states that it took him several years to recover the credibility he lost the day he "went crazy at the office." If the CIA was involved, it had neutralized a foe.

terror to insight. But in the end, the human psyche proved so complex that even the most skilled manipulator could not anticipate all the variables. He could use LSD and other drugs to chip away at free will. He could score temporary victories, and he could alter moods, perception—sometimes even beliefs. He had the power to cause great harm, but ultimately he could not conquer the human spirit.

CHAPTER
7
MUSHROOMS TO COUNTERCULTURE

The MKULTRA scientists reaped little but disaster, mischief, and disappointment from their efforts to use LSD as a miracle weapon against the minds of their opponents. Nevertheless, their insatiable need to try every possibility led them to test hundreds of other substances, including all the drugs that would later be called psychedelic. These drugs were known to have great potency. They were derived from natural botanical products, and the men from MKULTRA believed from the beginning that rare organic materials might somehow have the greatest effect on the human mind. The most amazing of the psychedelics came from odd corners of the natural world. Albert Hofmann created LSD largely out of ergot, a fungus that grows on rye; mescaline is nothing more than the synthetic essence of peyote cactus. Psilocybin, the drug that Timothy Leary preferred to LSD for his Harvard experiments, was synthesized from exotic Mexican mushrooms that occupy a special place in CIA history.

When the MKULTRA team first embarked on its mind-control explorations, the "magic mushroom" was only a rumor or fable in the linear history of the Western world. On nothing more than the possibility that the legend was based on fact, the Agency's scientists tracked the mushroom to the most remote parts of Mexico and then spent lavishly to test and develop its mind-altering properties. The results, like the LSD legacy, were as startling as they were unintended.

Among the botanicals that mankind has always turned to for intoxicants and poisons, mushrooms stand out. There is something enchantingly odd about the damp little buttons that can thrill a gourmet or kill one, depending on the subtle differences among the countless varieties. These fungi have a long record in unorthodox warfare. Two thousand years before the CIA looked to unleash powerful mushrooms in covert operations, the Roman Empress Agrippina eliminated her husband Claudius with a dish of poisonous mushrooms. According to Roman history, Agrippina wanted the emperor dead so that her son Nero could take the throne. She planned to take advantage of Claudius' love for the delicious *Amanita caesarea* mushroom, but she had to choose carefully among its deadly lookalikes. The poison could not be "sudden and instantaneous in its operation, lest the desperate achievement should be discovered," wrote Gordon and Valentina Wasson in their monumental and definitive work, *Mushrooms, Russia and History.* The Empress settled on the lethal *Amanita phalloides,* a fungus the Wassons considered well suited to the crime: "The victim would not give away the game by abnormal indispositions at the meal, but when the seizure came he would be so severely stricken that thereafter he would no longer be in command of his own affairs." Agrippina knew her mushrooms, and Nero became Emperor.

CIA mind-control specialists sought to emulate and surpass that kind of sophistication, as it might apply to any conceivable drug. Their fixation on the "magic mushroom" grew indirectly out of a meeting between drug experts and Morse Allen, head of the Agency's ARTICHOKE program, in October 1952. One expert told Allen about a shrub called piule, whose seeds had long been used as an intoxicant by Mexican Indians at religious ceremonies. Allen, who wanted to know about anything that distorted reality, immediately arranged for a young CIA scientist to take a Mexican field trip and gather samples of piule as well as other plants of "high narcotic and toxic value of interest to ARTICHOKE."

That young scientist arrived in Mexico City early in 1953. He could not advertise the true purpose of his trip because of ARTICHOKE's extreme secrecy, so he assumed cover as a researcher interested in finding native plants which were anesthetics. Fluent in Spanish and familiar with Mexico, he had no trouble moving around the country, meeting with leading experts on botanicals. Then he was off into the mountains south of the capital with his own field-testing equipment, gathering specimens and testing them crudely on the spot. By February, he had collected sacks full of material, including 10 pounds of piule. Before leaving Mexico to look for more samples around the Caribbean, the young scientist heard amazing tales about special mushrooms that grew only in the hot and rainy summer months. Such stories had circulated among Europeans in Mexico since Cortez had conquered the country early in the sixteenth century. Spanish friars had reported that the Aztecs used strange mushrooms in their religious ceremonies, which these converters of the heathens described as "demonic holy communions." Aztec priests called the special mushrooms *teonanactl,* "God's flesh." But Cortez's plunderers soon lost track of the rite, as did the traders and anthropologists who followed in their wake. Only the legend survived.

Back in Washington, the young scientist's samples went straight to the labs, and Agency officials scoured the historical record for accounts of the strange mushrooms. Morse Allen himself, though responsible in ARTICHOKE research for everything from the polygraph to hypnosis, took the trouble to go through the Indian lore. "Very early accounts of the ceremonies of some tribes of Mexican Indians show that mushrooms are used to produce hallucinations and to create intoxication in connection with religious festivals," he wrote. "In addition, this literature shows that witch doctors or 'divinators' used some types of mushrooms to produce confessions or to locate stolen objects or to predict the future." Here was a possible truth drug, Morse Allen reasoned. "Since it had been determined that no area of human knowledge is to be left unexplored in connection with the ARTICHOKE program, it was therefore regarded as essential that the peculiar qualities of the mushroom be explored. . . ." Allen declared. "Full consideration," he concluded, should be given to sending an Agency man back to Mexico during the summer. The CIA had begun its quest for "God's flesh."

Characteristically, Morse Allen was planning ahead in case the CIA's searchers came up with a mushroom worth having in large quantities. He knew that the supply from the tropics varied by season, and, anyway, it would be impractical to go to Mexico for fungi each time an operational need popped up. So

Allen decided to see if it were possible to grow the mushrooms at home, either outdoors or in hothouses. On June 24, 1953, he and an associate drove from Washington to Toughkenamon, Pennsylvania, in the heart of "the largest mushroom-growing area in the world." At a three-hour session with the captains of the mushroom industry, Allen explained the government's interest in poisonous and narcotic fungi. Allen reported that the meeting "was primarily designed to obtain a 'foothold' in the center of the mushroom-growing industry where, if requirements for mushroom growing were demanded, it would be done by professionals in the trade." The mushroom executives were quite reluctant to grow toxic products because they knew that any accidental publicity would scare their customers. In the end, however, their patriotism won out, and they agreed to grow any kind of fungus the government desired. Allen considered the trip a great success.

As useful as this commitment might be, an element of chance remained as long as the CIA had to depend on the natural process. But if the Agency could find synthetic equivalents for the active ingredients, it could manufacture rather than grow its own supply. Toward this goal of bypassing nature, Morse Allen had little choice but to turn for help to the man who the following year would wrest most of the ARTICHOKE functions from his grasp: Sid Gottlieb. Gottlieb, himself a Ph.D. in chemistry, had scientists working for him who knew what to do on the level of test tubes and beakers. Allen ran ARTICHOKE out of the Office of Security, which was not equipped for work on the frontiers of science.

Gottlieb and his colleagues moved quickly into the mysteries of the Mexican hallucinogens. They went to work on the chemical structures of the piule and other plants that Morse Allen's emissary brought back from his field trip, but they neglected to report their findings to the bureaucratically outflanked Allen. Gottlieb and the MKULTRA crew soon got caught up in the search for the magic mushroom. While TSS had its own limited laboratory facilities, it depended on secret contractors for most research and development. Working with an associate, a cadaverously thin chemistry Ph.D. named Henry Bortner, Gottlieb passed the tropical plants to a string of corporate and academic researchers. One of them, Dr. James Moore, a 29-year-old chemist at Parke, Davis & Company in Detroit, was destined to be the first man in the CIA camp to taste the magic mushroom.

Moore's career was typical of the specialists in the CIA's vast network of private contractors. His path to the mushroom led through several jobs and offbeat assignments, always with Agency funds and direction behind him. A precise, meticulous man of scientific habits, Moore was hardly the sort one would expect to find chasing psychedelic drugs. Such pursuits began for him in March 1953, when he had returned to his lab at Parke, Davis after a year of postdoctoral research at the University of Basel. His supervisor had called him in with an intriguing proposal: How would he like to work inside the company on a CIA contract? "Those were not particularly prosperous times, and the company was glad to get someone else to pay my salary [$8,000 a year]," notes Moore 25 years later. "If I had thought I was participating in a scheme run by a small band of mad individuals, I would have demurred."

He accepted the job.

The Agency contracted with Parke, Davis, as it did with numerous other drug companies, universities, and government agencies to develop behavioral products and poisons from botanicals. CIA-funded chemists extracted deadly substances like the arrow-poison curare from natural products, while others worked on ways to deliver these poisons most effectively, like the "nondiscernible microbioinoculator" (or dart gun) that the Army Chemical Corps invented. CIA-connected botanists collected—and then chemists analyzed—botanicals from all over the tropics: a leaf that killed cattle, several plants deadly to fish, another leaf that caused hair to fall out, sap that caused temporary blindness, and a host of other natural products that could alter moods, dull or stimulate nerves, or generally disorient people. Among the plants Moore investigated was Jamaica dogwood, a plant used by Caribbean natives to stun fish so they could be easily captured for food. This work resulted in the isolation of several new substances, one of which Moore named "lisetin," in honor of his daughter.

Moore had no trouble adjusting to the secrecy demanded by his CIA sponsors, having worked on the Manhattan Project as a graduate student. He dealt only with his own case officer, Henry Bortner, and two or three other CIA men in TSS. Once Moore completed his chemical work on a particular substance, he turned the results over to Bortner and apparently never learned of the follow-up. Moore worked in his own little isolated compartment, and he soon recognized that the Agency preferred contractors who did not ask questions about what was going on in the next box.

In 1955 Moore left private industry for academia, moving from Detroit to the relatively placid setting of the University of Delaware in Newark. The school made him an assistant professor, and he moved into a lab in the Georgian red-brick building that housed the chemistry department. Along with his family, Moore brought his CIA contract—then worth $16,000 a year, of which he received $650 per month, with the rest going to pay research assistants and overhead. Although the Agency allowed a few top university officials to be briefed on his secret connection, Moore appeared to his colleagues and students to be a normal professor who had a healthy research grant from the Geschickter Fund for Medical Research in Washington.

In the world of natural products—particularly mushrooms—the CIA soon made Moore a full-service agent. With some help from his CIA friends, he made contact with the leading lights in mycology (the study of mushrooms), attended professional meetings, and arranged for others to send him samples. From the CIA's point of view, he could not have had better cover. As Sid Gottlieb wrote, Moore "maintains the fiction that the botanical specimens he collects are for his own use since his field interest is natural-product chemistry." Under this pretext, Moore had a perfect excuse to make and purchase for the CIA chemicals that the Agency did not want traced. Over the years, Moore billed the Agency for hundreds of purchases, including 50 cents for an unidentified pamphlet, $433.13 for a particular shipment of mescaline, $1147.60 for a large quantity of mushrooms, and $12,000 for a quarter-ton of fluothane, an inhalation anesthetic. He shipped his purchases on as Bortner directed.

Moore eventually became a kind of short-order cook for what CIA documents call "offensive CW, BW" weapons at "very low cost and in a few days' time . . ." If there were an operational need, Bortner had only to call in the order, and Moore would whip up a batch of a "reputed depilatory" or hallucinogens like DMT or the incredibly potent BZ. On one occasion in 1963, Moore prepared a small dose of a very lethal carbamate poison —the same substance that OSS used two decades earlier to try to kill Adolf Hitler. Moore charged the Agency his regular consulting fee, $100, for this service.

"Did I ever consider what would have happened if this stuff were given to unwitting people?" Moore asks, reflecting on his

CIA days. "No. Particularly no. Had I been given that information, I think I would have been prepared to accept that. If I had been knee-jerk about testing on unwitting subjects, I wouldn't have been the type of person they would have used. There was nothing that I did that struck me as being so sinister and deadly. . . . It was all investigative."

James Moore was only one of many CIA specialists on the lookout for the magic mushroom. For three years after Morse Allen's man returned from Mexico with his tales of wonder, Moore and the others in the Agency's network pushed their lines of inquiry among contacts and travelers into Mexican villages so remote that Spanish had barely penetrated. Yet they found no magic mushrooms. Given their efforts, it was ironic that the man who beat them to "God's flesh" was neither a spy nor a scientist, but a banker. It was R. Gordon Wasson, vice-president of J. P. Morgan & Company, amateur mycologist, and co-author with his wife Valentina of *Mushrooms, Russia and History*. Nearly 30 years earlier, Wasson and his Russian-born wife had become fascinated by the different ways that societies deal with the mushroom, and they followed their lifelong obsession with these fungi, in all their glory, all over the globe.* They found whole nationalities, such as the Russians and the Catalans, were mycophiles, while others like the Spaniards and the Anglo-Saxons were not. They learned that in ancient Greece and Rome there was a belief that certain kinds of mushrooms were brought into being by lightning bolts. They discovered that widely scattered peoples, including desert Arabs, Siberians, Chinese, and Maoris of New Zealand, have shared

*On their honeymoon, in the summer of 1927, the Wassons were strolling along a mountain path when suddenly Valentina abandoned Gordon's side. "She had spied wild mushrooms in the forest," wrote Wasson, "and racing over the carpet of dried leaves in the woods, she knelt in poses of adoration before one cluster and then another of these growths. In ecstasy she called each kind by an endearing Russian name. Like all good Anglo-Saxons, I knew nothing about the fungal world and felt the less I knew about these putrid, treacherous excrescences the better. For her they were things of grace infinitely inviting to the perceptive mind." In spite of his protests, Valentina gathered up the mushrooms and brought them back to the lodge were she cooked them for dinner. She ate them all—alone. Wasson wanted no part of the fungi. While she mocked his horror, he predicted in the face of her laughter he would wake up a widower the next morning. When Valentina survived, the couple decided to find an explanation for "the strange cultural cleavage" that had caused them to react so differently to mushrooms. From then on, they were hooked, and the world became the richer.

the idea that mushrooms have supernatural connections. Their book appeared in limited edition, selling new in 1957 for $125. It contains facts and legends, lovingly told, as well as beautiful photographs of nearly every known species of mushroom.

Inevitably, the Wassons heard tell of "God's flesh," and in 1953 they started spending their vacations pursuing it. They took their first unsuccessful trek to Mexico about the time James Moore got connected to the CIA and Morse Allen met with the Pennsylvania mushroom executives. They had no luck until their third expedition, when Gordon Wasson and his traveling companion, Allan Richardson, found their holy grail high in the mountains above Oaxaca. On June 29, 1955, they entered the town hall in a village called Huautla de Jiménez. There, they found a young Indian about 35, sitting by a large table in an upstairs room. Unlike most people in the village, he spoke Spanish. "He had a friendly manner," Wasson later wrote, "and I took a chance. Leaning over the table, I asked him earnestly and in a low voice if I could speak to him in confidence. Instantly curious, he encouraged me. 'Will you,' I went on, 'help me learn the secrets of the divine mushroom?' and I used the Indian name *nti sheeto,* correctly pronouncing it with glottal stop and tonal differentiation of the syllables. When [he] recovered from his surprise he said warmly that nothing could be easier."

Shortly thereafter, the Indian led Wasson and Richardson down into a deep ravine where mushrooms were growing in abundance. The white men snapped picture after picture of the fungi and picked a cardboard box-full. Then, in the heavy humid heat of the afternoon, the Indian led them up the mountain to a woman who performed the ancient mushroom rite. Her name was Maria Sabina. She was not only a *curandera,* or shaman, of "the highest quality," wrote Wasson, but a *"señora sin mancha,* a woman without stain." Wasson described her as middle-aged and short, "with a spirituality in her expression that struck us at once. She had a presence. We showed our mushrooms to the woman and her daughter. They cried out in rapture over the firmness, the fresh beauty and abundance of our young specimens. Through the interpreter we asked if they would serve us that night. They said yes."

That night, Wasson, Richardson, and about 20 Indians gathered in one of the village's adobe houses. The natives wore their best clothes and were friendly to the white strangers. The host provided chocolate drinks, which evoked for Wasson accounts of similar beverages being served early Spanish writers. Maria Sabina sat on a mat before a simple altar table that was adorned with the images of the Child Jesus and the Baptism in Jordan. After cleaning the mushrooms, she handed them out to all the adults present, keeping 26 for herself and giving Wasson and Richardson 12 each.

Maria Sabina put out the last candle about midnight, and she chanted haunting, tightly measured melodies. The Indian celebrants responded with deep feeling. Both Wasson and Richardson began to experience intense hallucinations that did not diminish until about 4:00 A.M. "We were never more wide awake, and the visions came whether our eyes were open or closed," Wasson wrote:

> They emerged from the center of the field of our vision, opening up as they came, now rushing, now slowly at the pace that our will chose. They were vivid in color, always harmonious. They began with art motifs, such as might decorate carpets or textiles or wallpaper or the drawing board of an architect. Then they evolved into palaces with courts, arcades, gardens—resplendent palaces with semiprecious stones. . . . Could the miraculous mobility that I was now enjoying be the explanation for the flying witches that played some important part in the folklore and fairy tales of northern Europe? These reflections passed through my mind at the very time that I was seeing the vision, for the effect of the mushrooms is to bring about a fission of the spirit, a split in the person, a kind of schizophrenia, with the rational side continuing to reason and to observe the sensations that the other side is enjoying. The mind is attached by an elastic cord to the vagrant senses.

Thus Gordon Wasson described the first known mushroom trip by "outsiders" in recorded history. The CIA's men missed the event, but they quickly learned of it, even though Wasson's visit was a private noninstitutional one to a place where material civilization had not reached. Such swiftness was assured by the breadth of the Agency's informant network, which included formal liaison arrangements with agencies like the Agriculture Department and the FDA and informal contacts all over the world. A botanist in Mexico City sent the report that reached both CIA headquarters and then James Moore. In the best bureaucratic form, the CIA description of Wasson's visions stated sparsely that the New York banker thought he saw "a multitude of architectural forms." Still, "God's flesh" had been located, and the MKULTRA leaders snatched up information that Wasson planned to return the following summer and bring back some mushrooms.

During the intervening winter, James Moore wrote Wasson—"out of the blue," as Wasson recalls—and expressed a desire to look into the chemical properties of Mexican fungi. Moore eventually suggested that he would like to accompany Wasson's party, and, to sweeten the proposition, he mentioned that he knew a foundation that might be willing to help underwrite the expedition. Sure enough, the CIA's conduit, the Geschickter Fund, made a $2,000 grant. Inside the MKULTRA program, the quest for the divine mushroom became Subproject 58.

Joining Moore and Wasson on the 1956 trip were the world-renowned French mycologist Roger Heim and a colleague from the Sorbonne. The party made the final leg of the trip, one at a time, in a tiny Cessna, but when it was Moore's turn, the load proved too much for the plane. The pilot suddenly took a dramatic right angle turn through a narrow canyon and made an unscheduled stop on the side of a hill. Immediately on landing, an Indian girl ran out and slid blocks under the wheels, so the plane would not roll back into a ravine. The pilot decided to lighten the load by leaving Moore among the local Indians, who spoke neither English nor Spanish. Later in the day, the plane returned and picked up the shaken Moore.

Finally in Huautla, sleeping on a dirt floor and eating local food, everyone reveled in the primitiveness of the adventure except Moore, who suffered. In addition to diarrhea, he recalls, "I had a terribly bad cold, we damned near starved to death, and I itched all over." Beyond his physical woes, Moore became more and more alienated from the others, who got on famously. Moore was a "complainer," according to Wasson. "He had no empathy for what was going on," recalls Wasson. "He was like a landlubber at sea. He got sick to his stomach and hated it all." Moore states, "Our relationship deteriorated during the course of the trip."

Wasson returned to the same Maria Sabina who had led him to the high ground the year before. Again the ritual started well after dark and, for everyone but Moore, it was an enchanted evening. Sings Wasson: "I had the most superb feeling—a feeling of ecstasy. You're raised to a height where you have not been in everyday life—not ever." Moore, on the other hand, never left the lowlands. His description: "There was all this chanting in the dialect. Then they passed the mushrooms around, and we chewed them up. I did feel the hallucinogenic effect, although 'disoriented' would be a better word to describe my reaction."

Soon thereafter, Moore returned to Delaware with a bag of mushrooms—just in time to take his pregnant wife to the hospital for delivery. After dropping her off with the obstetrician, he continued down the hall to another doctor about his digestion. Already a thin man, Moore had lost 15 pounds. Over the next week, he slowly nursed himself back to health. He reported in to Bortner and started preliminary work in his lab to isolate the active ingredient in the mushrooms. Bortner urged him on; the men from MKULTRA were excited at the prospect that they might be able to create "a completely new chemical agent." They wanted their own private supply of "God's flesh." Sid Gottlieb wrote that if Moore succeeded, it was "quite possible" that the new drugs could "remain an Agency secret."

Gottlieb's dream of a CIA monopoly on the divine mushroom vanished quickly under the influence of unwanted competitors, and indeed, the Agency soon faced a control problem of burgeoning proportions. While Moore toiled in his lab, Roger Heim in Paris unexpectedly pulled off the remarkable feat of growing the mushrooms in artificial culture from spore prints he had made in Mexico. Heim then sent samples to none other than Albert Hofmann, the discoverer of LSD, who quickly isolated and chemically reproduced the active chemical ingredient. He named it psilocybin.

The dignified Swiss chemist had beaten out the CIA,* and the men from MKULTRA found themselves trying to obtain for-

---

*Within two years, Albert Hofmann would scoop the CIA once again, with some help from Gordon Wasson. In 1960 Hofmann broke down and chemically recreated the active ingredient in hallucinatory ololiuqui seeds sent him by Wasson before the Agency's contractor, William Boyd Cook of Montana State University, could do the job. Hofmann's and Wasson's professional relationship soon grew into friendship, and in 1962 they traveled together on horseback to Huautla de Jiménez to visit Maria Sabina. Hofmann presented the *curandera* with some genuine Sandoz psilocybin. Wasson recalls: "Of course, Albert Hofmann is so conservative he always gives too little a dose, and it didn't have any effect." The crestfallen Hofmann believed he had duplicated "God's flesh," and he doubled the dose. Then Maria Sabina had her customary visions, and she reported, according to Wasson, the drug was the "same" as the mushroom. States Wasson, whose prejudice for real mushrooms over chemicals is unmistakable, "I don't think she said it with very much enthusiasm."

mulas and supplies from overseas. Instead of locking up the world's supply of the drug in a safe somewhere, they had to keep track of disbursements from Sandoz, as they were doing with LSD. Defeated by the old master, Moore laid his own work aside and sent away to Sandoz for a supply of psilocybin.

This lapse in control still did not quash the hopes of Agency officials that the mushroom might become a powerful weapon in covert operations. Agency scientists rushed it into the experimental stage. Within three summers of the first trip with James Moore, the CIA's queasy professor from America, the mushroom had journeyed through laboratories on two continents, and its chemical essence had worked its way back to Agency conduits and a contractor who would test it. In Kentucky, Dr. Harris Isbell ordered psilocybin injected into nine black inmates at the narcotics prison. His staff laid the subjects out on beds as the drug took hold and measured physical symptoms every hour: blood pressure, knee-jerk reflexes, rectal temperature, precise diameter of eye pupils, and so on. In addition, they recorded the inmates' various subjective feelings:

> After 30 minutes, anxiety became quite definite and was expressed as consisting of fear that something evil was going to happen, fear of insanity, or of death.... At times patients had the sensation that they could see the blood and bones in their own body or in that of another person. They reported many fantasies or dreamlike states in which they seemed to be elsewhere. Fantastic experiences, such as trips to the moon or living in gorgeous castles were occasionally reported. . . . Two of the 9 patients . . . felt their experiences were caused by the experimenters controlling their minds. . . .

Experimental data piled up, with operational testing to follow.

But the magic mushroom never became a good spy weapon. It made people behave strangely but no one could predict where their trips would take them. Agency officials craved certainty.

On the other hand, Gordon Wasson found revelation. After a lifetime of exploring and adoring mushrooms, he had discovered the greatest wonder of all in that remote Indian village. His experience inspired him to write an account of his journey for the "Great Adventures" series in *Life* magazine. The story, spread across 17 pages of text and color photographs, was called "Seeking the Magic Mushroom: A New York banker goes to Mexico's mountains to participate in the age-old rituals of Indians who chew strange growths that produce visions." In 1957, before the Russian *sputnik* shook America later that year, *Life* introduced its millions of readers to the mysteries of hallucinogens, with a tone of glowing but dignified respect. Wasson wrote movingly of his long search for mushroom lore, and he became positively rhapsodic in reflecting on his Mexican "trip":

> In man's evolutionary past, as he groped his way out from his lowly past, there must have come a moment in time when he discovered the secret of the hallucinatory mushrooms. Their effect on him, as I see it, could only have been profound, a detonator to new ideas. For the mushrooms revealed to him worlds beyond the horizons known to him, in space and time, even worlds on a different plane of being, a heaven and perhaps a hell. For the credulous, primitive mind, the mushrooms must have reinforced mightily the idea of the miraculous. Many emotions are shared by men with the animal kingdom, but awe and reverence and the fear of God are peculiar to men. When we bear in mind the beatific sense of awe and ecstasy and *caritas* engendered by the divine mushrooms, one is emboldened to the point of asking whether they may not have planted in primitive man the very idea of God.

The article caused a sensation in the United States, where people had already been awakened to ideas like these by Aldous Huxley's *The Doors of Perception.* It lured waves of respectable adults—precursors of later hippie travelers—to Mexico in search of their own *curanderas.* (Wasson came to have mixed feelings about the response to his story, after several tiny Mexican villages were all but trampled by American tourists on the prowl for divinity.) One person whose curiosity was stimulated by the article was a young psychology professor named Timothy Leary. In 1959, in Mexico on vacation, he ate his first mushrooms. He recalls he "had no idea it was going to change my life." Leary had just been promised tenure at Harvard, but his life of conventional prestige lost appeal for him within five hours of swallowing the mushroom: "The revelation had come. The veil had been pulled back. . . . The prophetic call. The works. God had spoken."

Having responded to a *Life* article about an expedition that was partially funded by the CIA, Leary returned to a Harvard campus where students and professors had for years served as subjects for CIA- and military-funded LSD experiments. His career as a drug prophet lay before him. Soon he would be quoting in his own *Kamasutra* from the CIA's contractor Harold Abramson and others, brought together for scholarly drug conferences by the sometime Agency conduit, the Macy Foundation.

With LSD, as with mushrooms, the men from MKULTRA remained oblivious, for the most part, to the rebellious effect of the drug culture in the United States. "I don't think we were paying any attention to it," recalls a TSS official. The CIA's scientists looked at drugs from a different perspective and went on trying to fashion their spy arsenal. Through the entire 1960s and into the 1970s, the Agency would scour Latin America for poisonous and narcotic plants.* Earlier, TSS officials and contractors actually kept spreading the magic touch of drugs by forever pressing new university researchers into the field. Boston Psychopathic's Max Rinkel stirred up the interest of Rochester's Harold Hodge and told him how to get a grant from the Agency conduit, the Geschickter Fund. Hodge's group found a way to put a radioactive marker into LSD, and the MKULTRA crew made sure that the specially treated substance found its way to still more scientists. When a contractor like Harold Abramson spoke highly of the drug at a new conference or seminar, tens or hundreds of scientists, health professionals, and subjects—usually students—would wind up trying LSD.

One day in 1954, Ralph Blum, a senior at Harvard on his way to a career as a successful author, heard from a friend that doctors at Boston Psychopathic would pay $25 to anyone willing to spend a day as a happy schizophrenic. Blum could not resist. He applied, passed the screening process, took a whole battery of Wechsler psychological tests, and was told to report back on a given morning. That day, he was shown into a room with five other Harvard students. Project director Bob Hyde joined them and struck Blum as a reassuring father figure. Someone brought in a tray with six little glasses full of water and LSD. The students drank up. For Blum, the drug did not take hold for

*See Chapter 12.

about an hour and a half—somewhat longer than the average. While Hyde was in the process of interviewing him, Blum felt his mind shift gears. "I looked at the clock on the wall and thought how well behaved it was. It didn't pay attention to itself. It just stayed on the wall and told time." Blum felt that he was looking at everything around him from a new perspective. "It was a very subtle thing," he says. "My ego filter had been pretty much removed. I turned into a very accessible state —accessible to myself. I knew when someone was lying to me, and the richness of the experience was such that I didn't want to suffer fools gladly." Twenty-four years later, Blum concludes: "It was undeniably a very important experience for me. It made a difference in my life. It began to move the log jam of my old consciousness. You can't do it with just one blast. It was the beginning of realizing it was safe to love again. Although I wouldn't use them until much later, it gave me a new set of optics. It let me know there was something downstream."*

Many student subjects like Blum thought LSD transformed the quality of their lives. Others had no positive feelings, and some would later use the negative memories of their trips to invalidate the whole drug culture and stoned thinking process of the 1960s. In a university city like Boston where both the CIA and the Army were carrying on large testing programs at hospitals connected to Harvard, volunteering for an LSD trip became quite popular in academic circles. Similar reactions, although probably not as pronounced, occurred in other intellectual centers. The intelligence agencies turned to America's finest universities and hospitals to try LSD, which meant that the cream of the country's students and graduate assistants became the test subjects.

In 1969 the Bureau of Narcotics and Dangerous Drugs published a fascinating little study designed to curb illegal LSD

---

*Lincoln Clark, a psychiatrist who tested LSD for the Army at Massachusetts General Hospital, reflects a fairly common view among LSD researchers when he belittles drug-induced thinking of the sort described by Blum. "Everybody who takes LSD has an incredible experience that you can look at as having positive characteristics. I view it as pseudo-insight. This is part of the usual response of intellectually pretentious people." On the other hand, psychiatrist Sidney Cohen, who has written an important book on LSD, noted that to experience a visionary trip, "the devotee must have faith in, or at least be open to the possibility of the 'other state.' . . . He must 'let go,' not offer too much resistance to losing his personal identity. The ability to surrender oneself is probably the most important operation of all."

use. The authors wrote that the drug's "early use was among small groups of intellectuals at large Eastern and West Coast universities. It spread to undergraduate students, then to other campuses. Most often, users have been introduced to the drug by persons of higher status. Teachers have influenced students; upperclassmen have influenced lowerclassmen." Calling this a "trickle-down phenomenon," the authors seem to have correctly analyzed how LSD got around the country. They left out only one vital element, which they had no way of knowing: That somebody had to influence the teachers and that up there at the top of the LSD distribution system could be found the men of MKULTRA.

Harold Abramson apparently got a great kick out of getting his learned friends high on LSD. He first turned on Frank Fremont-Smith, head of the Macy Foundation which passed CIA money to Abramson. In this cozy little world where everyone knew everybody, Fremont-Smith organized the conferences that spread the word about LSD to the academic hinterlands. Abramson also gave Gregory Bateson, Margaret Mead's former husband, his first LSD. In 1959 Bateson, in turn, helped arrange for a beat poet friend of his named Allen Ginsberg to take the drug at a research program located off the Stanford campus. No stranger to the hallucinogenic effects of peyote, Ginsberg reacted badly to what he describes as "the closed little doctor's room full of instruments," where he took the drug. Although he was allowed to listen to records of his choice (he chose a Gertrude Stein reading, a Tibetan mandala, and Wagner), Ginsberg felt he "was being connected to Big Brother's brain." He says that the experience resulted in "a slight paranoia that hung on all my acid experiences through the mid-1960s until I learned from meditation how to disperse that."

Anthropologist and philosopher Gregory Bateson then worked at the Veterans Administration Hospital in Palo Alto. From 1959 on, Dr. Leo Hollister was testing LSD at that same hospital. Hollister says he entered the hallucinogenic field reluctantly because of the "unscientific" work of the early LSD researchers. He refers specifically to most of the people who attended Macy conferences. Thus, hoping to improve on CIA- and military-funded work, Hollister tried drugs out on student volunteers, including a certain Ken Kesey, in 1960. Kesey said he was a jock who had only been drunk once before, but on three successive Tuesdays, he tried different psychedelics. "Six weeks later I'd bought my first ounce of grass," Kesey later wrote, adding, "Six months later I had a job at that hospital as a psychiatric aide." Out of that experience, using drugs while he wrote, Kesey turned out *One Flew Over the Cuckoo's Nest.* He went on to become the counterculture's second most famous LSD visionary, spreading the creed throughout the land, as Tom Wolfe would chronicle in *The Electric Kool-Aid Acid Test.*

CIA officials never meant that the likes of Leary, Kesey, and Ginsberg should be turned on. Yet these men were, and they, along with many of the lesser-known experimental subjects, like Harvard's Ralph Blum, created the climate whereby LSD escaped the government's control and became available by the early sixties on the black market. No one at the Agency apparently foresaw that young Americans would voluntarily take the drug—whether for consciousness expansion or recreational purposes. The MKULTRA experts were mainly on a control trip, and they proved incapable of gaining insight from their own LSD experiences of how others less fixated on making people do their bidding would react to the drug.

It would be an exaggeration to put all the blame on—or give all the credit to—the CIA for the spread of LSD. One cannot forget the nature of the times, the Vietnam War, the breakdown in authority, and the wide availability of other drugs, especially marijuana. But the fact remains that LSD was one of the catalysts of the traumatic upheavals of the 1960s. No one could enter the world of psychedelics without first passing, unawares, through doors opened by the Agency. It would become a supreme irony that the CIA's enormous search for weapons among drugs—fueled by the hope that spies could, like Dr. Frankenstein, control life with genius and machines—would wind up helping to create the wandering, uncontrollable minds of the counterculture.

PART
III
SPELLS—
ELECTRODES AND
HYPNOSIS

It is possible that a certain amount of brain
damage is of therapeutic value.
—DR. PAUL HOCH, 1948

The whole history of scientific advance is
full of scientists investigating phenomena
the establishment did not even believe
were there.   —MARGARET MEAD, 1969

CHAPTER
8
BRAINWASHING

In September 1950, the Miami *News* published an article by Edward Hunter titled " 'Brain-Washing' Tactics Force Chinese into Ranks of Communist Party." It was the first printed use in any language of the term "brainwashing," which quickly became a stock phrase in Cold War headlines. Hunter, a CIA propaganda operator who worked under cover as a journalist, turned out a steady stream of books and articles on the subject. He made up his coined word from the Chinese *hsi-nao*—"to cleanse the mind"—which had no political meaning in Chinese.

American public opinion reacted strongly to Hunter's ideas, no doubt because of the hostility that prevailed toward communist foes, whose ways were perceived as mysterious and alien. Most Americans knew something about the famous trial of the Hungarian Josef Cardinal Mindszenty, at which the Cardinal appeared zombielike, as though drugged or hypnotized. Other defendants at Soviet "show trials" had displayed similar symptoms as they recited unbelievable confessions in dull, cliché-ridden monotones. Americans were familiar with the idea that the communists had ways to control hapless people, and Hunter's new word helped pull together the unsettling evidence into one sharp fear. The brainwashing controversy intensified during the heavy 1952 fighting in Korea, when the Chinese government launched a propaganda offensive that featured recorded statements by captured U.S. pilots, who "confessed" to a variety of war crimes including the use of germ warfare.

The official American position on prisoner confessions was that they were false and forced. As expressed in an Air Force Headquarters document, "Confessions can be of truthful details. . . . For purposes of this section, 'confessions' are considered as being the forced admission to a lie." But if the military had understandable reasons to gloss over the truth or falsity of the confessions, this still did not address the fact that confessions had been made at all. Nor did it lay to rest the fears of those like Edward Hunter who saw the confessions as proof that the communists now had techniques "to put a man's mind into a fog so that he will mistake what is true for what is untrue, what is right for what is wrong, and come to believe what did not happen actually had happened, until he ultimately becomes a robot for the Communist manipulator."

By the end of the Korean War, 70 percent of the 7,190 U.S. prisoners held in China had either made confessions or signed petitions calling for an end to the American war effort in Asia. Fifteen percent collaborated fully with the Chinese, and only 5 percent steadfastly resisted. The American performance contrasted poorly with that of the British, Australian, Turkish, and other United Nations prisoners—among whom collaboration was rare, even though studies showed they were treated about as badly as the Americans. Worse, an alarming number of the prisoners stuck by their confessions after returning to the United States. They did not, as expected, recant as soon as they stepped on U.S. soil. Puzzled and dismayed by this wholesale collapse of morale among the POWs, American opinion leaders settled in on Edward Hunter's explanation: The Chinese had somehow brainwashed our boys.

But how? At the height of the brainwashing furor, conservative spokesmen often seized upon the very mystery of it all to give a religious cast to the political debate. All communists have been, by definition, brainwashed through satanic forces, they argued—thereby making the enemy seem like robots completely devoid of ordinary human feelings and motivation. Liberals favored a more scientific view of the problem. Given the incontrovertible evidence that the Russians and the Chinese could, in a very short time and often under difficult circumstances, alter the basic belief and behavior patterns of both domestic and foreign captives, liberals argued that there must be a technique involved that would yield its secrets under objective investigation.

CIA Director Allen Dulles favored the scientific approach, although he naturally encouraged his propaganda experts to exploit the more emotional interpretations of brainwashing. Dulles and the heads of the other American security agencies became almost frantic in their efforts to find out more about the Soviet and Chinese successes in mind control. Under pressure for answers, Dulles turned to Dr. Harold Wolff, a world-famous neurologist with whom he had developed an intensely personal relationship. Wolff was then treating Dulles' own son for brain damage suffered from a Korean War head wound. Together they shared the trauma of the younger Dulles' fits and mental lapses. Wolff, a skinny little doctor with an overpowering personality, became fast friends with the tall, patrician CIA Director. Dulles may have seen brainwashing as an induced form of brain damage or mental illness. In any case, in late 1953, he asked Wolff to conduct an official study of communist brainwashing techniques for the CIA. Wolff, who had become fascinated by the Director's tales of the clandestine world, eagerly accepted.

Harold Wolff was known primarily as an expert on migraine headaches and pain, but he had served on enough military and intelligence advisory panels that he knew how to pick up Dulles' mandate and expand on it. He formed a working partnership with Lawrence Hinkle, his colleague at Cornell University Medical College in New York City. Hinkle handled the administrative part of the study and shared in the substance. Before going ahead, the two doctors made sure they had the approval of Cornell's president, Deane W. Malott and other high university officials who checked with their contacts in Washington to make sure the project did indeed have the great importance that Allen Dulles stated. Hinkle recalls a key White House aide urging Cornell to cooperate. The university administration agreed, and soon Wolff and Hinkle were poring over the Agency's classified files on brainwashing. CIA officials also helped arrange interviews with former communist interrogators and prisoners alike. "It was done with great secrecy," recalls Hinkle. "We went through a great deal of hoop-de-do and signed secrecy agreements, which everyone took very seriously."

* * *

The team of Wolff and Hinkle became the chief brainwashing studiers for the U.S. government, although the Air Force and Army ran parallel programs.* Their secret report to Allen Dulles, later published in a declassified version, was considered the definitive U.S. Government work on the subject. In fact, if allowances are made for the Cold War rhetoric of the fifties, the Wolff-Hinkle report still remains one of the better accounts of the massive political re-education programs in China and the Soviet Union. It stated flatly that neither the Soviets nor the Chinese had any magical weapons—no drugs, exotic mental ray-guns, or other fanciful machines. Instead, the report pictured communist interrogation methods resting on skillful, if brutal, application of police methods. Its portrait of the Soviet system anticipates, in dry and scholarly form, the work of novelist Alexander Solzhenitzyn in *The Gulag Archipelago.* Hinkle and Wolff showed that the Soviet technique rested on the cumulative weight of intense psychological pressure and human weakness, and this thesis alone earned the two Cornell doctors the enmity of the more right-wing CIA officials such as Edward Hunter. Several of his former acquaintances remember that Hunter was fond of saying that the Soviets brainwashed people the way Pavlov had conditioned dogs.

In spite of some dissenters like Hunter, the Wolff-Hinkle model became, with later refinements, the best available description of extreme forms of political indoctrination. According to the general consensus, the Soviets started a new prisoner off by putting him in solitary confinement. A rotating corps of guards watched him constantly, humiliating and demeaning him at every opportunity and making it clear he was totally cut off from all outside support. The guards ordered him to stand for long periods, let him sit, told him exactly the position he could take to lie down, and woke him if he moved in the slightest while sleeping. They banned all outside stimuli—books, conversation, or news of the world.

After four to six weeks of this mind-deadening routine, the prisoner usually found the stress unbearable and broke down. "He weeps, he mutters, and prays aloud in his cell," wrote Hinkle and Wolff. When the prisoner reached this stage, the inter-

---

*Among the Air Force and Army project leaders were Dr. Fred Williams of the Air Force Psychological Warfare Division, Robert Jay Lifton, Edgar Schein, Albert Biderman, and Lieutenant Colonel James Monroe (an Air Force officer who would later go to work full time in CIA behavioral programs).

rogation began. Night after night, the guards brought him into a special room to face the interrogator. Far from confronting his captive with specific misdeeds, the interrogator told him that he knew his own crimes—all too well. In the most harrowing Kafkaesque way, the prisoner tried to prove his innocence to he knew not what. Together the interrogator and prisoner reviewed the prisoner's life in detail. The interrogator seized on any inconsistency—no matter how minute—as further evidence of guilt, and he laughed at the prisoner's efforts to justify himself. But at least the prisoner was getting a response of some sort. The long weeks of isolation and uncertainty had made him grateful for human contact—even grateful that his case was moving toward resolution. True, it moved only as fast as he was willing to incriminate himself, but . . . Gradually, he came to see that he and his interrogator were working toward the same goal of wrapping up his case. In tandem, they ransacked his soul. The interrogator would periodically let up the pressure. He offered a cigarette, had a friendly chat, explained he had a job to do—making it all the more disappointing the next time he had to tell the prisoner that his confession was unsatisfactory.

As the charges against him began to take shape, the prisoner realized that he could end his ordeal only with a full confession. Otherwise the grueling sessions would go on forever. "The regimen of pressure has created an overall discomfort which is well nigh intolerable," wrote Hinkle and Wolff. "The prisoner invariably feels that 'something must be done to end this.' He must find a way out." A former KGB officer, one of many former interrogators and prisoners interviewed for the CIA study, said that more than 99 percent of all prisoners signed a confession at this stage.

In the Soviet system under Stalin, these confessions were the final step of the interrogation process, and the prisoners usually were shot or sent to a labor camp after sentencing. Today, Russian leaders seem much less insistent on exacting confessions before jailing their foes, but they still use the penal (and mental health) system to remove from the population classes of people hostile to their rule.

The Chinese took on the more ambitious task of re-educating their prisoners. For them, confession was only the beginning. Next, the Chinese authorities moved the prisoner into a group cell where his indoctrination began. From morning to night, he and his fellow prisoners studied Marx and Mao, listened to lectures, and engaged in self-criticism. Since the progress of each member depended on that of his cellmates, the group pounced on the slightest misconduct as an indication of backsliding. Prisoners demonstrated the zeal of their commitment by ferociously attacking deviations. Constant intimacy with people who reviled him pushed the resistant prisoner to the limits of his emotional endurance. Hinkle and Wolff found that "The prisoner must conform to the demands of the group sooner or later." As the prisoner developed genuine changes of attitude, pressure on him relaxed. His cellmates rewarded him with increasing acceptance and esteem. Their acceptance, in turn, reinforced his commitment to the Party, for he learned that only this commitment allowed him to live successfully in the cell. In many cases, this process produced an exultant sense of mission in the prisoner—a feeling of having finally straightened out his life and come to the truth. To be sure, this experience, which was not so different from religious conversion, did not occur in all cases or always last after the prisoner returned to a social group that did not reinforce it.

From the first preliminary studies of Wolff and Hinkle, the U.S. intelligence community moved toward the conclusion that neither the Chinese nor the Russians made appreciable use of drugs or hypnosis, and they certainly did not possess the brainwashing equivalent of the atomic bomb (as many feared). Most of their techniques were rooted in age-old methods, and CIA brainwashing researchers like psychologist John Gittinger found themselves poring over ancient documents on the Spanish Inquisition. Furthermore, the communists used no psychiatrists or other behavioral scientists to devise their interrogation system. The differences between the Soviet and Chinese systems seemed to grow out of their respective national cultures. The Soviet brainwashing system resembled a heavy-handed cop whose job was to isolate, break, and then subdue all the troublemakers in the neighborhood. The Chinese system was more like thousands of skilled acupuncturists, working on each other and relying on group pressure, ideology, and repetition. To understand further the Soviet or Chinese control systems, one had to plunge into the subtle mysteries of national and individual character.

While CIA researchers looked into those questions, the main thrust of the Agency's brainwashing studies veered off in a different direction. The logic behind the switch was familiar in the intelligence business. Just because the Soviets and the Chinese had not invented a brainwashing machine, officials reasoned, there was no reason to assume that the task was impossible. If such a machine were even remotely feasible, one had to assume the communists might discover it. And in that case, national security required that the United States invent the machine first. Therefore, the CIA built up its own elaborate brainwashing program, which, like the Soviet and Chinese versions, took its own special twist from *our* national character. It was a tiny replica of the Manhattan Project, grounded in the conviction that the keys to brainwashing lay in technology. Agency officials hoped to use old-fashioned American know-how to produce shortcuts and scientific breakthroughs. Instead of turning to tough cops, whose methods repelled American sensibilities, or the gurus of mass motivation, whose ideology Americans lacked, the Agency's brainwashing experts gravitated to people more in the mold of the brilliant—and sometimes mad—scientist, obsessed by the wonders of the brain.

In 1953 CIA Director Allen Dulles made a rare public statement on communist brainwashing: "We in the West are somewhat handicapped in getting all the details," Dulles declared. "There are few survivors, and we have no human guinea pigs to try these extraordinary techniques." Even as Dulles spoke, however, CIA officials acting under his orders had begun to find the scientists and the guinea pigs. Some of their experiments would wander so far across the ethical borders of experimental psychiatry (which are hazy in their own right) that Agency officials thought it prudent to have much of the work done outside the United States.

Call her Lauren G. For 19 years, her mind has been blank about her experience. She remembers her husband's driving her up to the old gray stone mansion that housed the hospital, Allan Memorial Institute, and putting her in the care of its director, Dr. D. Ewen Cameron. The next thing she recalls happened three weeks later:

> They gave me a dressing gown. It was way too big, and I was tripping all over it. I was mad. I asked why did I have to go round in this sloppy thing. I could hardly move because I was pretty weak. I remember trying to walk along the hall, and the walls

were all slanted. It was then that I said, "Holy Smokes, what a ghastly thing." I remember running out the door and going up the mountain in my long dressing gown.

The mountain, named *Mont Royal,* loomed high above Montreal. She stumbled and staggered as she tried to climb higher and higher. Hospital staff members had no trouble catching her and dragging her back to the Institute. In short order, they shot her full of sedatives, attached electrodes to her temples, and gave her a dose of electroshock. Soon she slept like a baby.

Gradually, over the next few weeks, Lauren G. began to function like a normal person again. She took basket-weaving therapy and played bridge with her fellow patients. The hospital released her, and she returned to her husband in another Canadian city.

Before her mental collapse in 1959, Lauren G. seemed to have everything going for her. A refined, glamorous horsewoman of 30, whom people often said looked like Elizabeth Taylor, she had auditioned for the lead in *National Velvet* at 13 and married the rich boy next door at 20. But she had never loved her husband and had let her domineering mother push her into his arms. He drank heavily. "I was really unhappy," she recalls. "I had a horrible marriage, and finally I had a nervous breakdown. It was a combination of my trying to lose weight, sleep loss, and my nerves."

The family doctor recommended that her husband send her to Dr. Cameron, which seemed like a logical thing to do, considering his wide fame as a psychiatrist. He had headed Allan Memorial since 1943, when the Rockefeller Foundation had donated funds to set up a psychiatric facility at McGill University. With continuing help from the Rockefellers, McGill had built a hospital known far beyond Canada's borders as innovative and exciting. Cameron was elected president of the American Psychiatric Association in 1953, and he became the first president of the World Psychiatric Association. His friends joked that they had run out of honors to give him.

Cameron's passion lay in the more "objective" forms of therapy, with which he could more easily and swiftly bring about improvements in patients than with the notoriously slow Freudian methods. An impatient man, he dreamed of finding a cure for schizophrenia. No one could tell him he was not on the right track. Cameron's supporter at the Rockefeller Foundation, Robert Morrison, recorded in his private papers that he found the psychiatrist tense and ill-at-ease, and Morrison ventured that this may account for "his lack of interest and effectiveness in psychotherapy and failure to establish warm personal relations with faculty members, both of which were mentioned repeatedly when I visited Montreal." Another Rockefeller observer noted that Cameron "appears to suffer from deep insecurity and has a need for power which he nourishes by maintaining an extraordinary aloofness from his associates."

When Lauren G.'s husband delivered her to Cameron, the psychiatrist told him she would receive some electroshock, a standard treatment at the time. Besides that, states her husband, "Cameron was not very communicative, but I didn't think she was getting anything out of the ordinary." The husband had no way of knowing that Cameron would use an unproved experimental technique on his wife—much less that the psychiatrist intended to "depattern" her. Nor did he realize that the CIA was supporting this work with about $19,000 a year in secret funds.*

Cameron defined "depatterning" as breaking up existing patterns of behavior, both the normal and the schizophrenic, by means of particularly intensive electroshocks, usually combined with prolonged, drug-induced sleep. Here was a psychiatrist willing—indeed, eager—to wipe the human mind totally clean. Back in 1951, ARTICHOKE's Morse Allen had likened the process to "creation of a vegetable." Cameron justified this *tabula rasa* approach because he had a theory of "differential amnesia," for which he provided no statistical evidence when he published it. He postulated that after he produced "complete amnesia" in a subject, the person would eventually recover memory of his normal but not his schizophrenic behavior. Thus, Cameron claimed he could generate "differential amnesia." Creating such a state in which a man who knew too much could be made to forget had long been a prime objective of the ARTICHOKE and MKULTRA programs.

Needless to say, Lauren G. does not recall a thing today about those weeks when Cameron depatterned her. Afterward, unlike

---

*Cameron himself may not have known that the Agency was the ultimate source of these funds which came through a conduit, the Society for the Investigation of Human Ecology. A CIA document stated he was unwitting when the grants started in 1957, and it cannot be said whether he ever found out.

over half of the psychiatrist's depatterning patients, Lauren G. gradually recovered full recall of her life before the treatment, but then, she remembered her mental problems, too.* Her husband says she came out of the hospital much improved. She declares the treatment had no effect one way or another on her mental condition, which she believes resulted directly from her miserable marriage. She stopped seeing Cameron after about a month of outpatient electroshock treatments, which she despised. Her relationship with her husband further deteriorated, and two years later she walked out on him. "I just got up on my own hind legs," she states. "I said the hell with it. I'm going to do what I want and take charge of my own life. I left and started over." Now divorced and remarried, she feels she has been happy ever since.

Cameron's depatterning, of which Lauren G. had a comparatively mild version, normally started with 15 to 30 days of "sleep therapy." As the name implies, the patient slept almost the whole day and night. According to a doctor at the hospital who used to administer what he calls the "sleep cocktail," a staff member woke up the patient three times a day for medication that consisted of a combination of 100 mg. Thorazine, 100 mg. Nembutal, 100 mg. Seconal, 150 mg. Veronal, and 10 mg. Phenergan. Another staff doctor would also awaken the patient two or sometimes three times daily for electroshock treatments.† This doctor and his assistant wheeled a portable machine into the "sleep room" and gave the subject a local anesthetic and muscle relaxant, so as not to cause damage with the convulsions that were to come. After attaching electrodes soaked in saline solution, the attendant held the patient down and the doctor turned on the current. In standard, professional electroshock, doctors gave the subject a single dose of 110 volts, lasting a fraction of a second, once a day or every other day. By

---

*Cameron wrote that when a patient remembered his schizophrenic symptoms, the schizophrenic behavior usually returned. If the amnesia held for these symptoms, as Cameron claimed it often did, the subject usually did not have a relapse. Even in his "cured" patients, Cameron found that Rorschach tests continued to show schizophrenic thinking despite the improvement in overt behavior. To a layman, this would seem to indicate that Cameron's approach got only at the symptoms, not the causes of mental problems. Not deterred, however, Cameron dismissed this inconsistency as a "persistent enigma."

†Cameron wrote in a professional journal that he gave only two electroshocks a day, but a doctor who actually administered the treatment for him says that three were common at the beginning of the therapy.

contrast, Cameron used a form 20 to 40 times more intense, two or three times daily, with the power turned up to 150 volts. Named the "Page–Russell" method after its British originators, this technique featured an initial one-second shock, which caused a major convulsion, and then five to nine additional shocks in the middle of the primary and follow-on convulsions. Even Drs. Page and Russell limited their treatment to once a day, and they always stopped as soon as their patient showed "pronounced confusion" and became "faulty in habits." Cameron, however, welcomed this kind of impairment as a sign the treatment was taking effect and plowed ahead through his routine.

The frequent screams of patients that echoed through the hospital did not deter Cameron or most of his associates in their attempts to "depattern" their subjects completely. Other hospital patients report being petrified by the "sleep rooms," where the treatment took place, and they would usually creep down the opposite side of the hall.

Cameron described this combined sleep-electroshock treatment as lasting between 15 to 30 days, with some subjects staying in up to 65 days (in which case, he reported, he awakened them for three days in the middle). Sometimes, as in the case of Lauren G., patients would try to escape when the sedatives wore thin, and the staff would have to chase after them. "It was a tremendous nursing job just to keep these people going during the treatment," recalls a doctor intimately familiar with Cameron's operation. This doctor paints a picture of dazed patients, incapable of taking care of themselves, often groping their way around the hospital and urinating on the floor.

Cameron wrote that his typical depatterning patient—usually a woman—moved through three distinct stages. In the first, the subject lost much of her memory. Yet she still knew where she was, why she was there, and who the people were who treated her. In the second phase, she lost her "space-time image," but still wanted to remember. In fact, not being able to answer questions like, "Where am I?" and "How did I get here?" caused her considerable anxiety. In the third stage, all that anxiety disappeared. Cameron described the state as "an extremely interesting constriction of the range of recollections which one ordinarily brings in to modify and enrich one's statements. Hence, what the patient talks about are only his sensations of the moment, and he talks about them almost exclu-

sively in highly concrete terms. His remarks are entirely unin-
fluenced by previous recollections—nor are they governed in
any way by his forward anticipations. He lives in the immediate present. All schizophrenic symptoms have disappeared.
There is complete amnesia for all events in his life."

Lauren G. and 52 other subjects at Allan Memorial received
this level of depatterning in 1958 and 1959. Cameron had already developed the technique when the CIA funding started.
The Agency sent the psychiatrist research money to take the
treatment *beyond this point.* Agency officials wanted to know
if, once Cameron had produced the blank mind, he could then
program in new patterns of behavior, as he claimed he could.
As early as 1953—the year he headed the American Psychiatric
Association—Cameron conceived a technique he called "psychic driving," by which he would bombard the subject with
repeated verbal messages. From tape recordings based on interviews with the patient, he selected emotionally loaded "cue
statements"—first negative ones to get rid of unwanted behavior and then positive to condition in desired personality traits.
On the negative side, for example, the patient would hear this
message as she lay in a stupor:

> Madeleine, you let your mother and father treat you as a child all
> through your single life. You let your mother check you up sexu-
> ally after every date you had with a boy. You hadn't enough
> determination to tell her to stop it. You never stood up for your-
> self against your mother or father but would run away from
> trouble. . . . They used to call you "crying Madeleine." Now that
> you have two children, you don't seem to be able to manage them
> and keep a good relationship with your husband. You are drifting
> apart. You don't go out together. You have not been able to keep
> him interested sexually.

Leonard Rubenstein, Cameron's principal assistant, whose
entire salary was paid from CIA-front funds, put the message
on a continuous tape loop and played it for 16 hours every day
for several weeks. An electronics technician, with no medical
or psychological background, Rubenstein, an electrical whiz,
designed a giant tape recorder that could play 8 loops for 8
patients at the same time. Cameron had the speakers installed
literally under the pillows in the "sleep rooms." "We made sure
they heard it," says a doctor who worked with Cameron. With

some patients, Cameron intensified the negative effect by running wires to their legs and shocking them at the end of the message.

When Cameron thought the negative "psychic driving" had gone far enough, he switched the patient over to 2 to 5 weeks of positive tapes:

> You mean to get well. To do this you must let your feelings come out. It is all right to express your anger.... You want to stop your mother bossing you around. Begin to assert yourself first in little things and soon you will be able to meet her on an equal basis. You will then be free to be a wife and mother just like other women.

Cameron wrote that psychic driving provided a way to make "direct, controlled changes in personality," without having to resolve the subject's conflicts or make her relive past experiences. As far as is known, no present-day psychologist or psychiatrist accepts this view. Dr. Donald Hebb, who headed McGill's psychology department at the time Cameron was in charge of psychiatry, minces no words when asked specifically about psychic driving: "That was an awful set of ideas Cameron was working with. It called for no intellectual respect. If you actually look at what he was doing and what he wrote, it would make you laugh. If I had a graduate student who talked like that, I'd throw him out." Warming to his subject, Hebb continues: "Look, Cameron was no good as a researcher.... He was eminent because of politics." Nobody said such things at the time, however. Cameron was a very powerful man.

The Scottish-born psychiatrist, who never lost the burr in his voice, kept searching for ways to perfect depatterning and psychic driving. He held out to the CIA front—the Society for the Investigation of Human Ecology—that he could find more rapid and less damaging ways to break down behavior. He sent the Society a proposal that combined his two techniques with sensory deprivation and strong drugs. His smorgasbord approach brought together virtually all possible techniques of mind control, which he tested individually and together. When his Agency grant came through in 1957, Cameron began work on sensory deprivation.

For several years, Agency officials had been interested in the interrogation possibilities of this technique that Hebb himself had pioneered at McGill with Canadian defense and Rockefeller money. It consisted of putting a subject in a sealed environment—a small room or even a large box—and depriving him of all sensory input: eyes covered with goggles, ears either covered with muffs or exposed to a constant, monotonous sound, padding to prevent touching, no smells—with this empty regime interrupted only by meal and bathroom breaks. In 1955 Morse Allen of ARTICHOKE made contact at the National Institutes of Health with Dr. Maitland Baldwin who had done a rather gruesome experiment in which an Army volunteer had stayed in the "box" for 40 hours until he kicked his way out after, in Baldwin's words, "an hour of crying loudly and sobbing in a most heartrending fashion." The experiment convinced Baldwin that the isolation technique could break any man, no matter how intelligent or strong-willed. Hebb, who unlike Baldwin released his subjects when they wanted, had never left anyone in "the box" for more than six days. Baldwin told Morse Allen that beyond that sensory deprivation would almost certainly cause irreparable damage. Nevertheless, Baldwin agreed that if the Agency could provide the cover and the subjects, he would do, according to Allen's report, "terminal type" experiments. After numerous meetings inside the CIA on how and where to fund Baldwin, an Agency medical officer finally shot down the project as being "immoral and inhuman," suggesting that those pushing the experiments might want to "volunteer their heads for use in Dr. Baldwin's 'noble' project."

With Cameron, Agency officials not only had a doctor willing to perform terminal experiments in sensory deprivation, but one with his own source of subjects. As part of his CIA-funded research, he had a "box" built in the converted stables behind the hospital that housed Leonard Rubenstein and his behavioral laboratory. Undaunted by the limits set in Hebb's work, Cameron left one woman in for 35 days, although he had so scrambled her mind with his other techniques that one cannot say, as Baldwin predicted to the Agency, if the prolonged deprivation did specific damage. This subject's name was Mary C., and, try as he might, Cameron could not get through to her. As the aloof psychiatrist wrote in his notes: "Although the patient was prepared by both prolonged sensory isolation (35 days) and by repeated depatterning, and although she received 101 days of positive driving, no favorable results were obtained."* Before prescribing this treatment, Cameron had diagnosed the

52-year-old Mary C.: "Conversion reaction in a woman of the involutional age with mental anxiety; hypochondriatic." In other words, Mary C. was going through menopause.

In his proposal to the CIA front, Cameron also said he would test curare, the South American arrow poison which, when liberally applied, kills by paralyzing internal body functions. In nonlethal doses, curare causes a limited paralysis which blocks but does not stop these functions. According to his papers, some of which wound up in the archives of the American Psychiatric Association, Cameron injected subjects with curare in conjunction with sensory deprivation, presumably to immobilize them further.

Cameron also tested LSD in combination with psychic driving and other techniques. In late 1956 and early 1957, one of his subjects was Val Orlikow, whose husband David has become a member of the Canadian parliament. Suffering from what she calls a "character neurosis that started with postpartum depression," she entered Allan Memorial as one of Cameron's personal patients. He soon put her under his version of LSD therapy. One to four times a week, he or another doctor would come into her room and give her a shot of LSD, mixed with either a stimulant or a depressant and then leave her alone with a tape recorder that played excerpts from her last session with him. As far as is known, no other LSD researcher ever subjected his patients to unsupervised trips—certainly not over the course of two months when her hospital records show she was given LSD 14 times. "It was terrifying," Mrs. Orlikow recalls. "You're afraid you've gone off somewhere and can't come back." She was supposed to write down on a pad whatever came into her head while listening to the tapes, but often she became so frightened that she could not write at all. "You become very small," she says, as her voice quickens and starts to reflect some of her horror. "You're going to fall off the step, and God, you're going down into hell because it's so far, and you are so little. Like Alice, where is the pill that makes you big, and you're a squirrel, and you can't get out of the cage, and somebody's going

---

*In his proposal to the Human Ecology group, Cameron wrote that his subjects would be spending *only* 16 hours a day in sensory deprivation, while they listened to psychic driving tapes (thus providing some outside stimuli). Nevertheless, one of Cameron's colleagues states that some patients, including Mary C. were in continuously. Always looking for a better way, Cameron almost certainly tried both variations.

to kill you." Then, suddenly, Mrs. Orlikow pulls out of it and lucidly states, "Some very weird things happened."

Mrs. Orlikow hated the LSD treatment. Several times she told Cameron she would take no more, and the psychiatrist would put his arm around her and ask, "Lassie," which he called all his women patients, "don't you want to get well, so you can go home and see your husband?" She remembers feeling guilty about not following the doctor's orders, and the thought of disappointing Cameron, whom she idolized, crushed her. Finally, after Cameron talked her out of quitting the treatment several times, she had to end it. She left the hospital but stayed under his private care. In 1963 he put her back in the hospital for more intensive psychic driving. "I thought he was God," she states. "I don't know how I could have been so stupid. . . . A lot of us were naïve. We thought psychiatrists had the answers. Here was the greatest in the world, with all these titles."

In defense of Cameron, a former associate says the man truly cared about the welfare of his patients. He wanted to make them well. As his former staff psychologist wrote:

> He abhorred the waste of human potential, seen most dramatically in the young people whose minds were distorted by what was then considered to be schizophrenia. He felt equally strongly about the loss of wisdom in the aged through memory malfunction. For him, the end justified the means, and when one is dealing with the waste of human potential, it is easy to adopt this stance.

Cameron retired abruptly in 1964, for unexplained reasons. His successor, Dr. Robert Cleghorn, made a virtually unprecedented move in the academic world of mutual back-scratching and praise. He commissioned a psychiatrist and a psychologist, unconnected to Cameron, to study his electroshock work. They found that 60 percent of Cameron's depatterned patients complained they still had amnesia for the period 6 months to 10 years before the therapy.* They could find no clinical proof that showed the treatment to be any more or less effective than other approaches. They concluded that "the incidence of physi-

---

*Cleghorn's team found little loss of memory on objective tests, like the Wechsler Memory Scale but speculated that these tests measured a different memory function—short-term recall—than that the subjects claimed to be missing.

cal complications and the anxiety generated in the patient because of real or imagined memory difficulty argue against" future use of the technique.

The study-team members couched their report in densely academic jargon, but one of them speaks more clearly now. He talks bitterly of one of Cameron's former patients who needs to keep a list of her simplest household chores to remember how to do them. Then he repeats several times how powerful a man Cameron was, how he was "the godfather of Canadian psychiatry." He continues, "I probably shouldn't talk about this, but Cameron—for him to do what he did—he was a very schizophrenic guy, who totally detached himself from the human implications of his work . . . God, we talk about concentration camps. I don't want to make this comparison, but God, you talk about 'we didn't know it was happening,' and it was—right in our back yard."

Cameron died in 1967, at age 66, while climbing a mountain. The *American Journal of Psychiatry* published a long and glowing obituary with a full-page picture of his not-unpleasant face.

D. Ewen Cameron did not need the CIA to corrupt him. He clearly had his mind set on doing unorthodox research long before the Agency front started to fund him. With his own hospital and source of subjects, he could have found elsewhere encouragement and money to replace the CIA's contribution, which never exceeded $20,000 a year. However, Agency officials knew exactly what they were paying for. They traveled periodically to Montreal to observe his work, and his proposal was chillingly explicit. In Cameron, they had a doctor, conveniently outside the United States, willing to do terminal experiments in electroshock, sensory deprivation, drug testing, and all of the above combined. By literally wiping the minds of his subjects clean by depatterning and then trying to program in new behavior, Cameron carried the process known as "brainwashing" to its logical extreme.

It cannot be said how many—if any—other Agency brainwashing projects reached the extremes of Cameron's work. Details are scarce, since many of the principal witnesses have died, will not talk about what went on, or lie about it. In what ways the CIA applied work like Cameron's is not known. What is known, however, is that the intelligence community, including the CIA, changed the face of the scientific community during the 1950s and early 1960s by its interest in such experiments. Nearly every scientist on the frontiers of brain research found men from the secret agencies looking over his shoulders, impinging on the research. The experience of Dr. John Lilly illustrates how this intrusion came about.

In 1953 Lilly worked at the National Institutes of Health, outside Washington, doing experimental studies in an effort to "map" the body functions controlled from various locations in the brain. He devised a method of pounding up to 600 tiny sections of hypodermic tubing into the skulls of monkeys, through which he could insert electrodes "into the brain to any desired distance and at any desired location from the cortex down to the bottom of the skull," he later wrote. Using electric stimulation, Lilly discovered precise centers of the monkeys' brains that caused pain, fear, anxiety, and anger. He also discovered precise, separate parts of the brain that controlled erection, ejaculation, and orgasm in male monkeys. Lilly found that a monkey, given access to a switch operating a correctly planted electrode, would reward himself with nearly continuous orgasms—at least once every 3 minutes—for up to 16 hours a day.

As Lilly refined his brain "maps," officials of the CIA and other agencies descended upon him with a request for a briefing. Having a phobia against secrecy, Lilly agreed to the briefing only under the condition that it and his work remain unclassified, completely open to outsiders. The intelligence officials submitted to the conditions most reluctantly, since they knew that Lilly's openness would not only ruin the spy value of anything they learned but could also reveal the identities and the interests of the intelligence officials to enemy agents. They considered Lilly annoying, uncooperative—possibly even suspicious.

Soon Lilly began to have trouble going to meetings and conferences with his colleagues. As part of the cooperation with the intelligence agencies, most of them had agreed to have their projects officially classified as SECRET, which meant that access to the information required a security clearance.* Lilly's security clearance was withdrawn for review, then tangled up

*Lilly and other veterans of government-supported research note that there is a practical advantage for the scientist who allows his work to be classified: it gives him an added claim on government funds. He is then in a position to argue that if his work is important enough to be SECRET, it deserves money.

and misplaced—all of which he took as pressure to cooperate with the CIA. Lilly, whose imagination needed no stimulation to conjure up pictures of CIA agents on deadly missions with remote-controlled electrodes strategically implanted in their brains, decided to withdraw from that field of research. He says he had decided that the physical intrusion of the electrodes did too much brain damage for him to tolerate.

In 1954 Lilly began trying to isolate the operations of the brain, free of outside stimulation, through sensory deprivation. He worked in an office next to Dr. Maitland Baldwin, who the following year agreed to perform terminal sensory deprivation experiments for ARTICHOKE's Morse Allen but who never told Lilly he was working in the field. While Baldwin experimented with his sensory-deprivation "box," Lilly invented a special "tank." Subjects floated in a tank of body-temperature water, wearing a face mask that provided air but cut off sight and sound. Inevitably, intelligence officials swooped down on Lilly again, interested in the use of his tank as an interrogation tool. Could involuntary subjects be placed in the tank and broken down to the point where their belief systems or personalities could be altered?

It was central to Lilly's ethic that he himself be the first subject of any experiment, and, in the case of the conscious-ness-exploring tank work, he and one colleague were the *only* ones. Lilly realized that the intelligence agencies were not in-terested in sensory deprivation because of its positive benefits, and he finally concluded that it was impossible for him to work at the National Institutes of Health without compromising his principles. He quit in 1958.

Contrary to most people's intuitive expectations, Lilly found sensory deprivation to be a profoundly integrating experience for himself personally. He considered himself to be a scientist who subjectively explored the far wanderings of the brain. In a series of private experiments, he pushed himself into the complete unknown by injecting pure Sandoz LSD into his thigh before climbing into the sensory-deprivation tank.* When the

---

*As was the case with LSD work, sensory deprivation research had both a mind control and a transcendental side. Aldous Huxley wrote thusly about the two pioneers in the field: "What men like Hebb and Lilly are doing in the laboratory was done by the Christian hermits in the Thebaid and elsewhere, and by Hindu and Tibetan hermits in the remote fastness of the Himalayas. My own belief is that these experiences really tell us something about the nature of the uni-

counterculture sprang up, Lilly became something of a cult figure, with his unique approach to scientific inquiry—though he was considered more of an outcast by many in the professional research community.

For most of the outside world, Lilly became famous with the release of the popular film, *The Day of the Dolphin,* which the filmmakers acknowledged was based on Lilly's work with dolphins after he left NIH. Actor George C. Scott portrayed a scientist, who, like Lilly, loved dolphins, did pioneering experiments on their intelligence, and tried to find ways to communicate with them. In the movie, Scott became dismayed when the government pounced on his breakthrough in talking to dolphins and turned it immediately to the service of war. In real life, Lilly was similarly dismayed when Navy and CIA scientists trained dolphins for special warfare in the waters off Vietnam.*

A few scientists like Lilly made up their minds not to cross certain ethical lines in their experimental work, while others were prepared to go further even than their sponsors from ARTICHOKE and MKULTRA. Within the Agency itself, there was only one final question: Will a technique work? CIA officials zealously tracked every lead, sparing no expense to check each angle many times over.

By the time the MKULTRA program ended in 1963, Agency researchers had found no foolproof way to brainwash another person.† "All experiments beyond a certain point always failed," says the MKULTRA veteran, "because the subject jerked himself back for some reason or the subject got amnesiac or catatonic." Agency officials found through work like

---

verse, that they are valuable in themselves and, above all, valuable when incorporated into our world-picture and acted upon [in] normal life."

*In a program called "swimmer nullification," government scientists trained dolphins to attack enemy frogmen with huge needles attached to their snouts. The dolphins carried tanks of compressed air, which when jabbed into a deep-diver caused him to pop dead to the surface. A scientist who worked in this CIA-Navy program states that some of the dolphins sent to Vietnam during the late 1960s got out of their pens and disappeared—unheard of behavior for trained dolphins. John Lilly confirms that a group of the marine mammals stationed at Cam Ranh Bay did go AWOL, and he adds that he heard that some eventually returned with their bodies and fins covered with attack marks made by other dolphins.

†After 1963 the Agency's Science and Technology Directorate continued brain research with unknown results. See Chapter 12.

Cameron's that they could create "vegetables," but such people served no operational use. People could be tortured into saying anything, but no science could guarantee that they would tell the truth.

The impotency of brainwashing techniques left the Agency in a difficult spot when Yuri Nosenko defected to the United States in February 1964. A ranking official of the Soviet KGB, Nosenko brought with him stunning information. He said the Russians had bugged the American embassy in Moscow, which turned out to be true. He named some Russian agents in the West. And he said that he had personally inspected the KGB file of Lee Harvey Oswald, who only a few months earlier had been murdered before he could be brought to trial for the assassination of President Kennedy. Nosenko said he learned that the KGB had had no interest in Oswald.

Was Nosenko telling the truth, or was he a KGB "plant" sent to throw the United States off track about Oswald? Was his information about penetration correct, or was Nosenko himself the penetration? Was he acting in good faith? Were the men within the CIA who believed he was acting in good faith themselves acting in good faith? These and a thousand other questions made up the classical trick deck for spies—each card having "true" on one side and "false" on the other.

Top CIA officials felt a desperate need to resolve the issue of Nosenko's legitimacy. With numerous Agency counterintelligence operations hanging in the balance, Richard Helms, first as Deputy Director and then as Director, allowed CIA operators to work Nosenko over with the interrogation method in which Helms apparently had the most faith. It turned out to be not any truth serum or electroshock depatterning program or anything else from the Agency's brainwashing search. Helms had Nosenko put through the tried-and-true Soviet method: isolate the prisoner, deaden his senses, break him. For more than three years—1,277 days, to be exact—Agency officers kept Nosenko in solitary confinement. As if they were using the Hinkle–Wolff study as their instruction manual and the Cardinal Mindszenty case as their success story, the CIA men had guards watch over Nosenko day and night, giving him not a moment of privacy. A light bulb burned continuously in his cell. He was allowed nothing to read—not even the labels on toothpaste boxes. When he tried to distract himself by making a chess set from pieces of lint in his cell, the guards discovered his game and swept the area clean. Nosenko had no window, and he was eventually put in a specially built 12′ × 12′ steel bank vault.

Nosenko broke down. He hallucinated. He talked his head off to his interrogators, who questioned him for 292 days, often while they had him strapped into a lie detector. If he told the truth, they did not believe him. While the Soviets and Chinese had shown that they could make a man admit anything, the CIA interrogators apparently lacked a clear idea of exactly what they wanted Nosenko to confess. When it was all over and Richard Helms ordered Nosenko freed after three and a half years of illegal detention, some key Agency officers still believed he was a KGB plant. Others thought he was on the level. Thus the big questions remained unresolved, and to this day, CIA men—past and present—are bitterly split over who Nosenko really is.

With the Nosenko case, the CIA's brainwashing programs had come full circle. Spurred by the widespread alarm over communist tactics, Agency officials had investigated the field, started their own projects, and looked to the latest technology to make improvements. After 10 years of research, with some rather gruesome results, CIA officials had come up with no techniques on which they felt they could rely. Thus, when the operational crunch came, they fell back on the basic brutality of the Soviet system.

CHAPTER
9
HUMAN ECOLOGY

Well before Harold Wolff and Lawrence Hinkle finished their brainwashing study for Allen Dulles in 1956, Wolff was trying to expand his role in CIA research and operations. He offered Agency officials the cooperation of his colleagues at Cornell University, where he taught neurology and psychiatry in the Medical College. In proposal after proposal, Wolff pressed upon the CIA his idea that to understand human behavior—and how governments might manipulate it—one had to study man in relationship to his total environment. Calling this field "human ecology," Wolff drew into it the disciplines of psychology, medicine, sociology, and anthropology. In the academic world of the early 1950s, this cross-disciplinary approach was somewhat new, as was the word "ecology," but it made sense to CIA officials. Like Wolff, they were far in advance of the trends in the behavioral sciences.

Wolff carved out vast tracts of human knowledge, some only freshly discovered, and proposed a partnership with the Agency for the task of mastering that knowledge for operational use. It was a time when knowledge itself seemed bountiful and promising, and Wolff was expansive about how the CIA could harness it. Once he figured out how the human mind really worked, he wrote, he would tell the Agency "how a man can be made to think, 'feel,' and behave according to the wishes of other men, and, conversely, how a man can avoid being influenced in this manner."

Such notions, which may now appear naïve or perverse, did

not seem so unlikely at the height of the Cold War. And Wolff's professional stature added weight to his ideas. Like D. Ewen Cameron, he was no obscure academic. He had been President of the New York Neurological Association and would become, in 1960, President of the American Neurological Association. He served for several years as editor-in-chief of the American Medical Association's *Archives of Neurology and Psychiatry.* Both by credentials and force of personality, Wolff was an impressive figure. CIA officials listened respectfully to his grand vision of how spies and doctors could work symbiotically to help—if not save—the world. Also, the Agency men never forgot that Wolff had become close to Director Allen Dulles while treating Dulles' son for brain damage.

Wolff's specialized neurological practice led him to believe that brain maladies, like migraine headaches, occurred because of disharmony between man and his environment. In this case, he wrote to the Agency, "The problem faced by the physician is quite similar to that faced by the Communist interrogator." Both would be trying to put their subject back in harmony with his environment whether the problem was headache or ideological dissent. Wolff believed that the beneficial effects of any new interrogation technique would naturally spill over into the treatment of his patients, and vice versa. Following the Soviet model, he felt he could help his patients by putting them into an isolated, disoriented state—from which it would be easier to create new behavior patterns. Although Russian-style isolation cells were impractical at Cornell, Wolff hoped to get the same effect more quickly through sensory deprivation. He told the Agency that sensory-deprivation chambers had "valid medical reason" as part of a treatment that relieved migraine symptoms and made the patient "more receptive to the suggestions of the psychotherapist." He proposed keeping his patients in sensory deprivation until they "show an increased desire to talk and to escape from the procedure." Then, he said, doctors could "utilize material from their own past experience in order to create psychological reactions within them." This procedure drew heavily on the Stalinist method. It cannot be said what success, if any, Wolff had with it to the benefit of his patients at Cornell.

Wolff offered to devise ways to use the broadest cultural and social processes in human ecology for covert operations. He understood that every country had unique customs for child rearing, military training, and nearly every other form of human intercourse. From the CIA's point of view, he noted, this kind of sociological information could be applied mainly to indoctrinating and motivating people. He distinguished these motivating techniques from the "special methods" that he felt were "more relevant to subversion, seduction, and interrogation." He offered to study those methods, too, and asked the Agency to give him access to everything in its files on "threats, coercion, imprisonment, isolation, deprivation, humiliation, torture, 'brainwashing,' 'black psychiatry,' hypnosis, and combinations of these with or without chemical agents." Beyond mere study, Wolff volunteered the unwitting use of Cornell patients for brainwashing experiments, so long as no one got hurt. He added, however, that he would advise the CIA on experiments that harmed their subjects if they were performed elsewhere. He obviously felt that only the grandest sweep of knowledge, flowing freely between scholar and spy, could bring the best available techniques to bear on their respective subjects.

In 1955 Wolff incorporated his CIA-funded study group as the Society for the Investigation of Human Ecology, with himself as president.* Through the Society, Wolff extended his efforts for the Agency, and his organization turned into a CIA-controlled funding mechanism for studies and experiments in the behavioral sciences.

In the early days of the Society, Agency officials trusted Wolff and his untried ideas with a sensitive espionage assignment. In effect, the new specialty of human ecology was going to telescope the stages of research and application into one continuing process. Speeding up the traditional academic method was required because the CIA men faced an urgent problem. "What was bothering them," Lawrence Hinkle explains, "was that the Chinese had cleaned up their agents in China. . . . What they really wanted to do was come up with some Chinese [in America], steer them to us, and make them into agents." Wolff accepted the challenge and suggested that the Cornell group hide its real purpose behind the cover of investigating "the ecological aspects of disease" among Chinese refugees. The Agency gave the project a budget of $84,175 (about 30 percent of the

*In 1961 the Society changed its name to the Human Ecology Fund, but for convenience sake it will be called the Society throughout the book.

money it put into Cornell in 1955) and supplied the study group with 100 Chinese refugees to work with. Nearly all these subjects had been studying in the United States when the communists took over the mainland in 1949, so they tended to be dislocated people in their thirties.

On the Agency side, the main concern, as expressed by one ARTICHOKE man, was the "security hazard" of bringing together so many potential agents in one place. Nevertheless, CIA officials decided to go ahead. Wolff promised to tell them about the inner reaches of the Chinese character, and they recognized the operational advantage that insight into Chinese behavior patterns could provide. Moreover, Wolff said he would pick out the most useful possible agents. The Human Ecology Society would then offer these candidates "fellowships" and subject them to more intensive interviews and "stress producing" situations. The idea was to find out about their personalities, past conditioning, and present motivations, in order to figure out how they might perform in future predicaments—such as finding themselves back in Mainland China as American agents. In the process, Wolff hoped to mold these Chinese into people willing to work for the CIA. Mindful of leaving some cover for Cornell, he was adamant that Agency operators not connected with the project make the actual recruitment pitch to those Chinese whom the Agency men wanted as agents.

As a final twist, Wolff planned to provide each agent with techniques to withstand the precise forms of hostile interrogation they could expect upon returning to China. CIA officials wanted to "precondition" the agents in order to create long-lasting motivation "impervious to lapse of time and direct psychological attacks by the enemy." In other words, Agency men planned to brainwash their agents in order to protect them against Chinese brainwashing.

Everything was covered—in theory, at least. Wolff was going to take a crew of 100 refugees and turn as many of them as possible into detection-proof, live agents inside China, and he planned to do the job quickly through human ecology. It was a heady chore for the Cornell professor to take on after classes.

Wolff hired a full complement of psychologists, psychiatrists, and anthropologists to work on the project. He bulldozed his way through his colleagues' qualms and government red tape alike. Having hired an anthropologist before learning that the CIA security office would not give her a clearance, Wolff simply lied to her about where the money came from. "It was a function of Wolff's imperious nature," says his partner Hinkle. "If a dog came in and threw up on the rug during a lecture, he would continue." Even the CIA men soon found that Harold Wolff was not to be trifled with. "From the Agency side, I don't know anyone who wasn't scared of him," recalls a longtime CIA associate. "He was an autocratic man. I never knew him to chew anyone out. He didn't have to. We were damned respectful. He moved in high places. He was just a skinny little man, but talk about mind control! He was one of the controllers."

In the name of the Human Ecology Society, the CIA paid $1,200 a month to rent a fancy town house on Manhattan's East 78th Street to house the Cornell group and its research projects. Agency technicians traveled to New York in December 1954 to install eavesdropping microphones around the building. These and other more obvious security devices—safes, guards, and the like—made the town house look different from the academic center it was supposed to be. CIA liaison personnel held meetings with Wolff and the staff in the secure confines of the town house, and they all carefully watched the 100 Chinese a few blocks away at the Cornell hospital. The Society paid each subject $25 a day so the researchers could test them, probe them, and generally learn all they could about Chinese people —or at least about middle-class, displaced, anticommunist ones.

It is doubtful that any of Wolff's Chinese ever returned to their homeland as CIA agents, or that all of Wolff's proposals were put into effect. In any case, the project was interrupted in midstream by a major shake-up in the CIA's entire mind-control effort. Early in 1955, Sid Gottlieb and his Ph.D. crew from TSS took over most of the ARTICHOKE functions, including the Society, from Morse Allen and the Pinkerton types in the Office of Security. The MKULTRA men moved quickly to turn the Society into an entity that looked and acted like a legitimate foundation. First they smoothed over the ragged covert edges. Out came the bugs and safes so dear to Morse Allen and company. The new crew even made some effort (largely unsuccessful) to attract non-CIA funds. The biggest change, however, was the Cornell professors now had to deal with Agency representatives who were scientists and who had strong ideas of their own on research questions. Up to this point, the Cornellians had been able to keep the CIA's involvement within bounds acceptable to them. While Harold Wolff never ceased wanting to explore the furthest reaches of behavior control, his colleagues were wary of going on to the outer limits—at least under Cornell cover.

No one would ever confuse MKULTRA projects with ivory-tower research, but Gottlieb's people did take a more academic —and sophisticated—approach to behavioral research than their predecessors. The MKULTRA men understood that not every project would have an immediate operational benefit, and they believed less and less in the existence of that one just-over-the-horizon technique that would turn men into puppets. They favored increasing their knowledge of human behavior in relatively small steps, and they concentrated on the reduced goal of influencing and manipulating their subjects. "You're ahead of the game if you can get people to do something ten percent more often than they would otherwise," says an MKULTRA veteran.

Accordingly, in 1956, Sid Gottlieb approved a $74,000 project to have the Human Ecology Society study the factors that caused men to defect from their countries and cooperate with foreign governments. MKULTRA officials reasoned that if they could understand what made old turncoats tick, it might help them entice new ones. While good case officers instinctively seemed to know how to handle a potential agent—or thought they did—the MKULTRA men hoped to come up with systematic, even scientific improvements. Overtly, Harold Wolff designed the program to look like a follow-up study to the Society's earlier programs, noting to the Agency that it was "feasible to study foreign nationals under the cover of a medical-sociological study." (He told his CIA funders that "while some information of general value to science should be produced, this in itself will not be a sufficient justification for carrying out a study of this nature.") Covertly, he declared the purpose of the research was to assess defectors' social and cultural background, their life experience, and their personality structure, in order to understand their motivations, value systems, and probable future reactions.

The 1956 Hungarian revolt occurred as the defector study was getting underway, and the Human Ecology group, with CIA headquarters approval, decided to turn the defector work into an investigation of 70 Hungarian refugees from that upheaval. By then, most of Harold Wolff's team had been together through the brainwashing and Chinese studies. While not all of them knew of the CIA's specific interests, they had streamlined their procedures for answering the questions that Agency officials found interesting. They ran the Hungarians through the battery of tests and observations in six months, compared to a year and a half for the Chinese project.

The Human Ecology Society reported that most of their Hungarian subjects had fought against the Russians during the Revolution and that they had lived through extraordinarily difficult circumstances, including arrest, mistreatment, and indoctrination. The psychologists and psychiatrists found that, often, those who had survived with the fewest problems had been those with markedly aberrant personalities. "This observation has added to the evidence that healthy people are not necessarily 'normal,' but are people particularly adapted to their special life situations," the group declared.

While CIA officials liked the idea that their Hungarian subjects had not knuckled under communist influence, they recognized that they were working with a skewed sample. American visa restrictions kept most of the refugee left-wingers and former communist officials out of the United States; so, as a later MKULTRA document would state, the Society wound up studying "western-tied rightist elements who had never been accepted completely" in postwar Hungary. Agency researchers realized that these people would "contribute little" toward increasing the CIA's knowledge of the processes that made a communist official change his loyalties.

In order to broaden their data base, MKULTRA officials decided in March 1957 to bring in some unwitting help. They gave a contract to Rutgers University sociologists Richard Stephenson and Jay Schulman "to throw as much light as possible on the sociology of the communist system in the throes of revolution." The Rutgers professors started out by interviewing the 70 Hungarians at Cornell in New York, and Schulman went on to Europe to talk to disillusioned Communists who had also fled their country. From an operational point of view, these were the people the Agency really cared about; but, as socialists, most of them probably would have resisted sharing their experiences with the CIA—if they had known.*

---

*Also to gain access to this same group of leftist Hungarian refugees in Europe,

Jay Schulman would have resisted, too. After discovering almost 20 years later that the Agency had paid his way and seen his confidential interviews, he feels misused. "In 1957 I was myself a quasi-Marxist and if I had known that this study was sponsored by the CIA, there is really, obviously, no way that I would have been associated with it," says Schulman. "My view is that social scientists have a deep personal responsibility for questioning the sources of funding; and the fact that I didn't do it at the time was simply, in my judgment, indication of my own naïveté and political innocence, in spite of my ideological bent."

Deceiving Schulman and his Hungarian subjects did not bother the men from MKULTRA in the slightest. According to a Gottlieb aide, one of the strong arguments inside the CIA for the whole Human Ecology program was that it gave the Agency a means of approaching and using political mavericks who could not otherwise get security clearances. "Sometimes," he chuckles, "these left-wing social scientists were damned good." This MKULTRA veteran scoffs at the displeasure Schulman expresses: "If we'd gone to a guy and said, 'We're CIA,' he never would have done it. They were glad to get the money in a world where damned few people were willing to support them. . . . They can't complain about how they were treated or that they were asked to do something they wouldn't have normally done."

The Human Ecology Society soon became a conduit for CIA money flowing to projects, like the Rutgers one, outside Cornell. For these grants, the Society provided only cover and administrative support behind the gold-plated names of Cornell and Harold Wolff. From 1955 to 1958, Agency officials passed funds through the Society for work on criminal sexual psychopaths at Ionia State Hospital,* a mental institution located on the

the Human Ecology Society put $15,000 in 1958 into an unwitting study by Dr. A. H. M. Struik of the University of Nijmegen in the Netherlands. An Agency document extolled this arrangement not only as a useful way of studying Hungarians but because it provided "entree" into a leading European university and psychological research center, adding "such a connection has manifold cover and testing possibilities as well as providing a base from which to take advantage of developments in that area of the world."

*Professor Laurence Hinkle states that it was never his or Cornell's intention that the Society would be used as a CIA funding conduit. When told that he himself had written letters on the Ionia project, he replied that the Society's CIA-supplied bookkeeper was always putting papers in front of him and that he must have signed without realizing the implications.

banks of the Grand River in the rolling farm country 120 miles northwest of Detroit. This project had an interesting hypothesis: That child molesters and rapists had ugly secrets buried deep within them and that their stake in not admitting their perversions approached that of spies not wanting to confess. The MKULTRA men reasoned that any technique that would work on a sexual psychopath would surely have a similar effect on a foreign agent. Using psychologists and psychiatrists connected to the Michigan mental health and the Detroit court systems, they set up a program to test LSD and marijuana, wittingly and unwittingly, alone and in combination with hypnosis. Because of administrative delays, the Michigan doctors managed to experiment only on 26 inmates in three years—all sexual offenders committed by judges without a trial under a Michigan law, since declared unconstitutional. The search for a truth drug went on, under the auspices of the Human Ecology Society, as well as in other MKULTRA channels.

The Ionia project was the kind of expansionist activity that made Cornell administrators, if not Harold Wolff, uneasy. By 1957, the Cornellians had had enough. At the same time, the Agency sponsors decided that the Society had outgrown its dependence on Cornell for academic credentials—that in fact the close ties to Cornell might inhibit the Society's future growth among academics notoriously sensitive to institutional conflicts. One CIA official wrote that the Society "must be given more established stature in the research community to be effective as a cover organization." Once the Society was cut loose in the foundation world, Agency men felt they would be freer to go anywhere in academia to buy research that might assist covert operations. So the CIA severed the Society's formal connection to Cornell.

The Human Ecology group moved out of its East 78th Street town house, which had always seem a little too plush for a university program, and opened up a new headquarters in Forest Hills, Queens, which was an inappropriate neighborhood for a well-connected foundation.* Agency officials hired a staff of four led by Lieutenant Colonel James Monroe, who had

---

*By 1961 the CIA staff had tired of Queens and moved the Society back into Manhattan to 201 East 57th Street. In 1965, as the Agency was closing down the front, it switched its headquarters to 1834 Connecticut Avenue N.W. in Washington, the same building owned by Dr. Charles Geschickter that housed another MKULTRA conduit, the Geschickter Fund for Medical Research.

worked closely with the CIA as head of the Air Force's study of Korean War prisoners. Sid Gottlieb and the TSS hierarchy in Washington still made the major decisions, but Monroe and the Society staff, whose salaries the Agency paid, took over the Society's dealings with the outside world and the monitoring of several hundred thousand dollars a year in research projects. Monroe personally supervised dozens of grants, including Dr. Ewen Cameron's brainwashing work in Montreal. Soon the Society was flourishing as an innovative foundation, attracting research proposals from a wide variety of behavioral scientists, at a time when these people—particularly the unorthodox ones —were still the step-children of the fund-granting world.

After the Society's exit from Cornell, Wolff and Hinkle stayed on as president and vice-president, respectively, of the Society's board of directors. Dr. Joseph Hinsey, head of the New York Hospital–Cornell Medical Center also remained on the board. Allen Dulles continued his personal interest in the Society's work and came to one of the first meetings of the new board, which, as was customary with CIA fronts, included some big outside names. These luminaries added worthiness to the enterprise while playing essentially figurehead roles. In 1957 the other board members were John Whitehorn, chairman of the psychiatry department at Johns Hopkins University, Carl Rogers, professor of psychology and psychiatry at the University of Wisconsin, and Adolf A. Berle, onetime Assistant Secretary of State and chairman of the New York Liberal Party.* Berle had originally put his close friend Harold Wolff in touch with the CIA, and at Wolff's request, he came on the Society board despite some reservations. "I am frightened about this one," Berle wrote in his diary. "If the scientists do what they have laid out for themselves, men will become manageable ants. But I don't think it will happen."

There was a lot of old-fashioned backscratching among the CIA people and the academics as they settled into the work of accommodating each other. Even Harold Wolff, the first and the most enthusistic of the scholar-spies, had made it clear from the beginning that he expected some practical rewards

*Other establishment figures who would grace the Human Ecology board over the years included Leonard Carmichael, head of the Smithsonian Institution, Barnaby Keeney, president of Brown University, and George A. Kelly, psychology professor and Society fund recipient at Ohio State University.

for his service. According to colleague Hinkle, who appreciated Wolff as one the great grantsmen of his time, Wolff expected that the Agency "would support our research and we would be their consultants." Wolff bluntly informed the CIA that some of his work would have no direct use "except that it vastly enhances our value . . . as consultants and advisers." In other words, Wolff felt that his worth to the CIA increased in proportion to his professional accomplishments and importance—which in turn depended partly on the resources he commanded. The Agency men understood, and over the last half of the 1950s, they were happy to contribute almost $300,000 to Wolff's own research on the brain and central nervous system. In turn, Wolff and his reputation helped them gain access to other leading lights in the academic world.

Another person who benefited from Human Ecology funds was Carl Rogers, whom Wolff had also asked to serve on the board. Rogers, who later would become famous for his nondirective, nonauthoritarian approach to psychotherapy, respected Wolff's work, and he had no objection to helping the ÇIA. Although he says he would have nothing to do with secret Agency activities today, he asks for understanding in light of the climate of the 1950s. "We really did regard Russia as the enemy," declares Rogers, "and we were trying to do various things to make sure the Russians did not get the upper hand." Rogers received an important professional reward for joining the Society board. Executive Director James Monroe had let him know that, once he agreed to serve, he could expect to receive a Society grant. "That appealed to me because I was having trouble getting funded," says Rogers. "Having gotten that grant [about $30,000 over three years], it made it possible to get other grants from Rockefeller and NIMH." Rogers still feels grateful to the Society for helping him establish a funding "track record," but he emphasizes that the Agency never had any effect on his research.

Although MKULTRA psychologist John Gittinger suspected that Rogers' work on psychotherapy might provide insight into interrogation methods, the Society did not give Rogers money because of the content of his work. The grant ensured his services as a consultant, if desired, and, according to a CIA document, "free access" to his project. But above all, the grant allowed the Agency to use Rogers' name. His standing in the academic community contributed to the layer of cover around the Society that Agency officials felt was crucial to mask their involvement.

Professor Charles Osgood's status in psychology also improved the Society's cover, but his research was more directly useful to the Agency, and the MKULTRA men paid much more to get it. In 1959 Osgood, who four years later became president of the American Psychological Association, wanted to push forward his work on how people in different societies express the same feelings, even when using different words and concepts. Osgood wrote in "an abstract conceptual framework," but Agency officials saw his research as "directly relevant" to covert activities. They believed they could transfer Osgood's knowledge of "hidden values and cues" in the way people communicate into more effective overseas propaganda. Osgood's work gave them a tool—called the "semantic differential"—to choose the right words in a foreign language to convey a particular meaning.

Like Carl Rogers, Osgood got his first outside funding for what became the most important work of his career from the Human Ecology Society. Osgood had written directly to the CIA for support, and the Society soon contacted him and furnished $192,975 for research over five years. The money allowed him to travel widely and to expand his work into 30 different cultures. Also like Rogers, Osgood eventually received NIMH money to finish his research, but he acknowledges that the Human Ecology grants played an important part in the progress of his work. He stresses that "there was none of the feeling then about the CIA that there is now, in terms of subversive activities," and he states that the Society had no influence on anything he produced. Yet Society men could and did talk to him about his findings. They asked questions that reflected their own covert interests, not his academic pursuits, and they drew him out, according to one of them, "at great length." Osgood had started studying cross-cultural meaning well before he received the Human Ecology money, but the Society's support ensured that he would continue his work on a scale that suited the Agency's purposes, as well as his own.

A whole category of Society funding, called "cover grants," served no other purpose than to build the Society's false front. These included a sociological study of Levittown, Long Island (about $4,500), an analysis of the Central Mongoloid skull ($700), and a look at the foreign-policy attitudes of people who owned fallout shelters, as opposed to people who did not ($2,-500). A $500 Human Ecology grant went to Istanbul University for a study of the effects of circumcision on Turkish boys. The researcher found that young Turks, usually circumcised between the ages of five and seven, felt "severe emotional impact with attending symptoms of withdrawal." The children saw the painful operations as "an act of aggression" that brought out previously hidden fears—or so the Human Ecology Society reported.

In other instances, the Society put money into projects whose covert application was so unlikely that only an expert could see the possibilities. Nonetheless, in 1958 the Society gave $5,570 to social psychologists Muzafer and Carolyn Wood Sherif of the University of Oklahoma for work on the behavior of teen-age boys in gangs. The Sherifs, both ignorant of the CIA connection,* studied the group structures and attitudes in the gangs and tried to devise ways to channel antisocial behavior into more constructive paths. Their results were filtered through clandestine minds at the Agency. "With gang warfare," says an MKULTRA source, "you tried to get some defectors-in-place who would like to modify some of the group behavior and cool it. Now, getting a juvenile delinquent defector was motivationally not all that much different from getting a Soviet one."

MKULTRA officials were clearly interested in using their grants to build contacts and associations with prestigious academics. The Society put $1,500 a year into the *Research in Mental Health Newsletter* published jointly at McGill University by the sociology and psychiatric departments. Anthropologist Margaret Mead, an international culture heroine, sat on the newsletter's advisory board (with, among others, D. Ewen Cameron), and the Society used her name in its biennial report. Similarly, the Society gave grants of $26,000 to the well-known University of London psychologist, H. J. Eysenck, for his work on motivation. An MKULTRA document acknowledged that this research would have "no immediate relevance for Agency needs," but that it would "lend prestige" to the Society. The

---

*According to Dr. Carolyn Sherif, who says she and her husband did not share the Cold War consensus and would never have knowingly taken CIA funds, Human Ecology executive director James Monroe lied directly about the source of the Society's money, claiming it came from rich New York doctors and Texas millionaires who gave it for tax purposes. Monroe used this standard cover story with other grantees.

grants to Eysenck also allowed the Society to take funding credit for no less than nine of his publications in its 1963 report. The following year, the Society managed to purchase a piece of the work of the most famous behaviorist of all, Harvard's B. F. Skinner. Skinner, who had tried to train pigeons to guide bombs for the military during World War II, received a $5,000 Human Ecology grant to pay the costs of a secretary and supplies for the research that led to his book, *Freedom and Dignity*. Skinner has no memory of the grant or its origins but says, "I don't like secret involvement of any kind. I can't see why it couldn't have been open and aboveboard."

A TSS source explains that grants like these "bought legitimacy" for the Society and made the recipients "grateful." He says that the money gave Agency employees at Human Ecology a reason to phone Skinner—or any of the other recipients—to pick his brain about a particular problem. In a similar vein, another MKULTRA man, psychologist John Gittinger mentions the Society's relationship with Erwin Goffman of the University of Pennsylvania, whom many consider today's leading sociological theorist. The Society gave him a small grant to help finish a book that would have been published anyway. As a result, Gittinger was able to spend hours talking with him about, among other things, an article he had written earlier on confidence men. These hucksters were experts at manipulating behavior, according to Gittinger, and Goffman unwittingly "gave us a better understanding of the techniques people use to establish phony relationships"—a subject of interest to the CIA.

To keep track of new developments in the behavioral sciences, Society representatives regularly visited grant recipients and found out what they and their colleagues were doing. Some of the knowing professors became conscious spies. Most simply relayed the latest professional gossip to their visitors and sent along unpublished papers. The prestige of the Human Ecology grantees also helped give the Agency access to behavioral scientists who had no connection to the Society. "You could walk into someone's office and say you were just talking to Skinner," says an MKULTRA veteran. "We didn't hesitate to do this. It was a way to name-drop."

The Society did not limit its intelligence gathering to the United States. As one Agency source puts it, "The Society gave us a legitimate basis to approach anyone in the academic community anywhere in the world." CIA officials regularly used it as cover when they traveled abroad to study the behavior of foreigners of interest to the Agency, including such leaders as Nikita Khrushchev. The Society funded foreign researchers and also gave money to American professors to collect information abroad. In 1960, for instance, the Society sponsored a survey of Soviet psychology through the simple device of putting up $15,000 through the official auspices of the American Psychological Association to send ten prominent psychologists on a tour of the Soviet Union. Nine of the ten had no idea of the Agency involvement, but CIA officials were apparently able to debrief everyone when the group returned. Then the Society sponsored a conference and book for which each psychologist contributed a chapter. The book added another $5,000 to the CIA's cost, but $20,000 all told seemed like a small price to pay for the information gathered. The psychologists—except perhaps the knowledgeable one—did nothing they would not ordinarily have done during their trip, and the scholarly community benefited from increased knowledge on an important subject. The only thing violated was the openness and trust normally associated with academic pursuits. By turning scholars into spies—even unknowing ones—CIA officials risked the reputation of American research work and contributed potential ammunition toward the belief in many countries that the U.S. notion of academic freedom and independence from the state is self-serving and hypocritical.

Secrecy allowed the Agency a measure of freedom from normal academic restrictions and red tape, and the men from MKULTRA used that freedom to make their projects more attractive. The Society demanded "no stupid progress reports," recalls psychologist and psychiatrist Martin Orne, who received a grant to support his Harvard research on hypnotism. As a further sign of generosity and trust, the Society gave Orne a follow-on $30,000 grant with no specified purpose.* Orne could use it as he wished. He believes the money was "a contingency investment" in his work, and MKULTRA officials agree. "We could go to Orne anytime," says one of them, "and say,

---

*A 1962 report of Orne's laboratory, the Institute for Experimental Psychiatry, showed that it received two sizable grants before the end of that year: $30,000 from Human Ecology and $30,000 from Scientific Engineering Institute, another CIA front organization. Orne says he was not aware of the latter group's Agency connection at the time, but learned of it later. He used its grant to study new ways of using the polygraph.

'Okay, here is a situation and here is a kind of guy. What would you expect we might be able to achieve if we could hypnotize him?' Through his massive knowledge, he could speculate and advise." A handful of other Society grantees also served in similar roles as covert Agency consultants in the field of their expertise.

In general, the Human Ecology Society served as the CIA's window on the world of behavioral research. No phenomenon was too arcane to escape a careful look from the Society, whether extrasensory perception or African witch doctors. "There were some unbelievable schemes," recalls an MKULTRA veteran, "but you also knew Einstein was considered crazy. You couldn't be so biased that you wouldn't leave open the possibility that some crazy idea might work." MKULTRA men realized, according to the veteran, that "ninety percent of what we were doing would fail" to be of any use to the Agency. Yet, with a spirit of inquiry much freer than that usually found in the academic world, the Society took early stabs at cracking the genetic code with computers and finding out whether animals could be controlled through electrodes placed in their brains.

The Society's unrestrained, scattershot approach to behavioral research went against the prevailing wisdom in American universities—both as to methods and to subjects of interest. During the 1950s one school of thought—so-called "behaviorism,"—was accepted on campus, virtually to the exclusion of all others. The "behaviorists," led by Harvard's B. F. Skinner, looked at psychology as the study of learned observable responses to outside stimulation. To oversimplify, they championed the approach in which psychologists gave rewards to rats scurrying through mazes, and they tended to dismiss matters of great interest to the Agency: e.g., the effect of drugs on the psyche, subjective phenomena like hypnosis, the inner workings of the mind, and personality theories that took genetic differences into account.

By investing up to $400,000 a year into the early, innovative work of men like Carl Rogers, Charles Osgood, and Martin Orne, the CIA's Human Ecology Society helped liberate the behavioral sciences from the world of rats and cheese. With a push from the Agency as well as other forces, the field opened up. Former iconoclasts became eminent, and, for better or worse, the Skinnerian near-monopoly gave way to a multiplication of contending schools. Eventually, a reputable behavioral scientist could be doing almost anything: holding hands with his students in sensitivity sessions, collecting survey data on spanking habits, or subjectively exploring new modes of consciousness. The CIA's money undoubtedly changed the academic world to some degree, though no one can say how much.

As usual, the CIA men were ahead of their time and had started to move on before the new approaches became established. In 1963, having sampled everything from palm reading to subliminal perception, Sid Gottlieb and his colleagues satisfied themselves that they had overlooked no area of knowledge—however esoteric—that might be promising for CIA operations. The Society had served its purpose; now the money could be better spent elsewhere. Agency officials transferred the still-useful projects to other covert channels and allowed the rest to die quietly. By the end of 1965, when the remaining research was completed, the Society for the Investigation of Human Ecology was gone.

CHAPTER
10
THE GITTINGER
ASSESSMENT SYSTEM

With one exception, the CIA's behavioral research—whether on LSD or on electroshock—seems to have had more impact on the outside world than on Agency operations. That exception grew out of the work of the MKULTRA program's resident genius, psychologist John Gittinger. While on the CIA payroll, toiling to find ways to manipulate people, Gittinger created a unique system for assessing personality and predicting future behavior. He called his method—appropriately—the Personality Assessment System (PAS). Top Agency officials have been so impressed that they have given the Gittinger system a place in most agent-connected activities. To be sure, most CIA operators would not go nearly so far as a former Gittinger aide who says, "The PAS was the key to the whole clandestine business." Still, after most of the touted mind controllers had given up or been sent back home, it was Gittinger, the staff psychologist, who sold his PAS system to cynical, anti-gimmick case officers in the Agency's Clandestine Services. And during the Cuban missile crisis, it was Gittinger who was summoned to the White House to give his advice on how Khrushchev would react to American pressure.

A heavy-set, goateed native of Oklahoma who in his later years came to resemble actor Walter Slezak, Gittinger looked much more like someone's kindly grandfather than a calculating theoretician. He had an almost insatiable curiosity about personality, and he spent most of his waking hours tinkering with and trying to perfect his system. So obsessed did he become that he always had the feeling—even after other researchers had verified large chunks of the PAS and after the CIA had put it into operational use—that the whole thing was "a kind of paranoid delusion."

Gittinger started working on his system even before he joined the CIA in 1950. Prior to that, he had been director of psychological services at the state hospital in Norman, Oklahoma. His high-sounding title did not reflect the fact that he was the only psychologist on the staff. A former high school guidance counselor and Naval lieutenant commander during World War II, he was starting out at age 30 with a master's degree. Every day he saw several hundred patients whose mental problems included virtually everything in the clinical textbooks.

Numerous tramps and other itinerants, heading West in search of the good life in California, got stuck in Oklahoma during the cold winter months and managed to get themselves admitted to Gittinger's hospital. In warmer seasons of the year, quite a few of them worked, when they had to, as cooks or dishwashers in the short-order hamburger stands that dotted the highways in the days before fast food. They functioned perfectly well in these jobs until freezing nights drove them from their outdoor beds. The hospital staff usually called them "seasonal schizophrenics" and gave them shelter until spring. Gittinger included them in the psychological tests he was so fond of running on his patients.

As he measured the itinerants on the Wechsler intelligence scale, a standard IQ test with 11 parts,* Gittinger made a chance observation that became, he says, the "bedrock" of his whole system. He noticed that the short-order cooks tended to do well on the digit-span subtest which rated their ability to remember numbers. The dishwashers, in contrast, had a poor memory for digits. Since the cooks had to keep track of many complex orders—with countless variations of medium rare, onions, and hold-the-mayo—their retentive quality served them well.

---

*Developed by psychologist David Wechsler, this testing system is called, in different versions, the Wechsler–Bellevue and the Wechsler Adult Intelligence Scale. As Gittinger worked with it over the years, he made modifications that he incorporated in what he named the Wechsler–Bellevue–G. For simplicity's sake, it is simply referred to as the Wechsler system throughout the book.

Gittinger also noticed that the cooks had different personality traits than the dishwashers. The cooks seemed able to maintain a high degree of efficiency in a distracting environment while customers were constantly barking new orders at them. They kept their composure by falling back on their internal resources and generally shutting themselves off from the commotion around them. Gittinger dubbed this personality type, which was basically inner-directed, an "Internalizer" (abbreviated "I"). The dishwashers, on the other hand, did not have the ability to separate themselves from the external world. In order to perform their jobs, they had to be placed off in some far corner of the kitchen with their dirty pots and pans, or else all the tumult of the place diverted them from their duty. Gittinger called the dishwasher type an "Externalizer" (E). He found that if he measured a high digit span in *any* person—not just a short-order cook—he could make a basic judgment about personality.

From observation, Gittinger concluded that babies were born with distinct personalities which then were modified by environmental factors. The Internalized—or I—baby was caught up in himself and tended to be seen as a passive child; hence, the world usually called him a "good baby." The E tot was more interested in outside stimuli and attention, and thus was more likely to cause his parents problems by making demands. Gittinger believed that the way parents and other authority figures reacted to the child helped to shape his personality. Adults often pressured or directed the I child to become more outgoing and the E one to become more self-sufficient. Gittinger found he could measure the compensations, or adjustments, the child made on another Wechsler subtest, the one that rated arithmetic ability. He noticed that in later life, when the person was subject to stress, these compensations tended to disappear, and the person reverted to his original personality type. Gittinger wrote that his system "makes possible the assessment of fundamental discrepancies between the surface personality and the underlying personality structure—discrepancies that produce tension, conflict, and anxiety."

Besides the E-I dimensions, Gittinger identified two other fundamental sets of personality characteristics that he could measure with still other Wechsler subtests. Depending on how a subject did on the block design subtest, Gittinger could tell if he were Regulated (R) or Flexible (F). The Regulated person had no trouble learning by rote but usually did not understand what he learned. The Flexible individual, on the other hand, had to understand something before he learned it. Gittinger noted that R children could learn to play the piano moderately well with comparatively little effort. The F child most often hated the drudgery of piano lessons, but Gittinger observed that the great concert pianists tended to be Fs who had persevered and mastered the instrument.

Other psychologists had thought up personality dimensions similar to Gittinger's E and I, R and F, even if they defined them somewhat differently. Gittinger's most original contribution came in a third personality dimension, which revealed how well people were able to adapt their social behavior to the demands of the culture they lived in. Gittinger found he could measure this dimension with the picture arrangement Wechsler subtest, and he called it the Role Adaptive (A) or Role Uniform (U). It corresponded to "charisma," since other people were naturally attracted to the A person while they tended to ignore the U.

All this became immensely more complicated as Gittinger measured compensations and modifications with other Wechsler subtests. This complexity alone worked against the acceptance of his system by the outside world, as did the fact that he based much of it on ideas that ran contrary to accepted psychological doctrine—such as his heretical notion that genetic differences existed. It did not help, either, that Gittinger was a non-Ph.D. whose theory sprang from the kitchen habits of vagrants in Oklahoma.

Any one of these drawbacks might have stifled Gittinger in the academic world, but to the pragmatists in the CIA, they were irrelevant. Gittinger's strange ideas seemed to work. With uncanny accuracy, he could look at nothing more than a subject's Wechsler numbers, pinpoint his weaknesses, and show how to turn him into an Agency spy. Once Gittinger's boss, Sid Gottlieb, and other high CIA officials realized how Gittinger's PAS could be used to help case officers handle agents, they gave the psychologist both the time and money to improve his system under the auspices of the Human Ecology Society.

Although he was a full-time CIA employee, Gittinger worked under Human Ecology cover through the 1950s. Agency officials considered the PAS to be one of the Society's greatest triumphs, definitely worth continuing after the Society was phased out. In 1962 Gittinger and his co-workers moved their base of operations from the Human Ecology headquarters in New York to a CIA proprietary company, set up especially for them in Washington and called Psychological Assessment Associates. Gittinger served as president of the company, whose cover was to provide psychological services to American firms overseas. He personally opened a branch office in Tokyo (later moved to Hong Kong) to service CIA stations in the Far East. The Washington staff, which grew to about 15 professionals during the 1960s, handled the rest of the world by sending assessment specialists off for temporary visits.

Hundreds of thousands of dollars in Human Ecology grants and then even more money in Psychological Assessment contracts—all CIA funds—flowed out to verify and expand the PAS. For example, the Society gave about $140,000 to David Saunders of the Educational Testing Service, the company that prepares the College Board exams. Saunders, who knew about the Agency's involvement, found a correlation between brain (EEG) patterns and results on the digit-span test, and he helped Gittinger apply the system to other countries. In this regard, Gittinger and his colleagues understood that the Wechsler battery of subtests had a cultural bias and that a Japanese E had a very different personality from, say, a Russian E. To compensate, they worked out localized versions of the PAS for various nations around the world.

While at the Human Ecology group, Gittinger supervised much of the Society's other research in the behavioral sciences, and he always tried to interest Society grantees in his system. He looked for ways to mesh their research with his theories—and vice versa. Some, like Carl Rogers and Charles Osgood, listened politely and did not follow up. Yet Gittinger would always learn something from their work that he could apply to the PAS. A charming man and a skillful raconteur, Gittinger convinced quite a few of the other grantees of the validity of his theories and the importance of his ideas. Careful not to threaten the egos of his fellow professionals, he never projected an air of superiority. Often he would leave people—even the skeptical—openmouthed in awe as he painted unnervingly accurate personality portraits of people he had never met. Indeed, people frequently accused him of somehow having cheated by knowing the subject in advance or peeking at his file.

Gittinger patiently and carefully taught his system to his

colleagues, who all seem to have views of him that range from great respect to pure idolatry. For all his willingness to share the PAS, Gittinger was never able to show anyone how to use the system as skillfully as he did. Not that he did not try; he simply was a more talented natural assessor than any of the others. Moreover, his system was full of interrelations and variables that he instinctively understood but had not bothered to articulate. As a result, he could look at Wechsler scores and pick out behavior patterns which would be valid and which no one else had seen. Even after Agency officials spent a small fortune trying to computerize the PAS, they found, as one psychologist puts it, the machine "couldn't tie down all the variables" that Gittinger was carrying around in his head.

Some Human Ecology grantees, like psychiatrist Robert Hyde, were so impressed with Gittinger's system that they made the PAS a major part of their own research. Hyde routinely gave Wechslers to his subjects before plying them with liquor, as part of the Agency's efforts to find out how people react to alcohol. In 1957 Hyde moved his research team from Boston Psychopathic Hospital, where he had been America's first LSD tripper, to Butler Health Center in Providence. There, with Agency funds, Hyde built an experimental party room in the hospital, complete with pinball machine, dartboard, and bamboo bar stools. From behind a two-way mirror, psychologists watched the subjects get tipsy and made careful notes on their reaction to alcohol. Not surprisingly, the observers found that pure Internalizers became more withdrawn after several drinks, and that uncompensated Es were more likely to become garrulous—in essence, sloppy drunks. Thus Gittinger was able to make generalizations about the different ways an I or an E responded to alcohol.* Simply by knowing how people scored on the Wechsler digit-span test, he could predict how they would react to liquor. Hyde and Harold Abramson at Mount Sinai Hospital made the same kind of observations for LSD, finding, among other things, that an E was more likely than an I to have a bad trip. (Apparently, an I is more accustomed than

---

*As with most of the descriptions of the PAS made in the book, this is an oversimplification of a more complicated process. The system, as Gittinger used it, yielded millions of distinct personality types. His observations on alcohol were based on much more than a straight I and E comparison. For the most complete description of the PAS in the open literature, see the article by Gittinger and Winne cited in the chapter notes.

an E to "being into his own head" and losing touch with external reality.)

At Gittinger's urging, other Human Ecology grantees gave the Wechsler battery to their experimental subjects and sent him the scores. He was building a unique data base on all phases of human behavior, and he needed samples of as many distinct groups as possible. By getting the scores of actors, he could make generalizations about what sort of people made good role-players. Martin Orne at Harvard sent in scores of hypnosis subjects, so Gittinger could separate the personality patterns of those who easily went into a trance from those who could not be hypnotized. Gittinger collected Wechslers of businessmen, students, high-priced fashion models, doctors, and just about any other discrete group he could find a way to have tested. In huge numbers, the Wechslers came flowing in—29,-000 sets in all by the early 1970s—each one accompanied by biographic data. With the 10 subtests he used and at least 10 possible scores on each of those, no two Wechsler results in the whole sample ever looked exactly the same. Gittinger kept a computer printout of all 29,000 on his desk, and he would fiddle with them almost every day—looking constantly for new truths that could be drawn out of them.

John Gittinger was interested in all facets of personality, but because he worked for the CIA, he emphasized deviant forms. He particularly sought out Wechslers of people who had rejected the values of their society or who had some vice—hidden or otherwise—that caused others to reject them. By studying the scores of the defectors who had come over to the West, Gittinger hoped to identify common characteristics of men who had become traitors to their governments. If there were identifiable traits, Agency operators could look for them in prospective spies. Harris Isbell, who ran the MKULTRA drug-testing program at the Lexington, Kentucky detention hospital, sent in the scores of heroin addicts. Gittinger wanted to know what to look for in people susceptible to drugs. The Human Ecology project at Ionia State Hospital in Michigan furnished Wechslers of sexual psychopaths. These scores showed that people with uncontrollable urges have different personality patterns than so-called normals. Gittinger himself journeyed to the West Coast to test homosexuals, lesbians, and the prostitutes he interviewed under George White's auspices in the San

Francisco safehouse. With each group, he separated out the telltale signs that might be a future indicator of their sexual preference in others. Gittinger understood that simply by looking at the Wechsler scores of someone newly tested, he could pick out patterns that corresponded to behavior of people in the data base.

The Gittinger system worked best when the TSS staff had a subject's Wechsler scores to analyze, but Agency officials could not very well ask a Russian diplomat or any other foreign target to sit down and take the tests. During World War II, OSS chief William Donovan had faced a similar problem in trying to find out about Adolf Hitler's personality, and Donovan had commisioned psychoanalyst Walter Langer to make a long-distance psychiatric profile of the German leader. Langer had sifted through all the available data on the Führer, and that was exactly what Gittinger's TSS assessments staff did when they lacked direct contact (and when they had it, too). They pored over all the intelligence gathered by operators, agents, bugs, and taps and looked at samples of a man's handwriting.* The CIA men took the the process of "indirect assessment" one step further than Langer had, however. They observed the target's behavior and looked for revealing patterns that corresponded with traits already recorded among the subjects of the 29,000 Wechsler samples.

Along this line, Gittinger and his staff had a good idea how various personality types acted after consuming a few drinks. Thus, they reasoned, if they watched a guest at a cocktail party and he started to behave in a recognizable way—by withdraw-

---

*Graphology (handwriting analysis) appealed to CIA officials as a way of supplementing PAS assessments or making judgments when only a written letter was available. Graphology was one of the seemingly arcane fields which the Human Ecology Society had investigated and found operational uses for. The Society wound up funding handwriting research and a publication in West Germany where the subject was taken much more seriously than in the United States, and it sponsored a study to compare handwriting analyses with Wechsler scores of actors (including some homosexuals), patients in psychotherapy, criminal psychopaths, and fashion models. Gittinger went on to hire a resident graphologist who could do the same sort of amazing things with handwriting as the Oklahoma psychologist could do with Wechsler scores. One former colleague recalls her spotting—accurately—a stomach ailment in a foreign leader simply by reading one letter. Asked in an interview about how the Agency used her work, she replied, "If they think they can manipulate a person, that's none of my business. I don't know what they do with it. My analysis was not done with that intention. . . . Something I learned very early in government was not to ask questions."

ing, for instance—they could make an educated guess about his personality type—in this case, that he was an I. In contrast, the drunken Russian diplomat who became louder and began pinching every woman who passed by probably was an E. Instead of using the test scores to predict how a person would behave, the assessments staff was, in effect, looking at behavior and working backward to predict how the person would have scored if he had taken the test. The Gittinger staff developed a whole checklist of 30 to 40 patterns that the skilled observer could look for. Each of these traits reflected one of the Wechsler subtests, and it corresponded to some insight picked up from the 29,000 scores in the data base.

Was the target sloppy or neat? Did he relate to women stiffly or easily? How did he hold a cigarette and put it into his mouth? When he went through a receiving line, did he immediately repeat the name of each person introduced to him? Taken as a whole, all these observations allowed Gittinger to make a reasoned estimate about a subject's personality, with emphasis on his vulnerabilities. As Gittinger describes the system, "If you could get a sample of several kinds of situations, you could begin to get some pretty good information." Nevertheless, Gittinger had his doubts about indirect assessment. "I never thought we were good at this," he says.

The TSS assessment staff, along with the Agency's medical office use the PAS indirectly to keep up the OSS tradition of making psychological portraits of world leaders like Hitler. Combining analytical techniques with gossipy intelligence, the assessors tried to give high-level U.S. officials a better idea of what moved the principal international political figures.* One such study of an American citizen spilled over into the legally forbidden domestic area when in 1971 the medical office prepared a profile of Daniel Ellsberg at the request of the White House. To get raw data for the Agency assessors, John Ehrlichman authorized a break-in at Ellsberg's psychiatrist's office in California. John Gittinger vehemently denies that his staff

---

*A profile of Ferdinand Marcos found the Filipino president's massive personal enrichment while in office to be a natural outgrowth of his country's tradition of putting loyalty to one's family and friends ahead of all other considerations. Agency assessors found the Shah of Iran to be a brilliant but dangerous megalomaniac whose problems resulted from an overbearing father, the humiliation of having served as a puppet ruler, and his inability for many years to produce a male heir.

played any role in preparing this profile, which the White House plumbers intended to use as a kind of psychological road map to compromise Ellsberg—just as CIA operators regularly worked from such assessments to exploit the weaknesses of foreigners.

Whether used directly or indirectly, the PAS gave Agency case officers a tool to get a better reading of the people with whom they dealt. CIA field stations overseas routinely sent all their findings on a target, along with indirect assessment checklists, back to Washington, so headquarters personnel could decide whether or not to try recruitment. The TSS assessment staff contributed to this process by attempting to predict what ploys would work best on the man in the case officers' sights. "Our job was to recommend what strategy to try," says a onetime Gittinger colleague. This source states he had direct knowledge of cases where TSS recommendations led to sexual entrapment operations, both hetero- and homosexual. "We had women ready—called them a stable," he says, and they found willing men when they had to.

One CIA psychologist stresses that the PAS only provided "clues" on how to compromise people. "If somebody's assessment came in like the sexual psychopaths', it would raise red flags," he notes. But TSS staff assessors could only conclude that the target had a potentially serious sex problem. They could by no means guarantee that the target's defenses could be broken. Nevertheless, the PAS helped dictate the best weapons for the attack. "I've heard John [Gittinger] say there's always something that someone wants," says another former Agency psychologist. "And with the PAS you can find out what it is. It's not necessarily sex or booze. Sometimes it's status or recognition or security." Yet another Gittinger colleague describes this process as "looking for soft spots." He states that after years of working with the system, he still bridled at a few of the more fiendish ways "to get at people" that his colleagues dreamed up. He stayed on until retirement, however, and he adds, "None of this was personal. It was for national security reasons."

A few years ago, ex-CIA psychologist James Keehner told reporter Maureen Orth that he personally went to New York in 1969 to give Wechsler tests to an American nurse who had volunteered her body for her country. "We wanted her to sleep with this Russian," explained Keehner. "Either the Russian would fall in love with her and defect, or we'd blackmail him.

I had to see if she could sleep with him over a period of time and not get involved emotionally. Boy, was she tough!" Keehner noted that he became disgusted with entrapment techniques, especially after watching a film of an agent in bed with a "recruitment target." He pointed out that Agency case officers, many of whom "got their jollies" from such work, used a hidden camera to get their shots. The sexual technology developed in the MKULTRA safehouses in New York and San Francisco had been put to work. The operation worked no better in the 1960s, however, than TSS officials predicted such activities would a decade earlier. "You don't really recruit agents with sexual blackmail," Keehner concluded. "That's why I couldn't even take reading the files after a while. I was sickened at seeing people take pleasure in other people's inadequacies. First of all, I thought it was just dumb. For all the money going out, nothing ever came back."

Keehner became disgusted by the picking-at-scabs aspect of TSS assessment work. Once the PAS had identified a target as having potential mental instabilities, staff members sometimes suggested ways to break him down, reasoning that by using a ratchetlike approach to put him under increased pressure, they might be able to break the lines that tied him to his country, if not to his sanity. Keehner stated, "I was sent to deal with the most negative aspects of the human condition. It was planned destructiveness. First, you'd check to see if you could destroy a man's marriage. If you could, then that would be enough to put a lot of stress on the individual, to break him down. Then you might start a minor rumor campaign against him. Harass him constantly. Bump his car in traffic. A lot of it is ridiculous, but it may have a cumulative effect." Agency case officers might also use this same sort of stress-producing campaign against a particularly effective enemy intelligence officer whom they knew they could never recruit but whom they hoped to neutralize.

Most operations—including most recruitments—did not rely on such nasty methods. The case officer still benefited from the TSS staff's assessment, but he usually wanted to minimize stress rather than accentuate it. CIA operators tended to agree that the best way to recruit an agent was to make the relationship as productive and satisfying as possible for him, operating from the old adage about catching more flies with honey than vinegar. "You pick the thing most fearful to him—the things which would cause him the most doubt," says the source. "If his greatest fear is that he can't trust you to protect him and his family, you overload your pitch with your ability to do it. Other people need structure, so you tell them exactly what they will need to do. If you leave it open-ended, they'll be scared you'll ask them to do things they're incapable of."*

Soon after the successful recruitment of a foreigner to spy for the CIA, either a CIA staff member or a specially trained case officer normally sat down with the new agent and gave him the full battery of Wechsler subtests—a process that took several hours. The tester never mentioned that the exercise had anything to do with personality but called it an "aptitude" test—which it also is. The assessments office in Washington then analyzed the results. As with the polygraph, the PAS helped tell if the agent were lying. It could often delve deeper than surface concepts of true and false. The PAS might show that the agent's motivations were not in line with his behavior. In that case, if the gap were too great, the case officer could expect to run up against considerable deception—resulting either from espionage motives or psychotic tendencies.

The TSS staff assessors sent a report back to the field on the best way to deal with the new agent and the most effective means to exploit him. They would recommend whether his case officer should treat him sternly or permissively. If the agent were an Externalizer who needed considerable companionship, the assessors might suggest that the case officer try to spend as much time with him as possible.† They would probably recommend against sending this E agent on a long mission

---

*This source reports that case officers usually used this sort of nonthreatening approach and switched to the rougher stuff if the target decided he did not want to spy for the CIA. In that case, says the ex-CIA man, "you don't want the person to say no and run off and tattle. You lose an asset that way—not in the sense of the case officer being shot, but by being nullified." The spurned operator might then offer not to reveal that the target was cheating on his wife or had had a homosexual affair, in return for the target not disclosing the recruitment attempt to his own intelligence service.

†While Agency officials might also have used the PAS to select the right case officer to deal with the E agent—one who would be able to sustain the agent's need for a close relationship over a long period of time—they almost never used the system with this degree of precision. An Agency office outside TSS did keep Wechslers and other test scores on file for most case officers, but the Clandestine Services management was not willing to turn over the selection of American personnel to the psychologists.

into a hostile country, where he could not have the friendly company he craved.

Without any help from John Gittinger or his system, covert operators had long been deciding matters like these, which were, after all, rooted in common sense. Most case officers prided themselves on their ability to play their agents like a musical instrument, at just the right tempo, and the Gittinger system did not shake their belief that nothing could beat their own intuition. Former CIA Deputy Director Ray Cline expresses a common view when he says the PAS "was part of the system—kind of a check-and-balance—a supposedly scientific tool that was not weighed very heavily. I never put as much weight on the psychological assessment reports as on a case officer's view. . . . In the end, people went with their own opinion." Former Director William Colby found the assessment reports particularly useful in smoothing over that "traumatic" period when a case officer had to pass on his agent to a replacement. Understandably, the agent often saw the switch as a danger or a hardship. "The new guy has to show some understanding and sympathy," says Colby, who had 30 years of operational experience himself, "but it doesn't work if these feelings are not real."

For those Agency officers who yearned to remove as much of the human element as possible from agent operations, Gittinger's system was a natural. It reduced behavior to a workable formula of shorthand letters that, while not insightful in all respects, gave a reasonably accurate description of a person. Like Social Security numbers, such formulas fitted well with a computerized approach. While not wanting to overemphasize the Agency's reliance on the PAS, former Director Colby states that the system made dealing with agents "more systematized, more professional."

In 1963 the CIA's Inspector General gave the TSS assessment staff high marks and described how it fit into operations:

> The [Clandestine Services] case officer is first and foremost, perhaps, a practitioner of the art of assessing and exploiting human personality and motivations for ulterior purposes. The ingredients of advanced skill in this art are highly individualistic in nature, including such qualities as perceptiveness and imagination. [The PAS] seeks to enhance the case officer's skill by bringing the methods and disciplines of psychology to bear. . . . The

prime objectives are control, exploitation, or neutralization. These objectives are innately anti-ethical rather than therapeutic in their intent.

In other words, the PAS is directed toward the relationship between the American case officer and his foreign agent, that lies at the heart of espionage. In that sense, it amounts to its own academic discipline—the psychology of spying—complete with axioms and reams of empirical data. The business of the PAS, like that of the CIA, is control.

One former CIA psychologist, who still feels guilty about his participation in certain Agency operations, believes that the CIA's fixation on control and manipulation mirrors, in a more virulent form, the way Americans deal with each other generally. "I don't think the CIA is too far removed from the culture," he says. "It's just a matter of degree. If you put a lot of money out there, there are many people who are lacking the ethics even of the CIA. At least the Agency had an ideological basis." This psychologist believes that the United States has become an extremely control-oriented society—from the classroom to politics to television advertising. Spying and the PAS techniques are unique only in that they are more systematic and secret.

Another TSS scientist believes that the Agency's behavioral research was a logical extension of the efforts of American psychologists, psychiatrists, and sociologists to change behavior—which he calls their "sole motivation." Such people manipulate their subjects in trying to make mentally disturbed people well, in turning criminals into law-abiding citizens, in improving the work of students, and in pushing poor people to get off welfare. The source cites all of these as examples of "behavior modification" for socially acceptable reasons, which, like public attitudes toward spying, change from time to time. "Don't get the idea that all these behavioral scientists were nice and pure, that they didn't want to change anything, and that they were detached in their science," he warns. "They were up to their necks in changing people. It just happened that the things they were interested in were not always the same as what we were." Perhaps the saving grace of the behavioral scientists is summed up by longtime MKULTRA consultant Martin Orne: "We are sufficiently ineffective so that our findings can be published."

With the PAS, CIA officials had a handy tool for social engineering. The Gittinger staff found one use for it in the sensitive area of selecting members of foreign police and intelligence agencies. All over the globe, Agency operators have frequently maintained intimate working relations with security services that have consistently mistreated their own citizens. The assessments staff played a key role in choosing members of the secret police in at least two countries whose human-rights records are among the world's worst.

In 1961, according to TSS psychologist John Winne, the CIA and the Korean government worked together to establish the newly created Korean Central Intelligence Agency (KCIA). The American CIA station in Seoul asked headquarters to send out an assessor to "select the initial cadre" of the KCIA. Off went Winne on temporary duty. "I set up an office with two translators," he recalls, "and used a Korean version of the Wechsler." The Agency psychologist gave the tests to 25 to 30 police and military officers and wrote up a half-page report on each, listing their strengths and weaknesses. Winne wanted to know about each candidate's "ability to follow orders, creativity, lack of personality disorders, motivation—why he wanted out of his current job. It was mostly for the money, especially with the civilians." The test results went to the Korean authorities, whom Winne believes made the personnel decisions "in conjunction with our operational people."

"We would do a job like this and never get feedback, so we were never sure we'd done a good job," Winne complains. Sixteen years after the end of his mission to Seoul and after news of KCIA repression at home and bribes to American congressmen abroad, Winne feels that his best efforts had "boomeranged." He states that Tongsun Park was not one of the KCIA men he tested.

In 1966 CIA staffers, including Gittinger himself, took part in selecting members of an equally controversial police unit in Uruguay—the anti-terrorist section that fought the Tupamaro urban guerrillas. According to John Cassidy, the CIA's deputy station chief there at the time, Agency operators worked to set up this special force together with the Agency for International Development's Public Safety Mission (whose members included Dan Mitrione, later kidnapped and killed by the Tupamaros). The CIA-assisted police claimed they were in a life-and-death struggle against the guerrillas, and they used incredibly brutal methods, including torture, to stamp out most of the Uruguayan left along with the guerrillas.

While the special police were being organized, "John [Gittinger] came down for three days to get the program underway," recalls Cassidy. Then Hans Greiner, a Gittinger associate, ran Wechslers on 20 Uruguayan candidates. One question on the information subtest was "How many weeks in the year?" Eighteen of the 20 said it was 48, and only one man got the answer right. (Later he was asked about his answer, and he said he had made a mistake; he meant 48.) But when Greiner asked this same group of police candidates, "Who wrote *Faust?*" 18 of the 20 knew it was Goethe. "This tells you something about the culture," notes Cassidy, who served the Agency all over Latin America. It also points up the difficulty Gittinger had in making the PAS work across cultural lines.

In any case, CIA man Cassidy found the assessment process most useful for showing how to train the anti-terrorist section. "According to the results, these men were shown to have very dependent psychologies and they needed strong direction," recalls the now-retired operator. Cassidy was quite pleased with the contribution Gittinger and Greiner made. "For years I had been dealing with Latin Americans," says Cassidy, "and here, largely by psychological tests, one of [Gittinger's] men was able to analyze people he had no experience with and give me some insight into them. . . . Ordinarily, we would have just selected the men and gone to work on them."

In helping countries like South Korea and Uruguay pick their secret police, TSS staff members often inserted a devilish twist with the PAS. They could not only choose candidates who would make good investigators, interrogators, or whatever, but they could also spot those who were most likely to succumb to future CIA blandishments. "Certain types were more recruitable," states a former assessor. "I looked for them when I wrote my reports. . . . Anytime the Company [the CIA] spent money for training a foreigner, the object was that he would ultimately serve our control purposes." Thus, CIA officials were not content simply to work closely with these foreign intelligence agencies; they insisted on penetrating them, and the PAS provided a useful aid.

In 1973 John Gittinger and his longtime associate John Winne, who picked KCIA men, published a basic description of the

PAS in a professional journal. Although others had written publicly about the system, this article apparently disturbed some of the Agency's powers, who were then cutting back on the number of CIA employees at the order of short-time Director James Schlesinger.

Shortly thereafter, Gittinger, then 56, stopped being president of Psychological Assessment Associates but stayed on as a consultant. In 1974 I wrote about Gittinger's work, albeit incompletely, in *Rolling Stone* magazine. Gittinger was disturbed that disclosure of his CIA connection would hurt his professional reputation. "Are we tarred by a brush because we worked for the CIA?" he asked during one of several rather emotional exchanges. "I'm proud of it." He saw no ethical problems in "looking for people's weaknesses" if it helped the CIA obtain information, and he declared that for many years most Americans thought this was a useful process. At first, he offered to give me the Wechsler tests and prepare a personality assessment to explain the system, but Agency officials prohibited his doing so. "I was given no explanation," said the obviously disappointed Gittinger. "I'm very proud of my professional work, and I had looked forward to being able to explain it."

In August 1977 Gittinger publicly testified in Senate hearings. While he obviously would have preferred talking about his psychological research, his most persistent questioner, Senator Edward Kennedy, was much more interested in bringing out sensational details about prostitutes and drug testing. A proud man, Gittinger felt "humiliated" by the experience, which ended with him looking foolish on national television. The next month, the testimony of his former associate, David Rhodes, further bruised Gittinger. Rhodes told the Kennedy subcommittee about Gittinger's role in leading the "Gang that Couldn't Spray Straight" in an abortive attempt to test LSD in aerosol cans on unwitting subjects. Gittinger does not want his place in history to be determined by this kind of activity. He would like to see his Personality Assessment System accepted as an important contribution to science.

Tired of the controversy and worn down by trying to explain the PAS, Gittinger has moved back to his native Oklahoma. He took a copy of the 29,000 Wechsler results with him, but he has lost his ardor for working with them. A handful of psychologists around the country still swear by the system and try to pass it on to others. One, who uses it in private practice, says that in therapy it saves six months in understanding the patient. This psychologist takes a full reading of his patient's personality with the PAS, and then he varies his treatment to fit the person's problems. He believes that most American psychologists and psychiatrists treat their patients the same, whereas the PAS is designed to identify the differences between people. Gittinger very much hopes that others will accept this view and move his system into the mainstream. "It means nothing unless I can get someone else to work on it," he declares. Given the preconceptions of the psychological community, the inevitable taint arising from the CIA's role in developing the system, and Gittinger's lack of academic credentials and energy, his wish will probably not be fulfilled.

CHAPTER
11
HYPNOSIS

No mind-control technique has more captured popular imagination—and kindled fears—than hypnosis. Men have long dreamed they could use overwhelming hypnotic powers to compel others to do their bidding. And when CIA officials institutionalized that dream in the early Cold War Days, they tried, like modern-day Svengalis, to use hypnosis to force their favors on unwitting victims.

One group of professional experts, as well as popular novelists, argued that hypnosis would lead to major breakthroughs in spying. Another body of experts believed the opposite. The Agency men, who did not fully trust the academics anyway, listened to both points of view and kept looking for applications which fit their own special needs. To them, hypnosis offered too much promise not to be pursued, but finding the answers was such an elusive and dangerous process that 10 years after the program started CIA officials were still searching for practical uses.

The CIA's first behavioral research czar, Morse Allen of AR-TICHOKE, was intrigued by hypnosis. He read everything he could get his hands on, and in 1951 he went to New York for a four-day course from a well-known stage hypnotist. This hypnotist had taken the Svengali legend to heart, and he bombarded Allen with tales of how he used hypnosis to seduce young women. He told the ARTICHOKE chief that he had convinced one mesmerized lady that he was her husband and that she desperately wanted him. That kind of deception has a place in covert operations, and Morse Allen was sufficiently impressed to report back to his bosses the hypnotist's claim that "he spent approximately five nights a week away from home engaging in sexual intercourse."

Apart from the bragging, the stage hypnotist did give Morse Allen a short education in how to capture a subject's attention and induce a trance. Allen returned to Washington more convinced than ever of the benefits of working hypnosis into the ARTICHOKE repertory and of the need to build a defense against it. With permission from above, he decided to take his hypnosis studies further, right in his own office. He asked young CIA secretaries to stay after work and ran them through the hypnotic paces—proving to his own satisfaction that he could make them do whatever he wanted. He had secretaries steal SECRET files and pass them on to total strangers, thus violating the most basic CIA security rules. He got them to steal from each other and to start fires. He made one of them report to the bedroom of a strange man and then go into a deep sleep. "This activity clearly indicates that individuals under hypnosis might be compromised and blackmailed," Allen wrote.

On February 19, 1954, Morse Allen simulated the ultimate experiment in hypnosis: the creation of a "Manchurian Candidate," or programmed assassin. Allen's "victim" was a secretary whom he put into a deep trance and told to keep sleeping until he ordered otherwise. He then hypnotized a second secretary and told her that if she could not wake up her friend, "her rage would be so great that she would not hesitate to 'kill.' " Allen left a pistol nearby, which the secretary had no way of knowing was unloaded. Even though she had earlier expressed a fear of firearms of any kind, she picked up the gun and "shot" her sleeping friend. After Allen brought the "killer" out of her trance, she had apparent amnesia for the event, denying she would ever shoot anyone.

With this experiment, Morse Allen took the testing as far as he could on a make-believe basis, but he was neither satisfied nor convinced that hypnosis would produce such spectacular results in an operational setting. All he felt he had proved was that an impressionable young volunteer would accept a command from a legitimate authority figure to take an action she may have sensed would not end in tragedy. She presumably trusted the CIA enough as an institution and Morse Allen as an individual to believe he would not let her do anything wrong.

The experimental setting, in effect, legitimated her behavior and prevented it from being truly antisocial.

Early in 1954, Allen almost got his chance to try the crucial test. According to a CIA document, the subject was to be a 35-year-old, well-educated foreigner who had once worked for a friendly secret service, probably the CIA itself. He had now shifted his loyalty to another government, and the CIA was quite upset with him. The Agency plan was to hypnotize him and program him into making an assassination attempt. He would then be arrested at the least for attempted murder and "thereby disposed of." The scenario had several holes in it, as the operators presented it to the ARTICHOKE team. First, the subject was to be involuntary and unwitting, and as yet no one had come up with a consistently effective way of hypnotizing such people. Second, the ARTICHOKE team would have only limited custody of the subject, who was to be snatched from a social event. Allen understood that it would probably take months of painstaking work to prepare the man for a sophisticated covert operation. The subject was highly unlikely to perform after just one command. Yet, so anxious were the ARTICHOKE men to try the experiment that they were willing to go ahead even under these unfavorable conditions: "The final answer was that in view of the fact that successful completion of this proposed act of attempted assassination was insignificant to the overall project; to wit, whether it was even carried out or not, that under 'crash conditions' and appropriate authority from Headquarters, the ARTICHOKE team *would* undertake the problem in spite of the operational limitations."

This operation never took place. Eager to be unleashed, Morse Allen kept requesting prolonged access to operational subjects, such as the double agents and defectors on whom he was allowed to work a day or two. Not every double agent would do. The candidate had to be among the one person in five who made a good hypnotic subject, and he needed to have a dissociative tendency to separate part of his personality from the main body of his consciousness. The hope was to take an existing ego state—such as an imaginary childhood playmate—and build it into a separate personality, unknown to the first. The hypnotist would communicate directly with this schizophrenic offshoot and command it to carry out specific deeds about which the main personality would know nothing. There would be inevitable leakage between the two personalities, particularly in dreams; but if the hypnotist were clever enough, he could build in cover stories and safety valves which would prevent the subject from acting inconsistently.

All during the spring and summer of 1954, Morse Allen lobbied for permission to try what he called "terminal experiments" in hypnosis, including one along the following scenario:

CIA officials would recruit an agent in a friendly foreign country where the Agency could count on the cooperation of the local police force. CIA case officers would train the agent to pose as a leftist and report on the local communist party. During training, a skilled hypnotist would hypnotize him under the guise of giving him medical treatment (the favorite ARTICHOKE cover for hypnosis). The hypnotist would then provide the agent with information and tell him to forget it all when he snapped out of the trance. Once the agent had been properly conditioned and prepared, he would be sent into action as a CIA spy. Then Agency officials would tip off the local police that the man was a dangerous communist agent, and he would be arrested. Through their liaison arrangement with the police, Agency case officers would be able to watch and even guide the course of the interrogation. In this way, they could answer many of their questions about hypnosis on a live guinea pig who believed his life was in danger. Specifically, the men from ARTICHOKE wanted to know how well hypnotic amnesia held up against torture. Could the amnesia be broken with drugs? One document noted that the Agency could even send in a new hypnotist to try his hand at cracking through the commands of the first one. Perhaps the most cynical part of the whole scheme came at the end of the proposal: "In the event that the agent should break down and admit his connection with US intelligence, we a) deny this absolutely and advise the agent's disposal, or b) indicate that the agent may have been dispatched by some other organ of US intelligence and that we should thereafter run the agent jointly with [the local intelligence service]."

An ARTICHOKE team was scheduled to carry out field tests along these lines in the summer of 1954. The planning got to an advanced stage, with the ARTICHOKE command center in Washington cabling overseas for the "time, place, and bodies available for terminal experiments." Then another cable complained of the "diminishing numbers" of subjects available for these tests. At this point, the available record becomes very fuzzy. The minutes of an ARTICHOKE working group meeting indicate that a key Agency official—probably the station chief in the country where the experiments were going to take place —had second thoughts. One participant at the meeting, obviously rankled by the obstructionism, said if this nay-sayer did not change his attitude, ARTICHOKE officials would have the Director himself order the official to go along.

Although short-term interrogations of unwitting subjects with drugs and hypnosis (the "A" treatment) continued, the more complicated tests apparently never did get going under the ARTICHOKE banner. By the end of the year, 1954, Allen Dulles took the behavioral-research function away from Morse Allen and gave it to Sid Gottlieb and the men from MKULTRA. Allen had directly pursued the goal of creating a Manchurian Candidate, which he clearly believed was possible. MKULTRA officials were just as interested in finding ways to assert control over people, but they had much less faith in the frontal-assault approach pushed by Allen. For them, finding the Manchurian Candidate became a figurative exercise. They did not give up the dream. They simply pursued it in smaller steps, always hoping to increase the percentages in their favor. John Gittinger, the MKULTRA case officer on hypnosis, states, "Predictable absolute control is not possible on a particular individual. Any psychologist, psychiatrist, or preacher can get control over certain kinds of individuals, but that's not a predictable, definite thing." Gittinger adds that despite his belief to this effect, he felt he had to give "a fair shake" to people who wanted to try out ideas to the contrary.

Gottlieb and his colleagues had already been doing hypnosis research for two years. They did a few basic experiments in the office, as Morse Allen did, but they farmed out most of the work to a young Ph.D. candidate at the University of Minnesota, Alden Sears. Sears, who later moved his CIA study project to the University of Denver, worked with student subjects to define the nature of hypnosis. Among many other things, he looked into several of the areas that would be building blocks in the creation of a Manchurian Candidate. Could a hypnotist induce a totally separate personality? Could a subject be sent on missions he would not remember unless cued by the hypnotist? Sears, who has since become a Methodist minister, refused to talk about methods he experimented with to build second identities.* By 1957, he wrote that the experiments that needed to be done "could not be handled in the University situation." Unlike Morse Allen, he did not want to perform the terminal experiments.

Milton Kline, a New York psychologist who says he also did not want to cross the ethical line but is sure the intelligence agencies have, served as an unpaid consultant to Sears and other CIA hypnosis research. Nothing Sears or others found disabused him of the idea that the Manchurian Candidate is possible. "It cannot be done by everyone," says Kline, "It cannot be done consistently, but it can be done."

A onetime president of the American Society for Clinical and Experimental Hypnosis, Kline was one of many outside experts to whom Gittinger and his colleagues talked. Other consultants, with equally impressive credentials, rejected Kline's views. In no other area of the behavioral sciences was there so little accord on basic questions. "You could find an expert who would agree with everything," says Gittinger. "Therefore, we tried to get everybody."

The MKULTRA men state that they got too many unsolicited suggestions on how to use hypnosis in covert operations. "The operators would ask us for easy solutions," recalls a veteran. "We therefore kept a laundry list of why they couldn't have what they wanted. We spent a lot of time telling some young kid whose idea we had heard a hundred times why it wouldn't work. We would wind up explaining why you couldn't have a free lunch." This veteran mentions an example: CIA operators put a great deal of time and money into servicing "dead drops" (covert mail pickup points, such as a hollow tree) in the Soviet Union. If a collector was captured, he was likely to give away the locations. Therefore Agency men suggested that TSS find a way to hypnotize these secret mailmen, so they could withstand interrogation and even torture if arrested.

Morse Allen had wanted to perform the "terminal experiment" to see if a hypnotically induced amnesia would stand up to torture. Gittinger says that as far as he knows, this experi-

*Sears still maintains the fiction that he thought he was dealing only with a private foundation, the Geschickter Fund, and that he knew nothing of the CIA involvement in funding his work. Yet a CIA document in his MKULTRA subproject says he was "aware of the real purpose" of the project." Moreover, Sid Gottlieb brought him to Washington in 1954 to demonstrate hypnosis to a select group of Agency officials.

ment was never carried out. "I still like to think we were human beings enough that this was not something we played with," says Gittinger. Such an experiment could have been performed, as Allen suggested, by friendly police in a country like Taiwan or Paraguay. CIA men did at least discuss joint work in hypnosis with a foreign secret service in 1962.* Whether they went further simply cannot be said.

Assuming the amnesia would hold, the MKULTRA veteran says the problem was how to trigger it. Perhaps the Russian phrase meaning "You're under arrest" could be used as a pre-programmed cue, but what if the police did not use these words as they captured the collector? Perhaps the physical sensation of handcuffs being snapped on could do it, but a metal watch-band could have the same effect. According to the veteran, in the abstract, the scheme sounded fine, but in practicality, a foolproof way of triggering the amnesia could not be found. "You had to accept that when someone is caught, they're going to tell some things," he says.

MKULTRA officials, including Gittinger, did recommend the use of hypnosis in operational experiments on at least one occasion. In 1959 an important double agent, operating outside his homeland, told his Agency case officer that he was afraid to go home again because he did not think he could withstand the tough interrogation that his government used on returning overseas agents. In Washington, the operators approached the TSS men about using hypnosis, backed up with drugs, to change the agent's attitude. They hoped they could instill in him the "ability or the necessary will" to hold up under questioning.

An MKULTRA official—almost certainly Gittinger—held a series of meetings over a two-week period with the operators and wrote that the agent was "a better than average" hypnotic subject, but that his goal was to get out of intelligence work: The agent "probably can be motivated to make at least one return visit to his homeland by application of any one of a

---

*Under my Freedom of Information suit, the CIA specifically denied access to the documents concerning the testing of hypnosis and psychedelic drugs in cooperation with foreign intelligence agencies. The justification given was that releasing such documents would reveal intelligence sources and methods, which are exempted by law. The hypnosis experiment was never carried out, according to the generic description of the document which the Agency had to provide in explaining why it had to be withheld.

number of techniques, including hypnosis, but he may redefect in the process." The MKULTRA official continued that hypnosis probably could not produce an "operationally useful" degree of amnesia for the events of the recent past or for the hypnotic treatment itself that the agent "probably has the native ability to withstand ordinary interrogation . . . provided it is to his advantage to do so."

The MKULTRA office recommended that despite the relatively negative outlook for the hypnosis, the Agency should proceed anyway. The operation had the advantage of having a "fail-safe" mechanism because the level of hypnosis could be tested out before the agent actually had to return. Moreover, the MKULTRA men felt "that a considerable amount of useful experience can be gained from this operation which could be used to improve Agency capability in future applications." In effect, they would be using hypnosis not as the linchpin of the operation, but as an adjunct to help motivate the agent.

Since the proposed operation involved the use of hypnosis and drugs, final approval could only be given by the high-level Clandestine Services committee set up for this purpose and chaired by Richard Helms. Permission was not forthcoming.

In June 1960 TSS officials launched an expanded program of operational experiments in hypnosis in cooperation with the Agency's Counterintelligence Staff. The legendary James Angleton—the prototype for the title character Saxonton in Aaron Latham's *Orchids for Mother* and for Wellington in Victor Marchetti's *The Rope Dancer*—headed Counterintelligence, which took on some of the CIA's most sensitive missions (including the illegal Agency spying against domestic dissidents). Counterintelligence officials wrote that the hypnosis program could provide a "potential breakthrough in clandestine technology." Their arrangement with TSS was that the MKULTRA men would develop the technique in the laboratory, while they took care of "field experimentation."

The Counterintelligence program had three goals: (1) to induce hypnosis very rapidly in unwitting subjects; (2) to create durable amnesia; and (3) to implant durable and operationally useful posthypnotic suggestion. The Agency released no information on any "field experimentation" of the latter two goals, which of course are the building blocks of the Manchurian Candidate. Agency officials provided only one heavily censored document on the first goal, rapid induction.

In October 1960 the MKULTRA program invested $9,000 in an outside consultant to develop a way of quickly hypnotizing an unwitting subject. John Gittinger says the process consisted of surprising "somebody sitting in a chair, putting your hands on his forehead, and telling the guy to go to sleep." The method worked "fantastically" on certain people, including some on whom no other technique was effective, and not on others. "It wasn't that predictable," notes Gittinger, who states he knows nothing about the field testing.

The test, noted in that one released document, did not take place until July 1963—a full three years after the Counterintelligence experimental program began, during which interval the Agency is claiming that no other field experiments took place. According to a CIA man who participated in this test, the Counterintelligence Staff in Washington asked the CIA station in Mexico City to find a suitable candidate for a rapid induction experiment. The station proposed a low-level agent, whom the Soviets had apparently doubled. A Counterintelligence man flew in from Washington and a hypnotic consultant arrived from California. Our source and a fellow case officer brought the agent to a motel room on a pretext. "I puffed him up with his importance," says the Agency man. "I said the bosses wanted to see him and of course give him more money." Waiting in an adjoining room was the hypnotic consultant. At a prearranged time, the two case officers gently grabbed hold of the agent and tipped his chair over until the back was touching the floor. The consultant was supposed to rush in at that precise moment and apply the technique. Nothing happened. The consultant froze, unable to do the deed. "You can imagine what we had to do to cover-up," says the official, who was literally left holding the agent. "We explained we had heard a noise, got excited, and tipped him down to protect him. He was so grubby for money he would have believed any excuse."

There certainly is a huge difference between the limited aim of this bungled operation and one aimed at building a Manchurian Candidate. The MKULTRA veteran maintains that he and his colleagues were not interested in a programmed assassin because they knew in general it would not work and, specifically, that they could not exert total control. "If you have one hundred percent control, you have one hundred percent dependency," he says. "If something happens and you haven't programmed it in, you've got a problem. If you try to put flexibility in, you lose control. To the extent you let the agent choose, you don't have control." He admits that he and his colleagues spent hours running the arguments on the Manchurian Candidate back and forth. "Castro was naturally our discussion point," he declares. "Could you get somebody gung-ho enough that they would go in and get him?" In the end, he states, they decided there were more reliable ways to kill people. "You can get exactly the same thing from people who are hypnotizable by many other ways, and you can't get anything out of people who are not hypnotizable, so it has no use," says Gittinger.

The only real gain in employing a hypnotized killer would be, in theory, that he would not remember who ordered him to pull the trigger. Yet, at least in the Castro case, the Cuban leader already knew who was after him. Moreover, there were plenty of people around willing to take on the Castro contract. "A well-trained person could do it without all this mumbo-jumbo," says the MKULTRA veteran. By going to the Mafia for hitmen, CIA officials in any case found killers who had a built-in amnesia mechanism that had nothing to do with hypnosis.*

The MKULTRA veteran gives many reasons why he believes the CIA never actually tried a Manchurian Candidate operation, but he acknowledges that he does not know.† If the ultimate experiments were performed, they would have been handled with incredible secrecy. It would seem, however, that the same kind of reasoning that impelled Sid Gottlieb to recommend testing powerful drugs on unwitting subjects would have led to experimentation along such lines, if not to create the Manchurian Candidate itself, on some of the building blocks,

---

*Referring to this CIA–mob relationship, author Robert Sam Anson has written, "It was inevitable: Gentlemen wishing to be killers gravitated to killers wishing to be gentlemen."

†The veteran admits that none of the arguments he uses against a conditioned assassin would apply to a programmed "patsy" whom a hypnotist could walk through a series of seemingly unrelated events—a visit to a store, a conversation with a mailman, picking a fight at a political rally. The subject would remember everything that happened to him and be amnesic only for the fact the hypnotist ordered him to do these things. There would be no gaping inconsistency in his life of the sort that can ruin an attempt by a hypnotist to create a second personality. The purpose of this exercise is to leave a circumstantial trail that will make the authorities think the patsy committed a particular crime. The weakness might well be that the amnesia would not hold up under police interrogation, but that would not matter if the police did not believe his preposterous story about being hypnotized or if he were shot resisting arrest. Hypnosis expert Milton Kline says he could create a patsy in three months; an assassin would take him six.

or lesser antisocial acts. Even if the MKULTRA men did not think hypnosis would work operationally, they had not let that consideration prevent them from trying out numerous other techniques. The MKULTRA chief could even have used a defensive rationale: He had to find out if the Russians could plant a "sleeper" killer in our midst, just as Richard Condon's novel discussed.

If the assassin scenario seemed exaggerated, Gottlieb still would have wanted to know what other uses the Russians might try. Certainly, he could have found relatively "expendable" subjects, as he and Morse Allen had for other behavior-control experiments. And even if the MKULTRA men really did restrain themselves, it is unlikely that James Angleton and his counterintelligence crew would have acted in such a limited fashion when they felt they were on the verge of a "breakthrough in clandestine technology."

PART

IV
CONCLUSIONS

I'm a professional and I just don't talk about these things. Lots of things are not fit for the public. This has nothing to do with democracy. It has to do with common sense. —GRATION H. YASETEVITCH, 1978 (explaining why he did not want to be interviewed for this book)

To hope that the power that is being made available by the behavioral sciences will be exercised by the scientists, or by a benevolent group, seems to me to be a hope little supported by either recent or distant history. It seems far more likely that behavioral scientists, holding their present attitudes, will be in the position of the German rocket scientists specializing in guided missiles. First they worked devotedly for Hitler to destroy the USSR and the United States. Now, depending on who captured them they work devotedly for the USSR in the interest of destroying the United States, or devotedly for the United States in the interest of destroying the USSR. If behavioral scientists are concerned solely with advancing their science, it seems most probable that they will serve the purpose of whatever group has the power. —CARL ROGERS, 1961

CHAPTER
12
THE SEARCH
FOR THE TRUTH

Sid Gottlieb was one of many CIA officials who tried to find a way to assassinate Fidel Castro. Castro survived, of course, and his victory over the Agency in April 1961 at the Bay of Pigs put the Agency in the headlines for the first time, in a very unfavorable light. Among the fiasco's many consequences was Gottlieb's loss of the research part of the CIA's behavior-control programs. Still, he and the others kept trying to kill Castro.

In the aftermath of the Bay of Pigs, President Kennedy reportedly vowed to splinter the CIA into a thousand pieces. In the end, he settled for firing Allen Dulles and his top deputies. To head the Agency, which lost none of its power, Kennedy brought in John McCone, a defense contractor and former head of the Atomic Energy Commission. With no operational background, McCone had a different notion than Dulles of how to manage the CIA, particularly in the scientific area. "McCone never felt akin to the covert way of doing things," recalls Ray Cline, whom the new Director made his Deputy for Intelligence. McCone apparently believed that science should be in the hands of the scientists, not the clandestine operators, and he brought in a fellow Californian, an aerospace "whiz kid" named Albert "Bud" Wheelon to head a new Agency Directorate for Science and Technology.

Before then, the Technical Services Staff (TSS), although located in the Clandestine Services, had been the Agency's largest scientific component. McCone decided to strip TSS of its main research functions—including the behavioral one—and let it concentrate solely on providing operational support. In 1962 he approved a reorganization of TSS that brought in Seymour Russell, a tough covert operator, as the new chief. "The idea was to get a close interface with operations," recalls an ex-CIA man. Experienced TSS technicians remained as deputies to the incoming field men, and the highest deputyship in all TSS went to Sid Gottlieb, who became number-two man under Russell. For Gottlieb, this was another significant promotion helped along by his old friend Richard Helms, whom McCone had elevated to be head of the Clandestine Services.

In his new job, Gottlieb kept control of MKULTRA. Yet, in order to comply with McCone's command on research programs, Gottlieb had to preside over the partial dismantling of his own program. The loss was not as difficult as it might have been, because, after 10 years of exploring the frontiers of the mind, Gottlieb had a clear idea of what worked and what did not in the behavioral field. Those areas that still were in the research stage tended to be extremely esoteric and technical, and Gottlieb must have known that if the Science Directorate scored any breakthroughs, he would be brought back into the picture immediately to apply the advances to covert operations.

"Sid was not the kind of bureaucrat who wanted to hold on to everything at all costs," recalls an admiring colleague. Gottlieb carefully pruned the MKULTRA lists, turning over to the Science Directorate the exotic subjects that showed no short-term operational promise and keeping for himself those psychological, chemical, and biological programs that had already passed the research stage. As previously stated, he moved John Gittinger and the personality-assessment staff out of the Human Ecology Society and kept them under TSS control in their own proprietary company.

While Gottlieb was effecting these changes, his programs were coming under attack from another quarter. In 1963 the CIA Inspector General did the study that led to the suspension of unwitting drug testing in the San Francisco and New York safehouses. This was a blow to Gottlieb, who clearly intended to hold on to *this* kind of research. At the same time, the Inspector General also recommended that Agency officials draft a new charter for the whole MKULTRA program, which still was exempt from most internal CIA controls. He found that many of the MKULTRA subprojects were of "insufficient sensitivity" to justify bypassing the Agency's normal procedures for approving and storing records of highly classified programs. Richard Helms, still the protector of unfettered behavioral research, responded by agreeing that there should be a new charter—on the condition that it be almost the same as the old one. "The basic reasons for requesting waiver of standardized administrative controls over these sensitive activities are as valid today as they were in April, 1953," Helms wrote. Helms agreed to such changes as having the CIA Director briefed on the programs twice a year, but he kept the approval process within his control and made sure that all the files would be retained inside TSS. And as government officials so often do when they do not wish to alter anything of substance, he proposed a new name for the activity. In June 1964 MKULTRA became MKSEARCH.*

Gottlieb acknowledged that security did not require transferring all the surviving MKULTRA subprojects over to MKSEARCH. He moved 18 subprojects back into regular Agency funding channels, including ones dealing with the sneezing powders, stink bombs, and other "harassment substances." TSS officials had encouraged the development of these as a way to make a target physically uncomfortable and hence to cause short-range changes in his behavior.

Other MKULTRA subprojects dealt with ways to maximize stress on whole societies. Just as Gittinger's Personality Assessment System provided a psychological road map for exploiting an individual's weaknesses, CIA "destabilization" plans provided guidelines for destroying the internal integrity of target countries like Castro's Cuba or Allende's Chile. Control— whether of individuals or nations—has been the Agency's main business, and TSS officials supplied tools for the "macro" as well as the "micro" attacks.

For example, under MKULTRA Subproject #143, the Agency gave Dr. Edward Bennett of the University of Houston about $20,000 a year to develop bacteria to sabotage petroleum pro-

---

*At 1977 Senate hearings, CIA Director Stansfield Turner summed up some of MKULTRA's accomplishments over its 11-year existence: The program contracted out work to 80 institutions, which included 44 colleges or universities, 15 research facilities or private companies, 12 hospitals or clinics, and 3 penal institutions. I estimate that MKULTRA cost the taxpayers somewhere in the neighborhood of $10 million.

ducts. Bennett found a substance that, when added to oil, fouled or destroyed any engine into which it was poured. CIA operators used exactly this kind of product in 1967 when they sent a sabotage team made up of Cuban exiles into France to pollute a shipment of lubricants bound for Cuba. The idea was that the tainted oil would "grind out motors and cause breakdowns," says an Agency man directly involved. This operation, which succeeded, was part of a worldwide CIA effort that lasted through the 1960s into the 1970s to destroy the Cuban economy.* Agency officials reasoned, at least in the first years, that it would be easier to overthrow Castro if Cubans could be made unhappy with their standard of living. "We wanted to keep bread out of the stores so people were hungry," says the CIA man who was assigned to anti-Castro operations. "We wanted to keep rationing in effect and keep leather out, so people got only one pair of shoes every 18 months."

Leaving this broader sort of program out of the new structure, Gottlieb regrouped the most sensitive behavioral activities under the MKSEARCH umbrella. He chose to continue seven projects, and the ones he picked give a good indication of those parts of MKULTRA that Gottlieb considered important enough to save. These included none of the sociological studies, nor the search for a truth drug. Gottlieb put the emphasis on chemical and biological substances—not because he thought these could be used to turn men into robots, but because he valued them for their predictable ability to disorient, discredit, injure, or kill people. He kept active two private labs to produce such substances, funded consultants who had secure ways to

---

*This economic sabotage program started in 1961, and the chain of command "ran up to the President," according to Kennedy adviser Richard Goodwin. On the CIA side, Agency Director John McCone "was very strong on it," says his former deputy Ray Cline. Cline notes that McCone had the standing orders to all CIA stations abroad rewritten to include "a sentence or two" authorizing a continuing program to disrupt the Cuban economy. Cuba's trade thus became a standing target for Agency operators, and with the authority on the books, CIA officials apparently never went back to the White House for renewed approval after Kennedy died, in Cline's opinion. Three former Assistant Secretaries of State in the Johnson and Nixon administrations say the sabotage, which included everything from driving down the price of Cuban sugar to tampering with cane-cutting equipment, was not brought to their attention. Former CIA Director William Colby states that the Agency finally stopped the economic sabotage program in the early 1970s. Cuban government officials counter that CIA agents were still working to create epidemics among Cuban cattle in 1973 and that as of spring 1978, Agency men were committing acts of sabotage against cargo destined for Cuba.

test them and ready access to subjects, and maintained a funding conduit to pass money on to these other contractors. Here are the seven surviving MKSEARCH subprojects:

• First on the TSS list was the safehouse program for drug testing run by George White and others in the Federal Bureau of Narcotics. Even in 1964, Gottlieb and Helms had not given up hope that unwitting experiments could be resumed, and the Agency paid out $30,000 that year to keep the safehouses open. In the meantime, something was going on at the "pad"—or at least George White kept on sending the CIA vouchers for unorthodox expenses—$1,100 worth in February 1965 alone under the old euphemism for prostitutes, "undercover agents for operations." What White was doing with or to these agents cannot be said, but he kept the San Francisco operation active right up until the time it finally closed in June. Gottlieb did not give up on the New York safehouse until the following year.*

• MKSEARCH Subproject #2 involved continuing a $150,000-a-year contract with a Baltimore biological laboratory. This lab, run by at least one former CIA germ expert, gave TSS "a quick-delivery capability to meet anticipated future operational needs," according to an Agency document. Among other things, it provided a private place for "large-scale production of microorganisms." The Agency was paying the Army Biological Laboratory at Fort Detrick about $100,000 a year for the same services. With its more complete facilities, Fort Detrick could be used to create and package more esoteric bacteria, but Gottlieb seems to have kept the Baltimore facility going in order to have a way of producing biological weapons without the Army's germ warriors knowing about it. This secrecy-within-in-secrecy was not unusual when TSS men were dealing with subjects as sensitive as infecting targets with diseases. Except on the most general level, no written records were kept on the

---

*In 1967 a Senate committee chaired by Senator Edward Long was inquiring into wiretapping by government agencies, including the Narcotics Bureau. The Commissioner of Narcotics, then Harry Giordano told a senior TSS man—almost certainly Gottlieb—that if CIA officials were "concerned" about its dealings with the Bureau involving the safehouses coming out during the hearings, the most "helpful thing" they could do would be to "turn the Long committee off." How the CIA men reacted to this not very subtle blackmail attempt is unclear from the documents, but what does come out is that the TSS man and another top-level CIA officer misled and lied to the top echelon of the Treasury Department (the Narcotics Bureau's parent organization) about the safehouses and how they were used.

subject. Whenever an operational unit in the Agency asked TSS about obtaining a biological weapon, Gottlieb or his aides automatically turned down the request unless the head of the Clandestine Services had given his prior approval. Gottlieb handled these operational needs personally, and during the early 1960s (when CIA assassination attempts probably were at their peak) even Gottlieb's boss, the TSS chief, was not told what was happening.

• With his biological arsenal assured, Gottlieb also secured his chemical flank in MKSEARCH. Another subproject continued a relationship set up in 1959 with a prominent industrialist who headed a complex of companies, including one that custom-manufactured rare chemicals for pharmaceutical producers. This man, whom on several occasions CIA officials gave $100 bills to pay for his products, was able to perform specific lab jobs for the Agency without consulting with his board of directors. In 1960 he supplied the Agency with 3 kilos (6.6 pounds) of a deadly carbamate—the same poison OSS's Stanley Lovell tried to use against Hitler.* This company president also was useful to the Agency because he was a ready source of information on what was going on in the chemical world. The chemical services he offered, coupled with his biological counterpart, gave the CIA the means to wage "instant" chemical and biological attacks—a capability that was frequently used, judging by the large numbers of receipts and invoices that the CIA released under the Freedom of Information Act.

• With new chemicals and drugs constantly coming to their attention through their continuing relations with the major pharmaceutical companies, TSS officials needed places to test them, particularly after the safehouses closed. Dr. James Hamilton, the San Francisco psychiatrist who worked with George White in the original OSS marijuana days, provided a way. He became MKSEARCH Subproject #3.

Hamilton had joined MKULTRA in its earliest days and had been used as a West Coast supervisor for Gottlieb and company. Hamilton was one of the renaissance men of the program, working on everything from psychochemicals to kinky sex to carbon-dioxide inhalation. By the early 1960s, he had arranged

---

*James Moore of the University of Delaware, who also produced carbamates when he was not seeking the magic mushroom, served at times as an intermediary between the industrialist and the CIA.

to get access to prisoners at the California Medical Facility at Vacaville.* Hamilton worked through a nonprofit research institute connected to the Facility to carry out, as a document puts it, "clinical testing of behavioral control materials" on inmates. Hamilton's job was to provide "answers to specific questions and solutions to specific problems of direct interest to the Agency." In a six-month span in 1967 and 1968, the psychiatrist spent over $10,000 in CIA funds simply to pay volunteers—which at normal rates meant he experimented on between 400 to 1,000 inmates in that time period alone.

• Another MKSEARCH subproject provided $20,000 to $25,000 a year to Dr. Carl Pfeiffer. Pfeiffer's Agency connection went back to 1951, when he headed the Pharmacology Department at the University of Illinois Medical School. He then moved to Emory University and tested LSD and other drugs on inmates of the Federal penitentiary in Atlanta. From there, he moved to New Jersey, where he continued drug experiments on the prisoners at the Bordentown reformatory. An internationally known pharmacologist, Pfeiffer provided the MKSEARCH program with data on the preparation, use, and effect of drugs. He was readily available if Gottlieb or a colleague wanted a study made of the properties of a particular substance, and like most of TSS's contractors, he also was an intelligence source. Pfeiffer was useful in this last capacity during the latter part of the 1960s because he sat on the Food and Drug Administration committee that allocated LSD for scientific research in the United States. By this time, LSD was so widely available on the black market that the Federal Government had replaced the CIA's informal controls of the 1950s with laws and procedures forbidding all but the most strictly regulated research. With Pfeiffer on the governing committee, the CIA could keep up its traditional role of monitoring above-ground LSD experimentation around the United States.

• To cover some of the more exotic behavioral fields, another MKSEARCH program continued TSS's relationship with Dr. Maitland Baldwin, the brain surgeon at the National Institutes of Health who had been so willing in 1955 to perform "terminal experiments" in sensory deprivation for Morse Allen and the

*During the late 1960s and early 1970s, it seemed that every radical on the West Coast was saying that the CIA was up to strange things in behavior modification at Vacaville. Like many of yesterday's conspiracy theories, this one turned out to be true.

ARTICHOKE program. After Allen was pushed aside by the men from MKULTRA, the new TSS team hired Baldwin as a consultant. According to one of them, he was full of bright ideas on how to control behavior, but they were wary of him because he was such an "eager beaver" with an obvious streak of "craziness." Under TSS auspices, Baldwin performed lobotomies on apes and then put these simian subjects into sensory deprivation—presumably in the same "box" he had built himself at NIH and then had to repair after a desperate soldier kicked his way out. There is no information available on whether Baldwin extended this work to humans, although he did discuss with an outside consultant how lobotomized patients reacted to prolonged isolation. Like Hamilton, Baldwin was a jack-of-all trades who in one experiment beamed radio frequency energy directly at the brain of a chimpanzee and in another cut off one monkey's head and tried to transplant it to the decapitated body of another monkey. Baldwin used $250 in Agency money to buy his own electroshock machine, and he did some kind of unspecified work at a TSS safehouse that caused the CIA to shell out $1450 to renovate and repair the place.

• The last MKSEARCH subproject covered the work of Dr. Charles Geschickter, who served TSS both as researcher and funding conduit. CIA documents show that Geschickter tested powerful drugs on mental defectives and terminal cancer patients, apparently at the Georgetown University Hospital in Washington. In all, the Agency put $655,000 into Geschickter's research on knockout drugs, stress-producing chemicals, and mind-altering substances. Nevertheless, the doctor's principal service to TSS officials seems to have been putting his family foundation at the disposal of the CIA—both to channel funds and to serve as a source of cover to Agency operators. About $2.1 million flowed through this tightly controlled foundation to other researchers.* Under MKSEARCH, Geschickter continued

---

*Geschickter was an extremely important TSS asset with connections in high places. In 1955 he convinced Agency officials to contribute $375,000 in secret funds toward the construction of a new research building at Georgetown University Hospital. (Since this money seemed to be coming from private sources, unwitting Federal bureaucrats doubled it under the matching grant program for hospital construction.) The Agency men had a clear understanding with Geschickter that in return for their contribution, he would make sure they received use of one-sixth of the beds and total space in the facility for their own "hospital safehouse." They then would have a ready source of "human patients and volunteers for experimental use," according to a CIA document, and the

to provide TSS with a means to assess drugs rapidly, and he branched out into trying to knock out monkeys with radar waves to the head (a technique which worked but risked frying vital parts of the brain). The Geschickter Fund for Medical Research remained available as a conduit until 1967.*

As part of the effort to keep finding new substances to test within MKSEARCH, Agency officials continued their search for magic mushrooms, leaves, roots, and barks. In 1966, with considerable CIA backing, J. C. King, the former head of the Agency's Western Hemisphere Division who was eased out after the Bay of Pigs, formed an ostensibly private firm called Amazon Natural Drug Company. King, who loved to float down jungle rivers on the deck of his houseboat with a glass of scotch in hand, searched the backwaters of South America for plants of interest to the Agency and/or medical science. To do the work, he hired Amazon men and women, plus at least two CIA paramilitary operators who worked out of Amazon offices in Iquitos, Peru. They shipped back to the United States finds that included *Chondodendron toxicoferum,* a paralytic agent which is "absolutely lethal in high doses," according to Dr. Timothy Plowman, a Harvard botanist who like most of the staff was unwitting of the CIA involvement. Another plant that was collected and grown by Amazon employees was the hallucinogen known as *yage,* which author William Burroughs has described as "the final fix."

MKSEARCH went on through the 1960s and into the early 1970s, but with a steadily decreasing budget. In 1964 it cost the

_____

research program in the building would provide cover for up to three TSS staff members. Allen Dulles personally approved the contribution and then, to make sure, he took it to President Eisenhower's special committee to review covert operations. The committee also gave its assent, with the understanding that Geschickter could provide "a reasonable expectation" that the Agency would indeed have use of the space he promised. He obviously did, because the CIA money was forthcoming. (This, incidentally, was the only time in a whole quarter-century of Agency behavior-control activities when the documents show that CIA officials went to the White House for approval of anything. The Church committee found no evidence that either the executive branch or Congress was informed of the programs.)

*In 1967, after *Ramparts* magazine exposed secret CIA funding of the National Student Association and numerous nonprofit organizations, President Johnson forbade CIA support of foundations or educational institutions. Inside the Agency there was no notion that this order meant ending relationships, such as the one with Geschickter. In his case, the agile CIA men simply transferred the funding from the foundation to a private company, of which his son was the secretary-treasurer.

Agency about $250,000. In 1972 it was down to four subprojects and $110,000. Gottlieb was a very busy man by then, having taken over all TSS in 1967 when his patron, Richard Helms finally made it to the top of the Agency. In June 1972 Gottlieb decided to end MKSEARCH, thus bringing down the curtain on the quest he himself had started two decades before. He wrote this epitaph for the program:

> As a final commentary, I would like to point out that, by means of Project MKSEARCH, the Clandestine Service has been able to maintain contact with the leading edge of developments in the field of biological and chemical control of human behavior. It has become increasingly obvious over the last several years that this general area had less and less relevance to current clandestine operations. The reasons for this are many and complex, but two of them are perhaps worth mentioning briefly. On the scientific side, it has become very clear that these materials and techniques are too unpredictable in their effect on individual human beings, under specific circumstances, to be operationally useful. Our operations officers, particularly the emerging group of new senior operations officers, have shown a discerning and perhaps commendable distaste for utilizing these materials and techniques. They seem to realize that, in addition to moral and ethical considerations, the extreme sensitivity and security constraints of such operations effectively rule them out.

About the time Gottlieb wrote these words, the Watergate break-in occurred, setting in train forces that would alter his life and that of Richard Helms. A few months later, Richard Nixon was re-elected. Soon after the election, Nixon, for reasons that have never been explained, decided to purge Helms. Before leaving to become Ambassador to Iran, Helms presided over a wholesale destruction of documents and tapes—presumably to minimize information that might later be used against him. Sid Gottlieb decided to follow Helms into retirement, and the two men mutually agreed to get rid of all the documentary traces of MKULTRA. They had never kept files on the safehouse testing or similarly sensitive operations in the first place, but they were determined to erase the existing records of their search to control human behavior. Gottlieb later told a Senate committee that he wanted to get rid of the material because of a "burgeoning paper problem" within the Agency, because the files were of "no constructive use" and might be "misunderstood," and because he wanted to protect the reputations of the researchers with whom he had collaborated on the assurance of secrecy. Gottlieb got in touch with the men who had physical custody of the records, the Agency's archivists, who proceeded to destroy what he and Helms thought were the only traces of the program. They made a mistake, however—or the archivists did. Seven boxes of substantive records and reports were incinerated, but seven more containing invoices and financial records survived—apparently due to misfiling.

Nixon named James Schlesinger to be the new head of the Agency, a post in which he stayed only a few months before the increasingly beleaguered President moved him over to be Secretary of Defense at the height of Watergate. During his short stop at CIA, Schlesinger sent an order to all Agency employees asking them to let his office know about any instances where Agency officials might have carried out any improper or illegal actions. Somebody mentioned Frank Olson's suicide, and it was duly included in the many hundreds of pages of misdeeds reported which became known within the CIA as the "family jewels."

Schlesinger, an outsider to the career CIA operators, had opened a Pandora's box that the professionals never managed to shut again. Samples of the "family jewels" were slipped out to *New York Times* reporter Seymour Hersh, who created a national furor in December 1974 when he wrote about the CIA's illegal spying on domestic dissidents during the Johnson and Nixon years. President Gerald Ford appointed a commission headed by Vice-President Nelson Rockefeller to investigate the past CIA abuses—and to limit the damage. Included in the final Rockefeller report was a section on how an unnamed Department of the Army employee had jumped out of a New York hotel window after Agency men had slipped him LSD. That revelation made headlines around the country. The press seized upon the sensational details and virtually ignored two even more revealing sentences buried in the Rockefeller text: "The drug program was part of a much larger CIA program to study possible means for controlling human behavior. Other studies explored the effects of radiation, electric-shock, psychology, psychiatry, sociology, and harassment substances."

At this point, I entered the story. I was intrigued by those two sentences, and I filed a Freedom of Information request with the CIA to obtain all the documents the Agency had furnished the Rockefeller Commission on behavior control. Although the law requires a government agency to respond within 10 days, it took the Agency more than a year to send me the first 50 documents on the subject, which turned out to be heavily censored.

In the meantime, the committee headed by Senator Frank Church was looking into the CIA, and it called in Sid Gottlieb, who was then spending his retirement working as a volunteer in a hospital in India. Gottlieb secretly testified about CIA assassination programs. (In describing his role in its final report, the Church Committee used a false name, "Victor Scheider.") Asked about the behavioral-control programs, Gottlieb apparently could not—or would not—remember most of the details. The committee had almost no documents to work with, since the main records had been destroyed in 1973 and the financial files had not yet been found.

The issue lay dormant until 1977, when, about June 1, CIA officials notified my lawyers that they had found the 7 boxes of MKULTRA financial records and that they would send me the releasable portions over the following months. As I waited, CIA Director Stansfield Turner notified President Carter and then the Senate Select Committee on Intelligence that an Agency official had located the 7 boxes. Admiral Turner publicly described MKULTRA as only a program of drug experimentation and not one aimed at behavior control. On July 20 I held a press conference at which I criticized Admiral Turner for his several distortions in describing the MKULTRA program. To prove my various points, I released to the reporters a score of the CIA documents that had already come to me and that gave the flavor of the behavioral efforts. Perhaps it was a slow news day, or perhaps people simply were interested in government attempts to tamper with the mind. In any event, the documents set off a media bandwagon that had the story reported on all three network television news shows and practically everywhere else.

The Senate Select Committee on Intelligence and Senator Edward Kennedy's Subcommittee on Health and Scientific Research soon announced they would hold public hearings on the subject. Both panels had looked into the secret research in 1975 but had been hampered by the lack of documents and forthcoming witnesses. At first the two committees agreed to work together, and they held one joint hearing. Then, Senator Barry Goldwater brought behind-the-scenes pressure to get the Intelligence panel, of which he was vice-chairman, to drop out of the proceedings. He claimed, among other things, that the committee was just rehashing old programs and that the time had come to stop dumping on the CIA. Senator Kennedy plowed ahead anyway. He was limited, however, by the small size of the staff he assigned to the investigation, and his people were literally buried in paper by CIA officials, who released 8,000 pages of documents in the weeks before the hearings. As the hearings started, the staff still not had read everything—let alone put it all in context.

As Kennedy's staff prepared for the public sessions, the former men from MKULTRA also got ready. According to one of them, they agreed among themselves to "keep the inquiry within bounds that would satisfy the committee." Specifically, he says that meant volunteering no more information than the Kennedy panel already had. Charles Siragusa, the narcotics agent who ran the New York safehouse, reports he got a telephone call during this period from Ray Treichler, the Stanford Ph.D. who specialized in chemical warfare for the MKULTRA program. "He wanted me to deny knowing about the safehouse," says Siragusa. "He didn't want me to admit that he was the guy. . . . I said there was no way I could do that." Whether any other ex-TSS men also suborned perjury cannot be said, but several of them appear to have committed perjury at the hearings.* As previously noted, Robert Lashbrook denied firsthand knowledge of the safehouse operation when, in fact, he had supervised one of the "pads" and been present, according to George White's diary, at the time of an "LSD surprise" experiment. Dr. Charles Geschickter testified he had not tested stress-producing drugs on human subjects while both his own 1960 proposal to the Agency and the CIA's documents indicate the opposite.

---

*Lying to Congress followed the pattern of lying to the press that some MKULTRA veterans adopted after the first revelations came out. For example, former Human Ecology Society director James Monroe told *The New York Times* on August 2, 1977 that "only about 25 to 30 percent" of the Society's budget came from the CIA—a statement he knew to be false since the actual figure was well over 90 percent. His untruth allowed some other grantees to claim that their particular project was funded out of the non-Agency part of the Society.

Despite the presence of a key aide who constantly cued him during the hearings, Senator Kennedy was not prepared to deal with these and other inconsistencies. He took no action to follow up obviously perjured testimony, and he seemed content to win headlines with reports of "The Gang That Couldn't Spray Straight." Although that particular testimony had been set up in advance by a Kennedy staffer, the Senator still managed to act surprised when ex-MKULTRA official David Rhodes told of the ill-fated LSD experiment at the Marin County safehouse.

The Kennedy hearings added little to the general state of knowledge on the CIA's behavior-control programs. CIA officials, both past and present, took the position that basically nothing of substance was learned during the 25-odd years of research, the bulk of which had ended in 1963, and they were not challenged. That proposition is, on its face, ridiculous, but neither Senator Kennedy nor any other investigator has yet put any real pressure on the Agency to reveal the content of the research—what was actually learned—as opposed to the experimental means of carrying it out. In this book, I have tried to get at some of the substantive questions, but I have had access to neither the scientific records, which Gottlieb and Helms destroyed, nor the principal people involved. Gottlieb, for instance, who moved from India to Santa Cruz, California and then to parts unknown, turned down repeated requests to be interviewed. "I am interested in very different matters than the subject of your book these days," he wrote, "and do not have either the time or the inclination to reprocess matters that happened a long time ago."

Faced with these obstacles, I have tried to weave together a representative sample of what went on, but having dealt with a group of people who regularly incorporated lying into their daily work, I cannot be sure. I cannot be positive that they never found a technique to control people, despite my definite bias in favor of the idea that the human spirit defeated the manipulators. Only a congressional committee could compel truthful testimony from people who have so far refused to be forthcoming, and even Congress' record has not been good so far. A determined investigative committee at least could make sure that the people being probed do not determine the "bounds" of the inquiry.

A new investigation would probably not be worth the effort just to take another stab at MKULTRA and ARTICHOKE. De-

THE SEARCH FOR THE TRUTH

spite my belief that there are some skeletons hidden—literally —the public probably now knows the basic parameters of these programs. The fact is, however, that CIA officials actively experimented with behavior-control methods for another decade *after* Sid Gottlieb and company lost the research action. The Directorate of Science and Technology—specifically its Office of Research and Development (ORD)—did not remain idle after Director McCone transferred the behavioral research function in 1962.

In ORD, Dr. Stephen Aldrich, a graduate of Amherst and Northwestern Medical School, took over the role that Morse Allen and then Sid Gottlieb had played before him. Aldrich had been the medical director of the Office of Scientific Intelligence back in the days when that office was jockeying with Morse Allen for control of ARTICHOKE, so he was no stranger to the programs. Under his leadership, ORD officials kept probing for ways to control human behavior, and they were doing so with space-age technology that made the days of MKULTRA look like the horse-and-buggy era. If man could get to the moon by the end of the 1960s, certainly the well-financed scientists of ORD could make a good shot at conquering inner space.

They brought their technology to bear on subjects like the electric stimulation of the brain. John Lilly had done extensive work in this field a decade earlier, before concluding that to maintain his integrity he must find another field. CIA men had no such qualms, however. They actively experimented with placing electrodes in the brain of animals and—probably— men. Then they used electric and radio signals to move their subjects around. The field went far beyond giving monkeys orgasms, as Lilly had done. In the CIA itself, Sid Gottlieb and the MKULTRA crew had made some preliminary studies of it. They started in 1960 by having a contractor search all the available literature, and then they had mapped out the parts of animals' brains that produced reactions when stimulated. By April 1961 the head of TSS was able to report "we now have a 'production capability' " in brain stimulation and "we are close to having debugged a prototype system whereby dogs can be guided along specific courses." Six months later, a CIA document noted, "The feasibility of remote control of activities in several species of animals has been demonstrated. . . . Special investigations and evaluations will be conducted toward the application of selected elements of these techniques to man."

Another six months later, TSS officials had found a use for electric stimulation: this time putting electrodes in the brains of cold-blooded animals—presumably reptiles. While much of the experimentation with dogs and cats was to find a way of wiring the animal and then directing it by remote control into, say, the office of the Soviet ambassador, this cold-blooded project was designed instead for the delivery of chemical and biological agents or for "executive action–type operations," according to a document. "Executive action" was the CIA's euphemism for assassination.

With the brain electrode technology at this level, Steve Aldrich and ORD took over the research function from TSS. What the ORD men found cannot be said, but the open literature would indicate that the field progressed considerably during the 1960s. Can the human brain be wired and controlled by a big enough computer? Aldrich certainly tried to find out.

Creating amnesia remained a "big goal" for the ORD researcher, states an ex-CIA man. Advances in brain surgery, such as the development of three-dimensional, "stereotaxic" techniques, made psychosurgery a much simpler matter and created the possibility that a precisely placed electrode probe could be used to cut the link between past memory and present recall. As for subjects to be used in behavioral experiments of this sort, the ex-CIA man states that ORD had access to prisoners in at least one American penal institution. A former Army doctor stationed at the Edgewood chemical laboratory states that the lab worked with CIA men to develop a drug that could be used to help program in new memories into the mind of an amnesic subject. How far did the Agency take this research? I don't know.

The men from ORD tried to create their own latter-day version of the Society for the Investigation of Human Ecology. Located outside Boston, it was called the Scientific Engineering Institute, and Agency officials had set it up originally in 1956 as a proprietary company to do research on radar and other technical matters that had nothing to do with human behavior. Its president, who says he was a "figurehead," was Dr. Edwin Land, the founder of Polaroid. In the early 1960s, ORD officials decided to bring it into the behavioral field and built a new wing to the Institute's modernistic building for the "life sciences." They hired a group of behavioral and medical scientists who were allowed to carry on their own independent research as long as it met Institute standards. These scientists were available to consult with frequent visitors from Washington, and they were encouraged to take long lunches in the Institute's dining room where they mixed with the physical scientists and brainstormed about virtually everything. One veteran recalls a colleague joking, "If you could find the natural radio frequency of a person's sphincter, you could make him run out of the room real fast." Turning serious, the veteran states the technique was "plausible," and he notes that many of the crazy ideas bandied about at lunch developed into concrete projects.

Some of these projects may have been worked on at the Institute's own several hundred–acre farm located in the Massachusetts countryside. But of the several dozen people contacted in an effort to find out what the Institute did, the most anyone would say about experiments at the farm was that one involved stimulating the pleasure centers of crows' brains in order to control their behavior. Presumably, ORD men did other things at their isolated rural lab.

Just as the MKULTRA program had been years ahead of the scientific community, ORD activities were similarly advanced. "We looked at the manipulation of genes," states one of the researchers. "We were interested in gene splintering. The rest of the world didn't ask until 1976 the type of questions we were facing in 1965. . . . Everybody was afraid of building the super-soldier who would take orders without questioning, like the kamikaze pilot. Creating a subservient society was not out of sight." Another Institute man describes the work of a colleague who bombarded bacteria with ultraviolet radiation in order to create deviant strains. ORD also sponsored work in parapsychology. Along with the military services, Agency officials wanted to know whether psychics could read minds or control them from afar (telepathy), if they could gain information about distant places or people (clairvoyance or remote viewing), if they could predict the future (precognition), or influence the movement of physical objects or even the human mind (photokinesis). The last could have incredibly destructive applications, if it worked. For instance, switches setting off nuclear bombs would have to be moved only a few inches to launch a holocaust. Or, enemy psychics, with minds honed to laser-beam sharpness, could launch attacks to burn out the brains of American nuclear scientists. Any or all of these techniques have numerous applications to the spy trade.

While ORD officials apparently left much of the drug work to Gottlieb, they could not keep their hands totally out of this field. In 1968 they set up a joint program, called Project OFTEN, with the Army Chemical Corps at Edgewood, Maryland to study the effects of various drugs on animals and humans. The Army helped the Agency put together a computerized data base for drug testing and supplied military volunteers for some of the experiments. In one case, with a particularly effective incapacitating agent, the Army arranged for inmate volunteers at the Holmesburg State Prison in Philadelphia. Project OFTEN had both offensive and defensive sides, according to an ORD man who described it in a memorandum. He cited as an example of what he and his coworkers hoped to find "a compound that could simulate a heart attack or a stroke in the targeted individual." In January 1973, just as Richard Helms was leaving the Agency and James Schlesinger was coming in, Project OFTEN was abruptly canceled.

What—if any—success the ORD men had in creating heart attacks or in any of their other behavioral experiments simply cannot be said. Like Sid Gottlieb, Steve Aldrich is not saying, and his colleagues seem even more closemouthed than Gottlieb's. In December 1977, having gotten wind of the ORD programs, I filed a Freedom of Information request for access to ORD files "on behavioral research, including but not limited to any research or operational activities related to bio-electrics, electric or radio stimulation of the brain, electronic destruction of memory, stereotaxic surgery, psychosurgery, hypnotism, parapsychology, radiation, microwaves, and ultrasonics." I also asked for documentation on behavioral testing in U.S. penal institutions, and I later added a request for all available files on amnesia. The Agency wrote back six months later that ORD had "identified 130 boxes (approximately 130 cubic feet) of material that are reasonably expected to contain behavioral research documents."

Considering that Admiral Turner and other CIA officials had tried to leave the impression with Congress and the public that behavioral research had almost all ended in 1963 with the phaseout of MKULTRA, this was an amazing admission. The sheer volume of material was staggering. This book is based on the 7 boxes of heavily censored MKULTRA financial records plus another 3 or so of ARTICHOKE documents, supplemented by interviews. It has taken me over a year, with significant research help, to digest this much smaller bulk. Clearly, greater resources than an individual writer can bring to bear will be needed to to get to the bottom of the ORD programs.

A free society's best defense against unethical behavior modification is public disclosure and awareness. The more people understand consciousness-altering technology, the more likely they are to recognize its application, and the less likely it will be used. When behavioral research is carried out in secret, it can be turned against the government's enemies, both foreign and domestic. No matter how pure or defense-oriented the motives of the researchers, once the technology exists, the decision to use it is out of their hands. Who can doubt that if the Nixon administration or J. Edgar Hoover had had some foolproof way to control people, they would not have used the technique against their political foes, just as the CIA for years tried to use similar tactics overseas?

As with the Agency's secrets, it is now too late to put behavioral technology back in the box. Researchers are bound to keep making advances. The technology has already spread to our schools, prisons, and mental hospitals, not to mention the advertising community, and it has also been picked up by police forces around the world. Placing hoods over the heads of political prisoners—a modified form of sensory deprivation—has become a standard tactic around the world, from Northern Ireland to Chile. The Soviet Union has consistently used psychiatric treatment as an instrument of repression. Such methods violate basic human rights just as much as physical abuse, even if they leave no marks on the body.

Totalitarian regimes will probably continue, as they have in the past, to search secretly for ways to manipulate the mind, no matter what the United States does. The prospect of being able to control people seems too enticing for most tyrants to give up. Yet, we as a country can defend ourselves without sending our own scientists—mad or otherwise—into a hidden war that violates our basic ethical and constitutional principles. After all, we created the Nuremberg Code to show there were limits on scientific research and its application. Admittedly, American intelligence officials have violated our own standard, but the U.S. Government has now officially declared violations will no longer be permitted. The time has come for the United States to lead by example in voluntarily renouncing secret government behavioral research. Other countries might even follow suit, particularly if we were to propose an international agreement which provides them with a framework to do so.

Tampering with the mind is much too dangerous to be left to the spies. Nor should it be the exclusive province of the behavioral scientists, who have given us cause for suspicion. Take this statement by their most famous member, B. F. Skinner: "My image in some places is of a monster of some kind who wants to pull a string and manipulate people. Nothing could be further from the truth. People are manipulated; I just want them to be manipulated more effectively." Such notions are much more acceptable in prestigious circles than people tend to think: D. Ewen Cameron read papers about "depatterning" with electroshock before meetings of his fellow psychiatrists, and they elected him their president. Human behavior is so important that it must concern us all. The more vigilant we and our representatives are, the less chance we will be unwitting victims.

NOTES

CHAPTER 1

The information on Albert Hofmann's first LSD trip and background on LSD came from an interview by the author with Hofmann, a paper by Hofmann called "The Discovery of LSD and Subsequent Investigations on Naturally Occurring Hallucinogens," another interview with Hofmann by Michael Horowitz printed in the June 1976 *High Times* magazine, and from a CIA document on LSD produced by the Office of Scientific Intelligence, August 30, 1955, titled "The Strategic Medical Significance of LSD-25."

Information on the German mescaline and hypnosis experiments at Dachau came from "Technical Report no. 331-45, German Aviation Research at the Dachau Concentration Camp," October, 1945, US Naval Technical Mission in Europe, found in the papers of Dr. Henry Beecher. Additional information came from *Trials of War Criminals Before the Nuremberg Tribunal,* the book *Doctors of Infamy* by Alexander Mitscherlich and Fred Mielke (New York: H. Schuman, 1949), interviews with prosecution team members Telford Taylor, Leo Alexander, and James McHaney, and an article by Dr. Leo Alexander, "Sociopsychologic Structure of the SS," *Archives of Neurology and Psychiatry,* May, 1948, Vol. 59, pp. 622–34.

The OSS experience in testing marijuana was described in interviews with several former Manhattan Project counterintelligence men, an OSS document dated June 21, 1943, Subject: Development of "truth drug," given the CIA identification number A/B, I, 12/1; from document A/B, I, 64/34, undated, Subject: Memorandum Relative to the use of truth drug in interrogation; document dated June 2, 1943, Subject: Memorandum on T. D. A "confidential memorandum," dated

April 4, 1954, found in the papers of George White, also was helpful.

The quote on US prisoners passing through Manchuria came from document 19, 18 June 1953, Subject: ARTICHOKE Conference.

The information on Stanley Lovell came from his book, *Of Spies and Strategems* (Englewood Cliffs, N.J.: Prentice-Hall, 1963), from interviews with his son Richard, a perusal of his remaining papers, interviews with George Kistiakowsky and several OSS veterans, and from "Science in World War II, the Office of Scientific Research and Development" in *Chemistry: A History of the Chemistry Components of the National Defense Research Committee,* edited by W. A. Noyes, Jr. (Boston: Little, Brown & Company, 1948).

Dr. Walter Langer provided information about his psychoanalytic portrait of Hitler, as did his book, *The Mind of Adolf Hitler* (New York: Basic Books, 1972). Dr. Henry Murray also gave an interview, as did several OSS men who had been through his assessment course. Murray's work is described at length in a book published after the war by the OSS Assessment staff, *Assessment of Men* (New York: Rinehart & Company, 1948).

Material on George Estabrooks came from his books, *Hypnotism* (New York: E. P. Dutton and Co., 1945) and *Death in the Mind,* co-authored with Richard Lockridge (New York: E. P. Dutton, 1945), and interviews with his daughter, Doreen Estabrooks Michl, former colleagues, and Dr. Milton Kline.

CHAPTER 2

The origins of the CIA's ARTICHOKE program and accounts of the early testing came from the following Agency Documents #192, 15 January 1953; #3, 17 May 1949; A/B, I, 8/1, 24 February 1949; February 10, 1951 memo on Special Interrogations (no document #); A/B, II, 30/2, 28 September 1949; #5, 15 August 1949; #8, 27 September 1949; #6, 23 August 1949; #13, 5 April 1950; #18, 9 May 1950; #142 (transmittal slip), 19 May 1952; #124, 25 January 1952; A/B, IV, 23/32, 3 March 1952; #23, 21 June 1950; #10, 27 February 1950; #37, 27 October 1950; A/B, I, 39/1, 12 December 1950; A/B, II, 2/2, 5 March 1952; A/B, II, 2/1, 15 February 1952; A/B, V, 134/3, 3 December 1951; A/B, I, 38/5, 1 June 1951; and #400, undated, "Specific Cases of Overseas Testing and Applications of Behavioral Drugs."

The documents were supplemented by interviews with Ray Cline, Harry Rositzke, Michael Burke, Hugh Cunningham, and several other ex-CIA men who asked to remain anonymous. *The Final Report of the Select Committee to Study Governmental Operations with Respect to Intelligence* (henceforth called the Church Committee Report) provided useful background.

Documents giving background on terminal experiments include #A/B, II, 10/57; #A/B, II, 10/58, 31 August, 1954; #A/B, II, 10/ 17, 27 September 1954; and #A/B, I, 76/4, 21 March 1955.

CHAPTER 3

The primary sources for the material on Professor Wendt's trip to Frankfurt were Dr. Samuel V. Thompson then of the Navy, the CIA psychiatric consultant, several of Wendt's former associates, as well as three CIA documents that described the testing: Document #168, 19 September 1952, Subject: "Project LGQ"; Document #168, 18 September 1952, Subject: Field Trip of ARTICHOKE team, 20 August-September 1952; and #A/B, II, 33/21, undated, Subject: Special Comments.

Information on the Navy's Project CHATTER came from the Church Committee Report, Book I, pp. 337–38. Declassified Navy Documents N-23, February 13, 1951, Subject: Procurement of Certain Drugs; N-27, undated, Subject: Project CHATTER; N-29, undated, Subject: Status Report: Studies of Motion Sickness, Vestibular Function, and Effects of Drugs; N-35, October 27, 1951, Interim Report; N-38, 30 September, 1952, Memorandum for File; and N-39, 28 October, 1952, Memorandum for File.

The information on the heroin found in Wendt's safe comes from the Rochester *Democrat and Chronicle,* October 2, 1977 and considerable background on Wendt's Rochester testing program was found in the Rochester *Times-Union,* January 28, 1955. The CIA quote on heroin came from May 15, 1952 OSI Memorandum to the Deputy Director, CIA, Subject: Special Interrogation.

Information on the Agency's interest in amnesia came from 14 January 1952 memo, Subject: BLUEBIRD/ARTICHOKE, Proposed Research; 7 March 1951, Subject: Informal Discussion with Chief [deleted] Regarding "Disposal"; 1 May 1951, Subject: Recommendation for Disposal of Maximum Custody Defectors; and #A/B, I, 75/13, undated, Subject: Amnesia.

The quote from Homer on nepenthe was found in Sidney Cohen's *The Beyond Within: The LSD Story* (New York: Atheneum, 1972).

The section on control came from interviews with John Stockwell and several other former CIA men.

CHAPTER 4

The description of Robert Hyde's first trip came from interviews with Dr. Milton Greenblatt, Dr. J. Herbert DeShon, and a talk by Max Rinkel at the 2nd Macy Conference on Neuropharmacology, pp. 235–36, edited by Harold A. Abramson, 1955: Madison Printing Company.

The descriptions of TSS and Sidney Gottlieb came from interviews with Ray Cline, John Stockwell, about 10 other ex-CIA officers, and other friends of Gottlieb.

Memos quoted on the early MKULTRA program include Memorandum from ADDP Helms to DCI Dulles, 4/3/53, Tab A, pp. 1–2 (quoted in Church Committee Report, Book I); APF A-1, April 13, 1953, Memorandum for Deputy Director (Administration, Subject: Project MKUL-TRA—Extremely Sensitive Research and Development Program; #A/B,I,64/6, 6 February 1952, Memorandum for the Record, Subject: Contract with [deleted] #A/B,I,64/29, undated, Memorandum for Technical Services Staff, Subject: Alcohol Antagonists and Accelerators, Research and Development Project. The Gottlieb quote is from Hearing before the Subcommittee on Health and Scientific Research of the Senate Committee on Human Resources, September 21, 1977, p. 206.

The background data on LSD came particularly from *The Beyond Within: The LSD Story* by Sidney Cohen (New York: Atheneum, 1972). Other sources included *Origins of Psychopharmacology: From CPZ to LSD* by Anne E. Caldwell (Springfield, Ill.: Charles C. Thomas, 1970) and Document 352, "An OSI Study of the Strategic Medical Importance of LSD-25," 30 August 1955.

TSS's use of outside researchers came from interviews with four former TSSers. MKULTRA Subprojects 8, 10, 63, and 66 described Robert Hyde's work. Subprojects 7, 27, and 40 concerned Harold Abramson. Hodge's work was in subprojects 17 and 46. Carl Pfeiffer's Agency connection, along with Hyde's, Abramson's, and Isbell's, was laid out by Lyman B. Kirkpatrick, Memorandum for the Record, 1 December 1953, Subject: Conversation with Dr. Willis Gibbons of TSS re Olson Case (found at p. 1030, Kennedy Subcommittee 1975 Biomedical and Behavioral Research Hearings). Isbell's testing program was also described at those hearings, as it was in Document #14, 24 July, 1953, Memo For: Liaison & Security Officer/TSS, Subject #71 An Account of the Chemical Division's Contacts in the National Institute of Health; Document #37, 14 July 1954, subject [deleted]; and Document #41, 31 August, 1956, subject; trip to Lexington, Ky., 21–23 August 1956. Isbell's program was further described in a "Report on ADAMHA Involvement in LSD Research," found at p. 993 of 1975 Kennedy subcommittee hearings. The firsthand account of the actual testing came from an interview with Edward M. Flowers, Washington, D.C.

The section on TSS's noncontract informants came from interviews with TSS sources, reading the proceedings of the Macy Conferences on "Problems of Consciousness" and "Neuropharmacology," and interviews with several participants including

Sidney Cohen, Humphrey Osmond, and Hudson Hoagland.

The material on CIA's relations with Sandoz and Eli Lilly came from Document #24, 16 November, 1953, Subject: ARTICHOKE Conference; Document #268, 23 October, 1953, Subject: Meeting in Director's Office at 1100 hours on 23 October with Mr. Wisner and [deleted]; Document #316, 6 January, 1954, Subject: Lysergic Acid Diethylamide (LSD-25); and Document #338, 26 October 1954, Subject: Potential Large Scale Availability of LSD through newly discovered synthesis by [deleted]; interviews with Sandoz and Lilly former executives; interviews with TSS sources; and Sidney Gottlieb's testimony before Kennedy subcommittee, 1977, p. 203.

Henry Beecher's US government connections were detailed in his private papers, in a report on the Swiss-LSD death to the CIA at p. 396, Church Committee Report, Book I, and in interviews with two of his former associates.

The description of TSS's internal testing progression comes from interviews with former staff members. The short reference to Sid Gottlieb's arranging for LSD to be given a speaker at a political rally comes from Document #A/B, II, 26/8, 9 June 1954, Subject: MKULTRA. Henry Beecher's report to the CIA on the Swiss suicide is at p. 396, Church Committee Report, Book I.

CHAPTER 5

The description of the CIA's relationship with SOD at Fort Detrick comes from interviews with several ex-Fort Detrick employees; Church Committee hearings on "Unauthorized Storage of Toxic Agents, Volume 1; Church Committee "Summary Report on CIA Investigation of MKNAOMI" found in Report, Book I, pp. 360–63; and/ Kennedy subcommittee hearings on Biological Testing Involving Human Subjects by the Department of Defense, 1977. The details of Sid Gottlieb's involvement in the plot to kill Patrice Lumumba are found in the Church Committee's Interim Report on "Alleged Assassination Plots Involving Foreign Leaders," pp. 20–21. The Church committee allowed Gottlieb to be listed under the pseudonym Victor Scheider, but several sources confirm Gottlieb's true identity, as does the biographic data on him submitted to the Kennedy subcommittee by the CIA, which puts him in the same job attributed to "Scheider" at the same time. The plot to give botulinum to Fidel Castro is outlined in the Assassination report, pp. 79–83. The incident with the Iraqi colonel is on p. 181 of the same report.

The several inches of CIA documents on the Olson case were released by the Olson family in 1976 and can be found in the printed volume of the 1975 Kennedy subcommittee hearings on Biomedical and Behavioral Resarch, pp.1005–1132. They form the base of much of the narrative, along with interviews with Alice Olson, Eric Olson, Benjamin Wilson, and several other ex-SOD men (who added next to nothing). Information also was gleaned from Vincent Ruwet's testimony before the Kennedy subcommittee in 1975, pp. 138–45 and the Church committee's summary of the affair, Book I, pp. 394–403. The quote on Harold Abramson's intention to give his patients unwitting doses of LSD is found in MKULTRA subproject 7, June 8, 1953, letter to Dr. [deleted]. Magician John Mulholland's work for the Agency is described in MKULTRA subprojects 19 and 34.

CHAPTER 6

The CIA's reaction to Frank Olson's death is described in numerous memos released by the Agency to the Olson family, which can be found at pp. 1005–1132 of the Kennedy Subcommittee 1975 hearings on Biomedical and Behavioral Research. See particularly at p. 1077, 18 December 1953, Subject: The Suicide of Frank Olson and at p. 1027, 1 December 1953, Subject: Use of LSD.

Richard Helms' views on unwitting testing are found in Document #448, 17 December 1963, Subject: Testing of Psychochemicals and Related Materials and in a memorandum to the CIA Director, June 9, 1964, quoted from on page 402 of the Church Committee Report, Book I.

George White's diary and letters were donated by his widow to Foothills Junior College, Los Altos, California and are the source of a treasure chest of material on him, including his letter to a friend explaining his almost being "blackballed" from the CIA, the various diary entries cited, including references to folk-dancing with Gottlieb, the interview with Hal Lipset where he explains his philosophy on chasing criminals, and his letter to Sid Gottlieb dated November 21, (probably) 1972.

The New York and San Francisco safehouses run by George White are the subjects of MKULTRA subprojects 3, 14, 16, 42, and 149. White's tips to the landlord are described in 42–156, his liquor bills in 42–157, "dry-runs" in 42–91. The New York safehouse run by Charles Siragusa is subproject 132. The "intermediate" tests are described in document 132–59.

Paul Avery, a San Francisco freelance writer associated with the Center for Investigative Reporting in Oakland, California interviewed William Hawkins and provided assistance on the details of the San Francisco safehouse and George White's background. Additional information on White came from interviews with his widow,

several former colleagues in the Narcotics Bureau, and other know-
ledgeable sources in various San Francisco law-enforcement agencies. An ex-Narcotics Bureau official told of Dr. James Hamilton's
study of unusual sexual practices and the description of his unwitting drug testing comes from MKULTRA subproject 2, which is his
subproject.

Ray Treichler discussed some of his work with harassment substances in testimony before the Kennedy subcommittee on September
20, 1977, pp. 105–8. He delivered his testimony under the pseudonym
"Philip Goldman."

"The Gang that Couldn't Spray Straight" article appeared in the
September 20, 1977 Washington *Post.*

Richard Helms' decision not to tell John McCone about the CIA's
connection to the Mafia in assassination attempts against Castro
is described in the Church Committee's Assassination report, pp.
102–3.

The 1957 Inspector General's Report on TSS, Document #417 and
the 1963 inspection of MKULTRA, 14 August 1963, Document #59
provided considerable detail throughout the entire chapter. The
Church Committee Report on MKULTRA in Book I, pp. 385–422 also
provided considerable information.

Sid Gottlieb's job as Assistant to the Clandestine Services chief for
Scientific Matters is described in Document #74 (operational series),
20 October 1959, Subject: Application of Imaginative Research on the
Behavioral and Physical Sciences to [deleted] Problems" and in the
1963 Inspector General's report.

Interviews with ex-CIA Inspector General Lyman Kirkpatrick, another former Inspector General's staff employee, and several ex-TSS
staffers contributed significantly to this chapter.

Helms' letter to the Warren Commission on "Soviet Brainwashing
Techniques," dated 19 June 1964, was obtained from the National
Archives.

The material on the CIA's operational use of LSD came from the
Church Committee Report, Book I, pp. 399–403 and from an affidavit filed in the Federal Court case of *John D. Marks* v. *Central Intelligence Agency, et. al.,* Civil Action No. 76–2073 by Eloise R.
Page, Chief, Policy and Coordination Staff of the CIA's Directorate
of Operations. In listing all the reasons why the Agency should not
provide the operational documents, Ms. Page gave some information on what was in the documents. The passages on TSS's and the
Medical Office's positions on the use of LSD came from a memo
written by James Angleton, Chief, Counterintelligence Staff on December 12, 1957 quoted in part at p. 401 of the Church Committee
Report, Book I.

CHAPTER 7

R. Gordon and Valentina Wasson's mammoth work, *Mushrooms, Russia and History,* (New York: Pantheon, 1957), was the source for the account of the Empress Agrippina's murderous use of mushrooms. Wasson told the story of his various journeys to Mexico in a series of interviews and in a May 27, 1957 *Life* magazine article, "Seeking the Magic Mushroom."

Morse Allen learned of piule in a sequence described in document #A/B,I,33/7, 14 November 1952, Subject: Piule. The sending of the young CIA scientist to Mexico was outlined in #A/B, I, 33/3, 5 December 1952. Morse Allen commented on mushroom history and covert possibilities in #A/B, I, 34/4, 26 June 1953, Subject: Mushrooms—Narcotic and Poisonous Varieties. His trip to the American mushroom-growing capital was described in Document [number illegible], 25 June 1953, Subject: Trip to Toughkenamon, Pennsylvania. The failure of TSS to tell Morse Allen about the results of the botanical lab work is outlined in #A/B, I, 39/5, 10 August 1954 Subject: Reports; Request for from TSS [deleted].

James Moore told much about himself in a long interview and in an exchange of correspondence. MKULTRA Subproject 51 dealt with Moore's consulting relationship with the Agency and Subproject 52 with his ties as a procurer of chemicals. See especially Document 51–46, 8 April 1963, Subject: MKULTRA Subproject 51; 51–24, 27 August 1956, Subject: MKULTRA Subproject 51-B; 52–94, 20 February 1963, Subject: (BB) Chemical and Physical Manipulants; 52–19, 20 December 1962; 52–17, 1 March 1963; 52–23, 6 December 1962; 52–64, 24 August 1959.

The CIA's arrangements with the Department of Agriculture are detailed in #A/B, I, 34/4, 26 June, 1953, Subject: Mushrooms—Narcotic and Poisonous varieties and Document [number illegible], 13 April 1953, Subject: Interview with Cleared Contacts.

Dr. Harris Isbell's work with psilocybin is detailed in Isbell document #155, "Comparison of the Reaction Induced by Psilocybin and LSD-25 in Man."

Information on the counterculture and its interface with CIA drug-testing came from interviews with Timothy Leary, Allen Ginsburg, Humphrey Osmond, John Lilly, Sidney Cohen, Ralph Blum, Herbert Kelman, Leo Hollister, Herbert DeShon, and numerous others. Ken Kesey described his first trip in *Garage Sale* (New York: Viking Press, 1973). Timothy Leary's *Kamasutra* was actually a book hand-produced in four copies and called *Psychedelic Theory: Working Papers from the Harvard IFIF Psychedelic Research Project, 1960–1963.* Susan Berns Wolf Rothchild kindly made her copy available. The material about Harold Abramson's turning on Frank Fremont-Smith and Gregory Bateson came from the proceedings of a conference on LSD sponsored by the Josiah Macy, Jr. Foundation on April 22, 23, and 24, 1959, pp. 8–22.

CHAPTER 8

Edward Hunter's article " 'Brain-Washing' Tactics Force Chinese into Ranks of Communist Party" appeared in the Miami *News* on September 24, 1950. His book was *Brainwashing in Red China* (New York: Vanguard Press, 1951). Other material came from several interviews with Hunter just before he died in June 1978.

The Air Force document cited on brainwashing was called "Air Force Headquarters Panel Convened to Record Air Force Position Regarding Conduct of Personnel in Event of Capture," December 14, 1953. Researcher Sam Zuckerman found it and showed it to me.

The figures on American prisoners in Korea and the quote from Edward Hunter came from hearings before the Senate Permanent Subcommittee on Investigations, 84th Congress, June 19, 20, 26, and 27, 1956.

The material on the setting up of the Cornell-Hinkle-Wolff study came from interviews with Hinkle, Helen Goodell, and several CIA sources. Hinkle's and Wolff's study on brainwashing appeared in classified form on 2 April 1956 as a Technical Services Division publication called *Communist Control Techniques* and in substantially the same form but unclassified as "Communist Interrogation and Indoctrination of 'Enemies of the State'—An Analysis of Methods Used by the Communist State Police." *AMA Archives of Neurology and Psychiatry,* August, 1956, Vol. 76.

Allen Dulles spoke on "Brain Warfare" before the Alumni Conference of Princeton University, Hot Springs, Virginia on April 10, 1953, and the quote on guinea pigs came from that speech.

The comments of Rockefeller Foundation officials about D. Ewen Cameron and the record of Rockefeller funding were found in Robert S. Morrison's diary, located in the Rockefeller Foundation Archives, Pocantico Hills, New York.

The key articles on Cameron's work on depatterning and psychic driving were "Production of Differential Amnesia as a Factor in the Treatment of Schizophrenia," *Comprehensive Psychiatry,* 1960, 1, p. 26 and "Effects of Repetition of Verbal Signals upon the Behavior of Chronic Psychoneurotic Patients" by Cameron, Leonard Levy, and Leonard Rubenstein, *Journal of Mental Science,* 1960, 106, 742. The background on Page-Russell electroshocks came from "Intensified Electrical Convulsive Therapy in the Treatment of Mental Disorders" by L. G. M. Page and R. J. Russell, *Lancet,* Volume 254, Jan.—June, 1948. Dr. John Cavanagh of Washington, D.C. provided background on the use of electroshock and sedatives in psychiatry.

Cameron's MKULTRA subproject was #68. See especially document 68–37, "Application for Grant to Study the Effects upon Human Behavior of the Repetition of Verbal Signals," January 21, 1957.

Part of Cameron's papers are in the archives of the American Psychiatric Association in Washington, and they provided considerable information on the treatment of Mary C., as well as a general look at his work. Interviews with at least a dozen of his former colleagues also provided considerable information.

Interviews with John Lilly and Donald Hebb provided background on sensory deprivation. Maitland Baldwin's work in the field was discussed in a whole series of ARTICHOKE documents including #A/B, I, 76/4, 21 March 1955, Subject: Total Isolation; #A/B, 1, 76/12, 19 May 1955, Subject: Total Isolation—Additional Comments; and #A/B, I, 76/17, 27 April 1955, Subject: Total Isolation, Supplemental Report #2. The quote from Aldous Huxley on sensory deprivation is taken from the book of his writings, *Moksha: Writings on Psychedelics and the Visionary Experience (1931–1963),* edited by Michael Horowitz and Cynthia Palmer (New York: Stonehill, 1978).

The material on Val Orlikow's experiences with Dr. Cameron came from interviews with her and her husband David and from portions of her hospital records, which she furnished.

Cameron's staff psychologist Barbara Winrib's comments on him were found in a letter to the Montreal *Star,* August 11, 1977.

The study of Cameron's electroshock work ordered by Dr. Cleghorn was published as "Intensive Electroconvulsive Therapy: A Follow-up Study," by A. E. Schwartzman and P. E. Termansen, *Canadian Psychiatric Association,* Volume 12, 1967.

In addition to several interviews, much material on John Lilly came from his autobiography, *The Scientist* (Philadelphia: J. B. Lippincott Company, 1978).

The CIA's handling of Yuri Nosenko was discussed at length in hearings before the House Assassinations Committee on September 15, 1978. The best press account of this testimony was written by Jeremiah O'Leary of the Washington *Star* on September 16, 1978: "How CIA Tried to Break Defector in Oswald Case."

CHAPTER 9

MKULTRA subprojects 48 and 60 provided the basic documents on the Society for the Investigation of Human Ecology. These were supplemented by the three biennial reports of the Society that could be found: 1957, 1961, and 1961–1963. Wolff's own research work is MKULTRA subproject 61. Wolff's proposals to the Agency are in #A/B, II,

10/68, undated "Proposed Plan for Implementing [deleted]" in two documents included in 48–29, March 5, 1956, "General Principles Upon Which these Proposals Are Based." The Agency's plans for the Chinese Project are described in #A/B, II, 10/48, undated, Subject: Cryptonym [deleted] A/B, II 10/72, 9 December, 1954, Subject: Letter of Instructions, and # A/B, II, 10/110, undated, untitled.

Details of the logistics of renting the Human Ecology headquarters and bugging it are in #A/B, II, 10/23, 30 August, 1954, Subject: Meeting of Working Committee of [deleted], No. 5 and #A/B, II, 10/92, 8 December, 1954, Subject: Technical Installation.

The Hungarian project, as well as being described in the 1957 biennial report, was dealt with in MKULTRA subprojects 65 and 82, especially 65-12, 28 June 1956, Subject: MKULTRA subproject 65; 65-11, undated, Subject: Dr. [deleted]'s Project—Plans for the Coming Year, July, 1957–June, 1958; and 82-15, 11 April 1958, Subject: Project MKULTRA, Subproject 82.

The Ionia State sexual psychopath research was MKULTRA Subproject 39, especially 39-4, 9 April 1958, Subject: Trip Report, Visit to [deleted], 7 April 1958. Paul Magnusson of the Detroit *Free Press* and David Pearl of the Detroit ACLU office both furnished information.

Carl Rogers' MKULTRA subproject was #97. He also received funds under Subproject 74. See especially 74-256, 7 October 1958, Supplement to Individual Grant under MKULTRA, Subproject No. 74 and 97-21, 6 August 1959, Subject: MKULTRA Subproject 97.

H. J. Eysenck's MKULTRA subproject was #111. See especially 111-3, 3 April 1961, Subject: Continuation of MKULTRA Subproject 111.

The American Psychological Association–sponsored trip to the Soviet Union was described in Subproject 107. The book that came out of the trip was called *Some Views on Soviet Psychology,* Raymond Bauer (editor), (Washington: American Psychological Association; 1962).

The Sherifs' research on teenage gangs was described in Subproject #102 and the 1961 Human Ecology biennial report. Dr. Carolyn Sherif also wrote a letter to the *American Psychological Association Monitor,* February 1978. Dr. Sherif talked about her work when she and I appeared on an August 1978 panel at the American Psychological Association's convention in Toronto.

Martin Orne's work for the Agency was described in Subproject 84. He contributed a chapter to the Society-funded book, *The Manipulation of Human Behavior,* edited by Albert Biderman and Herbert Zimmer-(New York: John Wiley & Sons; 1961), pp. 169–215. Financial data on Orne's Institute for Experimental Psychiatry came from a filing with the Commonwealth of Massachusetts, Attachment to Form 1023.

The quote from John Gittinger came from an interview with him conducted by Dr. Patricia Greenfield. Dr. Greenfield also interviewed Jay Schulman, Carl Rogers, and Charles Osgood for an article in the December 1977 issue of the *American Psychological Association Monitor,* from which my quotes of Schulman's comments are taken. She discussed Erving Goffman's role in a presentation to a panel of the American Psychological Association convention in Toronto in August 1978. The talk was titled "CIA Support of Basic Research in Psychology: Policy Implications."

CHAPTER 10

The material on the Gittinger Personality Assessment System (PAS) comes from "An Introduction to the Personality Assessment System" by John Winne and John Gittinger, Monograph Supplement No. 38, Clinical Psychology Publishing Co., Inc. 1973; an interview with John Winne; interviews with three other former CIA psychologists; 1974 interviews with John Gittinger by the author; and an extended interview with Gittinger by Dr. Patricia Greenfield, Associate Professor of Psychology at UCLA. Some of the material was used first in a *Rolling Stone* article, July 18, 1974, "The CIA Won't Quite Go Public." Robert Hyde's alcohol research at Butler Health Center was MKULTRA Subproject 66. See especially 66–17, 27 August, 1958. Subject: Proposed Alcohol Study—1958–1959 and 66–5. undated, Subject: Equipment—Ecology Laboratory.

The 1963 Inspector General's report on TSS, as first released under the Freedom of Information Act, did not include the section on personality assessment quoted from in the chapter. An undated, untitled document, which was obviously this section, was made available in one of the CIA's last releases.

MKULTRA subproject 83 dealt with graphology research, as did part of Subproject 60, which covered the whole Human Ecology Society. See especially 83-7, December 11, 1959, Subject: [deleted] Graphological Review and 60-28, undated, Subject [deleted] Activities Report, May, 1959–April, 1960.

Information on the psychological profile of Ferdinand Marcos came from a U.S. Government source who had read it. Information on the profile of the Shah of Iran came from a column by Jack Anderson and Les Whitten "CIA Study Finds Shah Insecure," Washington *Post,* July 11, 1975.

The quotes from James Keehner came from an article in *New Times* by Maureen Orth, "Memoirs of a CIA Psychologist," June 25, 1975.

For related reports on the CIA's role in training foreign police and its activities in Uruguay, see an article by Taylor Branch and John

Marks, "Tracking the CIA," *Harper's Weekly,* January 25, 1975 and Philip Agee's book, *Inside the Company: CIA Diary* (London: Penguin; 1975).

The quote from Martin Orne was taken from Patricia Greenfield's APA *Monitor* article cited in the last chapter's notes.

Gittinger's testimony before the Senate Select Committee on Intelligence and the Kennedy subcommittee on August 3, 1977 appeared on pages 50–63. David Rhodes' testimony on Gittinger's role in the abortive San Francisco LSD spraying appeared in hearings before the Kennedy subcommittee, September 20, 1977, pp. 100–110.

CHAPTER 11

Morse Allen's training in hypnosis was described in Document #A/B, V, 28/1, 9 July 1951, Subject [Deleted]. His hypnosis experiments in the office are described in a long series of memos. See especially #A/B, III, 2/18, 10 February 1954, Hypnotic Experimentation and Research and #A/B, II, 10/71, 19 August 1954, Subject: Operational/Security [deleted] and unnumbered document, 5 May 1955, Subject: Hypnotism and Covert Operations.

The quote on U.S. prisoners passing through Manchuria came from document #19, 18 June 1953, ARTICHOKE Conference.

Alden Sears' hypnosis work was the subject of MKULTRA subprojects 5, 25, 29, and 49. See especially 49–28, undated, Proposal for Research in Hypnosis at the [deleted], June 1, 1956 to May 31, 1957, 49–34, undated, Proposals for Research in Hypnosis at the [deleted], June 1, 1956 to May 31, 1957; 5–11, 28 May 1953, Project MKULTRA, Subproject 5 and 5-13, 20 April 1954, Subject: [deleted]. See also Patrick Oster's article in the Chicago *Sun-Times,* September 4, 1977, "How CIA 'Hid' Hypnosis Research."

General background on hypnosis came from interviews with Alden Sears, Martin Orne, Milton Kline, Ernest Hilgard, Herbert Spiegel, William Kroger, Jack Tracktir, John Watkins, and Harold Crasilneck. See Orne's chapter on hypnosis in *The Manipulation of Human Behavior,* edited by Albert Biderman and Herbert Zimmer (New York: John Wiley & Sons; 1961), pp. 169–215.

The contemplated use of hypnosis in an operation involving a foreign intelligence service is referred to in the Affidavit by Eloise R. Page, in the case *John D. Marks* v. *Central Intelligence Agency et al.* Civil Action no. 76-2073.

The 1959 proposed use of hypnosis that was approved by TSS is described in documents #433, 21 August 1959, Possible Use of Drugs and Hypnosis in [deleted] Operational Case; #434, 27 August 1959, Comments on [deleted]; and #435, 15 September 1959, Possible Use of

Drugs and Hypnosis in [deleted] Operational Case.

MKULTRA Subproject 128 dealt with the rapid induction technique. See especially 128-1, undated, Subject: To test a method of rapid hypnotic induction in simulated and real operational settings (MKULTRA 128).

A long interview with John Gittinger added considerably to this chapter. Mr. Gittinger had refused earlier to be interviewed directly by me for this book. Our conversation was limited solely to hypnosis.

CHAPTER 12

The reorganization of TSS was described in document #59, 26 July 1963, Report of the Inspection of MKULTRA and in interviews with Ray Cline, Herbert Scoville, and several other former CIA officials.

Richard Helms' recommendations for a new MKULTRA charter were described in document #450, 9 June, 1964, Sensitive Research Programs (MKULTRA).

Admiral Stansfield Turner's statement on the MKULTRA program was made before a joint session of the Kennedy subcommittee and the Senate Select Committee on Intelligence, August 3, 1977, pp. 4-8.

MKSEARCH programs and their origins in MKULTRA are described in documents #449, 8 April 1964, Revision of Project MKULTRA and #S-1-7, untitled, undated.

Dr. Edward Bennett's work is the subject of MKULTRA subprojects 104 and 143. See especially 143-23, 11 December 1962, Subject: MKULTRA Subproject 143. Other information on the CIA's economic sabotage program against Cuba came from interviews with Major General Edward Lansdale, Ray Cline, William Colby, Lincoln Gordon, Covey Oliver, Charles Meyer, Richard Goodwin, Roger Morris, several former CIA and State Department officials, and Cuban government officials.

The continued safehouse operation is MKSEARCH subproject 4. See especially S-12-1, bank statements and receipts of safehouse. The CIA's dealings with the Treasury Department over the Long committee's investigations of wiretaps are detailed in documents #451, 30 January 1967, A Report on a Series of Meetings with Department of the Treasury officials and #452, undated, Meeting with Department of Treasury Official.

The biological laboratory is the subject of MKULTRA subprojects 78 and 110 and MKSEARCH 2. See especially Documents 78-28, September 28, 1962, Subject: PM Support and Biological [deleted] and S-5-6, 8 September 1965, Subject: Hiring by Chief TSD/BB of [deleted], Former Staff Employee in a Consultant Capacity on an Agency Contract. The costs of the Fort Detrick operations came from p. 18 and p. 204 of the

Church committee hearings on Unauthorized Storage of Toxic Agents, September 16, 17, and 18, 1975. The description of TSS's procedures for dealing with biological weapons came from Document 78-28 (cited above) and document #509, undated (but clearly June 1975), Subject: Discussions of MKNAOMI with [deleted]

The chemical company subproject is MKULTRA subproject 116 and MKSEARCH 5. See especially 116-57, 30 January 1961, Subject: MKUL-TRA, Subproject 116; 116-62, October 28, 1960, shipping invoice; and 116-61, 4 November 1960, Subject: MKULTRA Subproject 116. Also see James Moore's subproject, MKULTRA 52; especially 52-53, invoice #3, 1125-009-1902, April 27, 1960.

James Hamilton's work is the subject of MKULTRA subprojects 124 and 140 and MKSEARCH Subproject 3. See especially 140-57, 6 May 1965, Subject: Behavioral Control and 140-83, 29 May 1963, Subject: MKULTRA Subproject 140.

Carl Pfeiffer's subprojects are MKULTRA 9, 26, 28, and 47 and MKSEARCH 7. See especially S-7-4, undated, Subject: Approval of Project [deleted].

Maitland Baldwin's Subprojects are MKULTRA 62 and MKSEARCH 1. See especially 62-2, undated [deleted] Special Budget and 62-3, undated, 1956, Subject: Re: Trip to [deleted], October 10-14, 1956.

Charles Geschickter's subprojects are MKULTRA 23, 35, and 45 and MKSEARCH 6. See especially 35-10, May 16, 1955, Subject: To provide for Agency-Sponsored Research Involving Covert Biological and Chemical Warfare; 45-78, undated, Research Proposal: 1960; 45-104, undated, Subject: Research Proposal: 1958-1959; 45-95, 26 January 1959, Coninuation of MKULTRA, Subproject No. 45; 45-104, 21 January 1958, Continuation of MKULTRA, Subproject No. 45; 45-52, 8 February 1962, Continuation of MKULTRA, Subproject No. 45; S-13-7, 13 August Subject, Approval of [deleted]; and S-13-9, 13 September 1967, Subject: Approval of [deleted]. See also Geschickter's testimony before the Kennedy subcommittee, September 20, 1977, pp. 44–49.

The lack of congressional or executive branch knowledge of CIA behavioral activities was mentioned on p. 386, Church Committee Report, Book I.

Amazon Natural Drug's CIA connection was described by an ex-CIA official and confirmed by the mother of another former Agency man. Several former employees described its activities in interviews.

Gottlieb's termination of MKSEARCH came from Document S-14-3, 10 July 1972, Termination of MKSEARCH.

The destruction of MKULTRA documents was described in Document #419, 3 October, 1975, Subject: Destruction of Drug and Toxin Related Files and 460, 31 January, 1973, Subject: Project Files: (1951–1967).

The MKULTRA subprojects on electric stimulation of the brain are

106 and 142. See especially 106-1, undated, Subject: Proposal; 142-14, 22 May 1962, Subject: Project MKULTRA, Subproject No. 142; and document #76 (MKDELTA release), 21 April 1961, Subject: "Guided Animal" Studies.

The list of parapsychology goals was taken from an excellent article by John Wilhelm in the August 2, 1977 Washington *Post:* "Psychic Spying?"

Project OFTEN information was taken from document #455, 6 May 1974, Subject: Project OFTEN and Memorandum for the Secretary of Defense from Deanne P. Siemer, September 20, 1977, Subject: Experimentation Programs Conducted by the Department of Defense That Had CIA Sponsorship or Participation and That Involved the Administration to Human Subjects of Drugs Intended for Mind-control or Behavior-modification Purposes.

The quote from B. F. Skinner was taken from Peter Schrag's book, *Mind Control* (New York: Pantheon, 1978) p. 10.

INDEX

A-bomb, 35
"A" treatment, 40-41, 44, 186
Abourezk, Sen. James, ix
Abramson, Harold, 59-62
  LSD psychosis victim, 62n, 64,
    68, 118, 120, 169
  treats Dr. Frank Olson for
    accidental LSD dose, 79-82
Abramson, Mrs. Harold, 62n
Acupuncture, 130
Addiction Research Center, 59
Agency for International
    Development (AID)
  Public Safety Mission, 178-179
Agrippina, 106
Albania, 44
Alcohol, 35, 70, 91-92
  "Extender," 58n
Aldrich, Dr. Stephen, 209, 210, 212
Alexander, Dr. Leo, ix, 10
Allan Memorial Institute, 131-132,
    136, 139
Allen, Morse, 23-26, 32, 38, 41n,
    42-43, 106-108, 111-113, 133,
    138, 143, 157, 182-192,
    201-202, 209
Allende, Salvador, 197
Altmeyer, Paul, ix
Amanita caesarea, 106
Amanita phalloides, 106
Amazon Natural Drug Company,
    203
American Journal of Psychiatry, 141

American Medical Association,
    Archives of Neurology and
    Psychiatry, 148
American Neurological Association,
    148
American Psychiatric Assoc., 132,
    136
  archives, 139
American Psychological Association,
    158, 161
American Society for Clinical and
    Experimental Hypnosis, 187
American Telephone and Telegraph,
    (AT&T), 18
Amherst College, 209
Amnesia, 17, 48, 210, 212
  "complete," 133
  "differential," 133
  induction by drugs, 41
  induction by hypnosis, 42, 183,
    185, 187-189
  produced by electroshock, 23, 133,
    140
Amphetamines, 35
Andres, Monica, viii
Angleton, James, 189, 192
Angola, 46
Anslinger, Harry, 89
Anson, Robert Sam, 191n
Anthrax, 76, 78
Anthropology, 15, 147
Army Biological Laboratory.
  See U.S. Army

Army Chemical Corps.
  See U.S. Army
Army Intelligence.
  See U.S. Army
ARTICHOKE, 29-33, 37-43, 55,
  106-108, 133, 138, 143-144,
  182-186, 202, 208-209, 212
  difficulty recruiting phychiatrist,
    30-31
  ethical and moral considerations,
    32-33
  women excluded as experi-
    menters, 43
  work with Chinese refugees,
    150-151, 153
  use of college students in tests, 31
Atomic Energy Commission, 195
"Aunt Jemima," 14
Avery, Paul, ix
Azores, 34
Aztecs, 107

Badalamenti, Rosalyn T., ix
Baldwin, Dr. Maitland, 138, 143,
  201-202
Barbiturates, 6, 35
Basel, Switzerland, 3
Bateson, Gregory, 120
Baylor University, 67n
Bay of Pigs, 195, 203
Becker, Eddie, ix
Beecher, Henry, 67n, 72n
Behavior
  "behaviorism," 162
  -control, 29, 30
    modification, unethical, 213
    See also mind-control
  manipulation, 147
  research, 30
  sciences, 147
Bennett, Dr. Edward, 197-198
Benzedrine, 40, 80
Berle, Adolf A., 156
Berlin airlift, 57
Bevis, Penny, viii
Biderman, Albert, 128n
Bio-electrics, 212
Bissell, Richard, 76
Blackmail, 46-47
Blauer, Harold, 67n
Blowback, 48
BLUEBIRD, 22-26, 28-29
  renamed ARTICHOKE, 29
Blum, Ralph, 118-119, 121
Bordentown, N.J., reformatory, 201

Borosage, Robert, viii
Bortner, Henry, 86, 108-110, 115
Boston Psychopathic Hospital, 53,
  54, 58, 59, 118, 169
Botanicals, 109
Botulinum, 74-75
Botulinus toxin, 16
Brainwashing, 28
  Chinese credited with, 125-126
  CIA investigations, 127-146
    methods, 128-130
  tested by Dr. D. E. Cameron,
    139-141
Branch, Taylor, viii
Brandt, Dr. Karl, 10
Braun, Wernher von, 9
Brothel, 93-96
Brown University, 156n
Brucellosis, 75
Bufontenine, 63
"Bugs," 58
Burch, Neil, 67n
Bureau of Narcotics and Dangerous
  Drugs. *See* Federal Bureau of
  Narcotics
Bureau of Prisons. *See* U.S. Bureau
  of Prisons
Burke, Michael, 28
Burroughs, William, 84n, 203
Butler Health Center (Providence),
  169
BZ (psychochemical), 102, 110

California Medical Facility
  (Vacaville), 201
Cal Tech (California Institute of
  Technology), 55
Cameras, in tobacco pouches, 55
Cameron, Dr. D. Ewen, viii, 131-139,
  145, 148, 156, 159, 214
  LSD testing, 139-141
Cam Ranh Bay, 144n
Cannabis indica, 6
  See also Marijuana
Carbamate poison, 110, 200
Carbon-dioxide inhalation, 200
Carmichael, Leonard, 156n
Carter, Pres. Jimmy, 206
Cassidy, John, 178-179
CASTIGATE, 37
Castro, Fidel, 17, 74-76, 98, 191,
  195, 197, 198
Cattell, James, 67n
Cavanagh, Dr. John, ix
Central Mongoloid skull, 158

Center for National Security Studies, viii

Central Intelligence Agency (CIA)
abuses investigated, 109, 205-207
Army Chemical Corps
Special Operations Division (SOD) work for, 73-86
ARTICHOKE, 29, 33, 55, 88
auditors, 99
behavioral research, 164, 206-209
BLUEBIRD, 22-26, 28-29
brainwashing studies, 127-146
funding of, 132, 133, 136, 137-138, 141
carnal operations, 95
CASTIGATE, 37
CHATTER, 35-39, 43
Clandestine Services division (Directorate of Operations), *also* "dirty tricks department," 56-57, 73-75, 101, 103, 164, 176-177, 189, 195-196, 200, 204
Assistant for Scientific Matters, 103
Health Alteration Committee, 75n
cooperation with British and Canadian governments, 30
Counterintelligence, 145, 189-190
D-lysergic acid diethylamide (LSD), use of
experiments, 61-73, 119-122, 169, 180
accidental, 70-72
funding of research, 58-59, 79, 111
military services interest, 59
National Institute of Mental Health interest, 59
testing, 73-86, 87-97, 99-104, 105, 154-155, 164
drugs, use of, 21-33, 34-44
experiments with Mexican mushrooms, 106-117
use of prison inmates in, 117
Frankfurt base, 35-38
funding of botanical poison research, 111
funding of Society for the Investigation of Human Ecology, 149
General Counsel, 83
human behavior manipulation, 147-163, 164-181
hypnosis experiments, 182-192

informants, 64
Inspector General, 98, 100-101, 102n, 176, 196
liason with Army, Navy, and Air Force Intelligence, 30
Mafia operations, 22, 101
material deleted from OSS documents, 7
medical staff, 29
Medical Office, 102n
methods after World War II, 20
mind-control work, vii, 8-13, 17, 18, 21-33, 34-44
MKDELTA, 57, 103
MKNAOMI, 57, 73-74
MKSEARCH, 197-200
MKULTRA, 57 et al
Office of Security, 22-24, 29, 30-32, 38, 55, 80, 82, 108, 150-157
Office of Scientific Intelligence, 21-23, 26, 28, 29, 209
Office of Technical Services, 29n
"Operation Midnight Climax," 100
Personality Assessment System, ix
Research Chairman, 84-85
responsibility in Dr. Frank Olson's death, 85, 87
Science and Technology Directorate, 144n, 196, 209
Office of Research and Development (ORD) 209, 213
Security Memorandum, 1949, 21
Soviet Division, 28
"Special" interrogation, 22
Technical Services Division. 29n
Technical Services Staff (TSS), 29, 55, 57-58, 61-62, 64-65, 67, 70-72 et al
assessment staff, 172-175, 179
Chemical Division, 55
perjury questioned, 207
tests with dolphins, 144
use of college students in tests, 31
Western Hemisphere Division, 203
with respect to Freedom of Information Act, 211
work with Navy, 1952, 34-44
"Charisma," 167
CHATTER, 35-39, 43
CIA psychiatric consultants' report on, 43-44
Chemical and biological warfare (CBW), 16-17, 55, 57, 74n
Cheshire, Mark, ix
Chestnut Lodge, 81-84
Chile, 197, 213

China
  credited with brainwashing, 125-
    126, 131, 150
  use of drugs in, 130
  political re-education programs
    in, 128-130
Chondodendron toxicoferum, 203
Church, Sen. Frank, 206
  Committee. *See* U.S. Senate
Circumcision, effect on Turkish
  boys, 159
City College (College of the City of
  New York, CCNY), 56
Civil Service Commission, 23
Clandestine Services, 74-76
  Health Alteration Committee, 76n
Clark, Lincoln, 119n
Claudius, 106
Cleghorn, Dr. Robert, 140
Cline, Ray, 28, 56, 176, 198n
Cocaine, 57n
Cohen, Sidney, ix, 119n
Cointreau, 77
Colby, William, 76, 176, 198n
Cold War, viii, 9, 11, 125, 128, 148
  hysteria, 27
  influence on mind-control
    experiments, 26-27, 57
  use of hypnotism in, 182
Colgate University, 19
College Board exams, 168
Columbia College, 12
  Law School, 12
  University, 59
Commissioner of Narcotics, 36
Conant, James, 14
Condon, Richard, 9n, 192
Congo, 17, 75
Conklin, M. J., ix
Cook, William Boyd, 115n
Cooper, Gary, 34
Cornell University, 13, 127
  Medical School, 33, 127-128,
    147-153, 154-156
  patients used in experiments, 149
Cortez, 107
Corynanthine, 61
Counterintelligence, 48
"Cover grants," 158
Cuba, 197, 198
  missile crisis, 164
Cummins, Ken, viii
Cunningham, Hugh, 28
Curandera (shaman), 112, 115n,
  117
Curare, 109, 139

Dachau, 4-6, 8-11
Day of the Dolphin, The, 144
"Dead drops," 187
Death in the Mind, 20
Deep Creek Lodge, Md., 73-74, 79
deFlorez, Adm. Luis, 84
Del Gracio, August, 6-7, 88, 93
Delaney, Hannah, viii
Democrat and Chronicle
  (Rochester, N.Y.), 36n
Department of the Army, 205
"Depatterning," viii, 133-136, 214
DeShon, H. Jackson, 54, 60
Destruction of memory, 212
Dewey, Gov. Thomas, 7n, 90, 93
Dexamyl, 38
Dexedrine, 38, 39, 40, 42
Diarrhea inducers, 99
"Differential amnesia," 133
Dille, James, 67n
Dishwashers, 165-166
D-lysergic acid diethylamide (LSD)
  CIA experiments with, 61-73,
    119-122, 169, 180
    accidental, 70-72
  CIA funding of research, 58-59
  CIA interest peak, 55-58
  CIA testing, 73-86, 87-97, 99-104,
    105, 154-155, 164
  Corynanthine as possible
    antidote, 61
  discovery of, 3-4, 8-9
  effects on Siamese fighting fish
    and snails documented, 61
  fear of Russian possession, 65
  importation to U.S., 54
  Kauders' lecture on in Boston, 53
  Lilly manufacture of, 66-67
  Military services' interest, 59
  National Institute of Mental
    Health interest, 59
  paranoia from, 54
  Pfeiffer's test with, 201
  practical joke with, 77, 86
    dose to Dr. Frank Olson called
      "therapeutic," 83
  radioactive marker for, 118
  reaction of schizophrenics to, 60
  scientists' reports published, 61
  studies at Lexington Federal drug
    hospital, 62-64
  use in covert operations, 61
DMT, 110
Dolphins, 144
Donovan, Gen. William "Wild Bill,"
  12-18, 27, 171

Doors of Perception, The, 117
Drugs
 CIA use of, 21-33, 34-44,
 memory destroying, 41
 testing, 180
Drum, James "Trapper," 83-84
Dulles, Allen, 27, 48, 56-57, 66-67,
 72, 82, 84, 87, 127, 131,
 147-148, 156, 186, 195, 203n

Eagleton, Thomas, 103
Earman, John, 98, 100
Edgewood Arsenal (Md.), 74n
 chemical laboratory, 210
Educational Testing Service, 168
Edwards, Sheffield, 221
EEG tests, 26, 168
Ehrlichman, John, 172
Einstein, Albert, 8, 9
Eisenhower, Pres. Dwight D., 14,
 203n
Electric Kool-Aid Acid Test, The, 121
Electric stimulation, 212
Electrodes
 experiments with, 142-143, 210
"Electro-sleep" machine
 danger of temporary brain
 damage, 25
Electroshock, 133, 134, 140, 145,
 202, 214
 amnesia from, 25
 battery driven, 26
 continued treatments, 25-26
 EEG tests to determine effects, 26
 "excruciating pain," 25
 in CIA behavioral research, 164
 "Page-Russell" method, 135
 Reiter machine, 25
 sleep-, 135
Ellsberg, Daniel, 172-173
Emory University, 201
Epidemics, 77
Ergot, 4, 66, 105
Estabrooks, George "Esty," 19-20
"Executive action," 210
Explorations of Personality, 17
EXPLOSIVE, 41-42
Explosive seashells, 55
"Externalizer" (E), 166-167, 168,
 169, 172, 175-176
Eysenck, H. J., 159-160

False papers, 55
Faust, 179
Federal Bureau of Investigation
 (FBI), 8, 30

Federal Bureau of Narcotics, 7, 36,
 88, 89-90, 91, 92-93, 199
 and Dangerous Drugs, 119-120
Feldman, Ira "Ike," 94, 98
Fiore, Nick, viii
Flagrante delicto, 92
"Flexible" (F), 166-167
Flowers, Eddie, 63-64
Foothills College, 7n
Food and Drug Administration,
 67-68, 201
Ford, Pres. Gerald, 85n-86n, 205
Forest Hills, Queens, N.Y., 155
Fort Detrick, Md., 57, 73-79, 85,
 199-200
Frankenstein, Dr. 9, 121
Freedom and Dignity, 160
Freedom of Information Act, vii-viii,
 7n, 188n, 200, 206, 212
Fremont-Smith, Frank, 120
Fried, Frank, Shriver, Harris and
 Kampelman (law firm), viii

Gallagher, John, ix
"Gang that Couldn't Spray Straight,"
 100n, 180, 208
Gardner, John, 18
Gaynor, Paul, 25, 38
Georgetown University Hospital, 202
Germ warfare, 125-126
Geschickter, Dr. Charles, 59, 155n,
 202, 207
Geschickter Fund for Medical
 Research, 59, 110, 114, 118,
 155n, 187n, 202-203
Gestapo, 4, 19
Gibbons, Willis, 57, 83-84
Ginsberg, Allen, 120-121
Giordano, Harry, 199n
Gittinger, John, ix, 18, 20, 94, 100,
 130, 157, 160, 186, 187, 188,
 190, 191
 Personality Assessment System
 (PAS), 164-181, 196-197
"God's Flesh," 107-111, 112, 114, 115
 See also Teonanactl
Goethe, Johann von, 179
Goffman, Erwin, 160
Goldwater, Sen. Barry, 207
Goodwin, Richard, 198n
"Goofball." *See* Dexamyl
Goldstein, Bonnie, ix
Göring, Hermann, 10
Gottlieb, Dr. Sidney, 17, 20, 55-72,
 73-75, 97-98, 100-103, 108,
 110, 115, 151-162, 167, 186·

192, 195-206, 208-209, 212
Graphology (handwriting analysis),
171n
Great Britain, 12
Greenblatt, Milton, ix, 53
Greene, Bob, viii
Greenfield, Dr. Patricia, ix
Greiner, Hans, 179
Gulag Archipelago, The, 128
Gypsies, 5, 10

Haggerty, Julie, ix
Hair, 54
Hallucinogens, 117
Halperin, Morton, viii
Hamilton, Dr. James, 91n, 97
200-202
Hammerstein, Oscar II, 81
Handwriting analysis, 17
"Harassment substances," 100, 197
Harvard, 14, 105, 118, 119, 160, 161,
162, 170, 203
Medical School, 53, 72n
Harvey, Laurence, 9n
Hashish, 58
Hawkins, William, 94
Hayward, Lisa Olson, 84
Hebb, Dr. Donald, 137-138, 143n
Heim, Roger, 114-115
Helms, Richard, 13, 17, 20, 44, 48,
56-57, 72, 87, 97, 100-101,
145-146, 189, 196-197, 199,
204-205, 208, 212
Heroin, 35, 62, 64, 91, 94
Hersh, Seymour, 205
Hidden microphones, 39
High Noon, 34
Hinkle, Laurence, ix, 127-130, 147,
149, 151, 154n, 156, 157
Hinsey, Dr. Joseph, 156
Hillenkoetter, Roscoe, 22-23
Hilton, James, 13
Himmler, Heinrich, 5
Hite Report, The, 94
Hitler, Adolf, 10, 13, 15-16, 17,
18-19, 26, 53, 110, 171, 172,
200
Hoch, Paul, 67n
Hodge, Harold, 59, 118
Hofmann, Dr. Albert, ix, 3-4, 5, 8-9,
53-54, 58, 105, 115
Holliday, Billie, 91n
Hollister, Dr. Leo, 120-121
Holmesburg State Prison (Pa.), 212
Homer, 41n
Homosexuals, 170, 175n

entrapment of, 96-97, 173
Hood, William, ix
Hoover, Pres. Herbert, 27
Hoover, J. Edgar, 30, 90, 213
Hsi-nao, 125
Huaulta de Jiménez, 112, 114, 115n
"Human ecology," 147-163
defined, 147
"special methods," 149
Human Ecology Fund, 149n
Human Ecology Society. *See* Society
For the Investigation of
Human Ecology
Hungarian revolt, 1956, 152-154
Hunt, Howard, 55
Hunter, Edward, 125-126, 128
Huxley, Aldous, 117, 143n
Hyde, Robert, 54, 59-61, 64, 69, 119,
169
Hypnosis, 5, 11, 18-19, 21, 24, 40-42,
154, 162, 182-192, 212
methods, 55
"terminal experiment," 185-187

Institute for Experimental
Psychiatry, 161n
"Internalizer (I)," 166-167, 169, 172
Interrogation techniques, 30
Investigative Reporters and Editors,
Inc., viii
Invisible inks, 55
Ionia State Hospital (Michigan),
154-155, 170
Iguitos, Peru, 203
Isabell, Dr. Harris, 59, 62-64, 116,
170
Istanbul University, 159
Itching powder, 100
Ivy Leaguer, 91

Jamaica dogwood, 109
Jellinek, Roger, ix
Jews, 5, 10
"Johnny Evans," 20
Johns Hopkins University, 156
Johnson, Pres. Lyndon, 198n, 203n,
205
Jones, Janet, 94
Justice Department, 93n

Kamasutra, 118
Kauders, Otto, 53
Keehner, James, 173-175
Keeney, Barnaby, 156n
Kelly, George A., 156n
Kempster, Norman, ix

Kennedy, Sen. Edward, 93n, 100n,
     180, 206-208
Kennedy, Pres. John F., 14, 100, 145,
     195, 198n
Kesey, Ken, 120-121
KGB, 96, 129, 145-146
Khrushchev, Nikita, 161, 164
King, J. C., 203
Kirkpatrick, Gen. Lyman, 82-83, 85,
     100n, 102n
Kistiakowsky, Dr. George, 14
Klee, Gerald, 67n
Kleiner, Elsa, ix
Kleiner, Fred, ix
Kline, Milton, ix, 187, 191n, 195
Knockout drops, 89, 93
Kohan, Jeff, ix
Korean Central Intelligence Agency
     (KCIA), 178, 179-180
Korean War, 23, 26, 28, 34, 43, 57,
     125-127
Kubie, Dr. Lawrence, 19

Langer, Walter, ix, 15-16, 15-16n,
     18, 171
Langer, William, 15
Land, Dr. Edwin, 210
Lashbrook, Robert, 74, 79-83, 85-86,
     93, 207
Latham, Aaron, 189
Lauren G., 131-135
Leary, Timothy, 105, 117-118, 122
Lee, Marty, ix
Lenzner, Terry, 63n
Le Rosey, 13
Lesbians, 170
Levittown, L.I., N.Y., 158
Lexington, Kentucky, Federal drug
     hospital, 62-64, 89, 116, 170
Life magazine, 116-117, 118
Lifton, Robert Jay, 128n
Lilly, Eli & Company, 66-68
Lilly, Dr. John, ix, 62, 142-144, 209
Lipscomb, Tom, ix
"Lisetin," 109
Long, Sen. Edward, 199n
Lovell, Stanley, 13-17, 55, 75, 88, 200
LSD. *See* D-lysergic acid diethyla-
     mide
Luciano, Charles "Lucky," 7n, 88, 93
Lumumba, Patrice, 17, 75
Luther, 79

McCarthy, Sen. Joseph, 26, 69
McCone, John, 100-101, 195, 196,
     198n, 209

McGill University, 132, 138, 159
     psychology department, 137
Macy, Josiah J., Foundation, 59,
     64-65, 118, 120-121
McQuown, Judith H., ix
Madeleine, 136
Mafia, 7, 22, 74
     CIA-Mafia assassination plots,
     100, 191
Magnusson, Paul, ix
Malott, Deane W., 127
Manchuria, Japanese use of biologi-
     cal warfare in, 77n
Manchurian Candidate
     defined, 9, 9n
     hypnosis to create, 183, 186-187,
     189, 191
Mandala, Tibetan, 121
Manhattan Project, 109, 131
     involvement with OSS drug
     experiments, 6-8, 88
Mao Tse-tung, 130
Marchetti, Victor, 189
Marcos, Ferdinand, 172n
Maria Sabina, 112-114, 115n
Marijuana, 6-8, 38, 40, 42, 88, 91,
     154
     "Mexican grown" in Project
     CHATTER, 36
Marin County, 99, 208
Marines, 24
Marrazzi, Amedeo, 67n
Marx, Karl, 130
Mary, C., 138-139
Massachusetts General Hospital
     67n, 119n
Massachusetts Mental Health
     Center, 53n
Mata Hari, 96
Mead, Margaret, 65, 120, 159
Me and Juliet, 81
Medicine, 147
Menninger, Karl, 19
Menninger, William, 19
Menopause, 139
Mescaline, 4-6, 11, 58, 106, 111
     forced injections of derivatives,
     67n
Meselson, Matthew, ix
Miami *News*, 125
"Microbioinoculator, non-
     discernible," 77
Microphones, 92, 94
Microwaves, 212
Migraine headaches, 127, 148
Mills, Bill, ix

Mind-control, vii
    BLUEBIRD program, 22-26, 28
    bureaucratic squabbling and
        conflict over, 29, 30
    defense against, 23
    "gap," 28
    rationalizations for, 30-31
    research, 13
Mindszenty, Josef Cardinal, 21-22,
    28, 125, 145
Mintz, Jim, viii
Missouri Institute of Psychiatry, 67n
Mitrione, Dan, 178
Mitty, Walter, 47
MKDELTA, 57, 103
MKNAOMI, 57, 73-74
MKSEARCH, 197, 198-204
    Subproject #2, 199
    Subproject #3, 200
MKULTRA, 57-61, 67-69, 71-72, et al
    safehouses, 174
    subproject #3 (George White),
        92-95, 98-104
    subproject #58, 114, 115-116
    subproject #143, 197-198
"Model psychosis," 53
Monroe, Dr. James, 128n, 155-157,
    159n, 207n
Montana State University, 115n
Montreal, Quebec, 132-133, 141, 156
Mont Royal, 132
Moore, Dr. James, ix, 108, 112, 116,
    200n
"Morgan Hall," 92
Morgan, J. P., & Company, 111
Morphine, 62
Morrison, Robert, 133
Moscow purge trials of 1937 and
    1938, 21
Mount Holyoke College, 18n
Mt. Sinai Hospital, 59, 169
Mulholland, John, 80
Murray, Henry "Harry," 17-18
Mushrooms
    CIA experiments with, 105-121
    "magic," 105-107, 112, 117-118,
        200n
Mushrooms, Russia and History,
    106, 111
Mycology, 111

Naked Lunch, 84n
Narcohypnosis, 23n
Narcotherapy, 23n, 40
National Institutes of Health, 62, 67,
    138, 142-144, 201-202

National Institute of Mental Health
    (NIMH), 59, 63, 157-158
    Addiction Research Center, 59
National Security Act of 1947, 27
National Security Council, 27
National Student Association, 203n
National Velvet, 132
Naval intelligence, 24, 34-43
Naval Medical Research Institute,
    35, 67n
Nazis
    experiments with drugs, 5, 8-10
    "aviation medicine," 5, 9
    war criminals, 10-11
Neff, Walter, 5
Nembutal, 80, 134
Nepenthe, 41n
"Neurosurgical techniques"
    (lobotomy-related), 26
New York Hospital-Cornell Medical
    Center, 156
New York Liberal Party, 156
New York Neurological Association,
    148
New York State Psychiatric Institute,
    67n
New York Times, 205, 207n
Newsday, viii
Nicotine, 57n
1984, 96n
Nixon, Pres. Richard, 86, 198n, 204,
    205, 213
"Nondiscernible microbioinoculator"
    (dart gun), 76, 109
Norman, Okla., state hospital, 165
Northern Ireland, 213
Northwestern University Medical
    School, 209
Nosenko, Yuri, 145-146
Nti sheeto, 112
    See also Mushrooms
Nuremburg trial, 10
    code, 10-11, 213
    Tribunal records, 22

Oaxaca, Mexico, 112
Office of Strategic Services (OSS)
    agent network, 16
    creation of, 12-13
    drug experiments, 6-8, 11-12, 55,
        89
    during World War II, 12-20, 40,
        76, 89-90
    mind-control research, 13, 16
    National Defense Research
        Committee, 14

Research and Analysis, 15
Research, Development, 13, 55
    Division 19, 14
    testing programs, 17-18
        methods used in corporations, 18
    "truth drug" committee, 6-7
    use of carbamate poison in Hitler assassination attempt, 110
Of Spies and Strategems, 16n
Ohio State University, 156n
"Old boys," 13
Oliver, Florence, viii
Ololiuqui seeds, 115n
Olson, Alice (Mrs. Frank), 77-78, 79, 81-85, 86
Olson, Eric, 81-85
Olson, Dr. Frank, 73-86, 87-88, 93, 97, 100n, 205
"Operation Midnight Climax," 99
Opium, 91n
Orchids for Mother, 189
Orlikow, David, 139
Orlikow, Val, 139-140
Orne, Martin, 161-162, 170, 177
Orth, Maureen, 173-174
Orwell, George, 96n
Osgood, Charles, ix, 158, 162, 168
Osmond, Humphrey, ix
Oster, Patrick, ix
Oswald, Lee Harvey, 145
Overholser, Dr. Winfred, 6

"Page-Russell" method, 135
Paraguay, 188
Parapsychology, 211, 212
Park, Tongsun, 178
Parke, Davis & Company, 108, 109
Pasternak, Walter, 99
Pavlov, Ivan Petrovich, 128
Pecks' Bad Boy, 14, 55
Personality Assessment System, ix
Peterzell, Jay, viii
Petrillo, Joseph, viii
Peyote cactus, 105, 120
Pfeiffer, Carl, 59, 201
Pharmaceutical companies, 65
Phenergan, 134
Philby, Harold "Kim," 44n
Piaget, Jean, 65
Picrotoxin, 23
Piule, 106-108
Placebos, 37
Plötner, Dr. Kurt, 5
Plowman, Dr. Timothy, 203
Poison gas, 16

Polaroid, 210
Political warfare, 30
Polygraph (lie detector), 22, 24, 146, 161n
    in detection of homosexuality, 24n
    in detection of theft of cash, 24n
    "super," 25
Powers, Francis Gary, 74
Princeton, 90
    Inn, 65
Project OFTEN, 212
Prostitutes, 91, 93n, 94-97, 99, 170, 180, 199
Psilocybin, 105, 115-116
Psychedelic drugs, 105, 109
Psychiatry, 15
"Psychic driving," 136-137, 140
Psychological Assessment Associates, 168, 180
Psychology, 15, 147
Psychosurgery, 212

Radar waves, 203
Radiation, 212
Radio stimulation of the brain, 212
Ramparts magazine, 203
Research in Mental Health Newsletter, 159
"Relugated" (R), 166-167
Rhodes, David, 99-100, 180, 208
Richards, Bill, ix
Richardson, Allan, 112-113
Rinkel, Max, 53, 54, 118
Rivea seeds, 63
Robinson, Julian, ix
Rockefeller Commission, 84, 206
    Foundation, 132-133, 138, 157
    Vice-President Nelson, 205
Rodgers, Richard, 81
Rogers, Carl, 156, 157, 158, 162, 168
"Role Adaptive" (R), 167
"Role Uniform" (U), 167
Rolling Stone magazine, 180
Roosevelt Hotel (New Orleans), 8
Roosevelt, Pres. Franklin D., 12
Rope Dancer, The, 189
Rositzke, Harry, 28
Rubenstein, Leonard, 136-138
Russell, Seymour, 196
Russians, 5
Rutgers University, 153, 154
Ruwet, Lt. Col. Vincent, 74, 77, 79, 81, 83-85, 86

Sadism, 97

"Safehouses," 39, 41, 69, 92-94, 101-102, 199-200, 202
St. Anthony's Fire, 4
St. Clair, Diane, viii
St. Elizabeth's Hospital, 6
Sandoz drug and chemical empire, 3, 54, 58-59, 65-66, 68, 115n, 116, 119, 143
San Francisco safehouse, 93-99, 101, 102, 170-171, 174, 194, 199
Saunders, David, 168
"Saucepan chemist," 13
Savage, Charles, 67n
Schacht, Hjalmar, 75
Scheflin, Alan, ix
"Scheider, Victor," 206
Schein, Edgar, 128n
Schizophrenia,   53, 132-133, 140
  induced by hallacinogenic mushrooms, 114
Schizophrenics
  behavior of, 134n
  electroshock in treatment of, 133
  reaction to LSD, 60
  symptoms, 134n, 136
Schlesinger, James, 180, 205, 212
Schulman, Jay, 153-154
Schwab, Dr. John, 74
Scientific Engineering Institute, 161n, 210-211
Scopolamine, 6, 63
Scott, George C., 144
Sears, Alden, 186-187
Seconal, 38, 39, 42, 134
Secretary of Defense, 36
"Seeking the Magic Mushroom," 117
See-through mirrors, 92
"Semantic differential," 158
"Señora sin mancha," 112
Sensory deprivation, 128, 138n, 141 143, 148, 201-202
"Serunim," 72
Sex, 47-48, 93-97
  kinky, 200
Sexual entrapment, 173
Shah of Iran, 13, 172n
Shelley, Mary, 9
Shellfish toxin, 74
Sherif, Carolyn Wood, 159
Sherif, Muzafer, 159
Short-order cooks, 165-166
Simon, John J., ix
Sinatra, Frank, 9n
Siragusa, Charles, 99n, 207
Skinner, B. F., 160, 162, 214
"Sleep cocktail," 134

"Sleep room," 134, 135
"Sleep therapy," 134
Slezak, Walter, 164
Smithsonian Institution, 156n
Sneezing powder, 99, 197
Society for the Investigation of Human Ecology, 133n, 137, 139n, 149, 163, 167-168, 170, 171n, 196, 207n, 210
Sociology, 15, 147
Sodium amytal, 23
Sodium pentothal, 40
Sokolow, Richard, viii
Solzhenitzyn, Alexander, 128
Sommer, Andy, ix
Sorbonne, 114
South Korea, 178, 179-180
Soviet Union (Russia), 26-28, 74-77, 101, 129-131, 157, 161, 213
  behavior-control programs, 28n
  behavioral research, 30, 102n
    use of drugs in, 130
  brainwashing, 129
  political re-education programs, 128
"Space-time image," 135
Spanish Inquisition, 130
Speer, Albert, 10
Sputnik, 117
Spy tradecraft
  alternatives to physical torture in obtaining information, 45-49
  blackmail, 46-47
  entrapment, 47
  limited usefulness of physical torture in obtaining information, 44-45
  sex, 48
  uselessness against well-intentioned agent, 49
S. S. (Schutzstaffel), 4-6
Stalin, Josef, 26, 69, 129, 148
Stanford University, 99, 120, 207
  Medical School, 97
Staph. enterotoxin, 75
State Department, 24
Statler Hotel, 81-83
Stein, Gertrude, 120
Stephenson, Richard, 153
Stereotoxic Surgery, 210, 212
Stink bombs, 99, 197
Stockwell, John, ix, 46-48
Stress creation, 17, 174
Struik, Dr. A. H. M., 154n
Suicide pills, 55, 74
Sullivan, Timothy, viii

Svengali, 182
"Swimmer nullification," 144n

Tabula rasa, 133
Taiwan, 188
Taylor, Elizabeth, 132
Taylor, Telford, ix
Technical Services Staff (TSS), 29
Teonanactl, 107
Tetrahydrocannabinol, 38
THIRD CHANCE, 62n
Thompson, Hunter S., 63
Thompson, Dr. Samuel, ix, 34-35,
    37-38, 40, 42-43
Thorazine, 134
Thornwell, James, 62n-63n
Times Books, ix
Toughkenamon, Pa., 108
Toulouse-Lautrec, Henri, 93
Transmitters
  in false teeth, 55
Treichler, Ray, 65, 86, 99, 207
"Trickle-down phenomenon," 120
Truth drugs, 30, 36, 48, 55, 155, 198
  serum, 145
Tupamaro urban guerrillas, 178-179
Turner, Stansfield, 197n, 206, 212
Two-way mirrors, 37, 39

Ultrasonics, 212
Ultraviolet radiation, 211
U.S. Air Force, 67, 128
  Psychological Warfare Div., 128n
  study of Korean War prisoners,
    156
U.S. Army
  Biological Laboratory, 199-200
  Chemical corps, 58, 65, 67, 74,
    109, 212
    Special Operations Division
      (SOD) of biological research
      center, 57, 74, 82
  clandestine services, 74
  Intelligence, 43
  studies of brainwashing, 128
  THIRD CHANCE, 62n
U.S. Bureau of Prisons, 89
U.S. Rubber, 57
U.S. Senate, 44, 180
  Church committee, 76n, 100n,
    102-103, 206
  Select Committee on Intelligence,
    206
  Subcommittee on Health and
    Scientific Research, 206-207
University of Basel, 109

University of California at Berkley,
  18
University of Delaware, 110, 115,
  200n
University of Denver, 186
University of Houston, 197
University of Illinois Medical School,
  59
  Pharmacology Dept., 201
University of London, 159
University of Maryland Medical
  School, 67n
University of Minnesota, 67n, 186
University of Nijmegen, 154n
University of Oklahoma, 59, 159
University of Pennsylvania, 160
University of Rochester, 35, 59
University of Washington, 67n
University of Wisconsin, 77, 156
ULTRA program, 57n
Uruguay, 178-179

Venezuelan equine encephalo-
  myelitis, 75-76
Verne, Jules, 8-9
Veronal, 134
Veterans Administration Hospital,
  Palo Alto, Ca., 120-121
Vietnam War, 122

Wagner, Richard, 120
Warren Commission, 101n
Washington *Post,* 77, 85, 100n
Wasson, R. Gordon, ix, 106, 111-117
Wasson, Valentina, 106, 111-112
Watergate, 204-205
Wechsler, David, 165n
  Adult Intelligence Scale, 165n
  battery, 170-171, 173, 178-180
  -Bellevue-G., 165n
  digit-span test, 169
  intelligence scale, 165
  psychological tests, 118
  subtests, 166-169, 172, 175
Wendt, G. Richard, 35-43
  presumed addition to heroin, 36n
Wendt, Mrs. G. Richard, 42
West, Louis Jolyon, 59
Wheelon, Albert "Bud," 195
White, George, 6-8, 12, 20, 88, 97-99,
  102, 170-171, 199-200, 207
Whitehorn, John, 156
Whittaker, Florence, viii
"Who? Me?," 14-15
Whores. *See* Prostitutes
Williams College, 13

Williams, Dr. Fred, 128n
Wilson, Benjamin, 77-78
Winkle, Owen, 93
Winne, John, 178, 179-180
Wiretapping, 55, 199n
Wolfe, Tom, 121
Wolff, Harold, 33, 127-130, 147

Wolff-Hinkle report, 128
  study, 145
World Psychiatric Assoc., 132

Yage, 203

Zuckerman, Sam, ix